Counselling Skills i
Applied Sport Psyc

Learning How to Counsel

Paul McCarthy and Zoe Moffat

Routledge
Taylor & Francis Group

NEW YORK AND LONDON

Designed cover image: Getty images

First published 2024
by Routledge
605 Third Avenue, New York, NY 10158

and by Routledge
4 Park Square, Milton Park, Abingdon, Oxon, OX14 4RN

Routledge is an imprint of the Taylor & Francis Group, an informa business

ISBN: 978-1-032-59258-9 (hbk)
ISBN: 978-1-032-59257-2 (pbk)
ISBN: 978-1-003-45385-7 (ebk)

DOI: 10.4324/9781003453857

Typeset in Galliard
by Apex CoVantage, LLC

Counselling Skills in Applied Sport Psychology

Counselling Skills in Applied Sport Psychology is a new text that provides a 'how to' in basic counselling skills for sport psychology students and practitioners. The book supports scholarship in applied sport psychology at the upper undergraduate and postgraduate levels, especially for those training to become sport psychology practitioners.

Presented in ten chapters and an extensive appendix (of forms and letters) to cater to the ranging needs of students, the book addresses basic counselling skills, their place in applied sport psychology, and personal development. The core of the book lies in exploring counselling models and how to counsel client-athletes through beginnings, middles, and endings. It delves more deeply into personal and professional development, especially understanding therapeutic modalities, supervision, and self-care.

Providing a unique focus of basic counselling skills in applied sport psychology, concentrating on the professional relationship between the sport psychology practitioner and client-athlete in applied sport psychology practice, *Counselling Skills in Applied Sport Psychology* is essential reading and practice for upper undergraduates and postgraduates in applied sport psychology and sport and exercise psychology.

Paul McCarthy, PhD leads the taught doctorate in Sport and Exercise Psychology at Glasgow Caledonian University, Scotland. He is a British Psychological Society (BPS)-chartered psychologist, Health and Care Professions Council (HCPC)-registered sport and exercise psychologist and Senior Teaching Fellow. He developed the first taught doctorate in sport and exercise psychology in Scotland and the UK in 2017. Most of his research explores emotion, attention, and motivation among sport performers and the practice of applied sport psychology. He served as editor of *Sport and Exercise Psychology Review* from 2013–2017. He has run his own private practice for the past 20 years, splitting his work time between academic teaching, researching, writing, and supporting clients from amateur to professional levels, especially in golf, football, rugby, gymnastics, and athletics.

Zoe Moffat, PhD is a practitioner psychologist working at the Scottish Institute of Sport. Zoe is a chartered sport and exercise psychologist with the BPS and a practitioner psychologist with the HCPC. Zoe has published several peer-reviewed papers in sport and exercise psychology. She works with Paralympians, Olympians, and professional athletes in several sports, including rugby, golf, and netball.

To Lesley, Liam, Euan, and Niamh, for all time.

Contents

3 Understanding people from a psychological perspective   39

Tables

Acknowledgements

Thank you to David Varley and Megan Smith from Routledge for their encouragement, support, and guidance. Thank you also to the students and staff in the Department of Psychology at Glasgow Caledonian University.

Preface

We are passionate about educating and training aspiring sport psychology practitioners. Our passion for the field of applied sport psychology means we present this book as a first step on the road to becoming a sport psychology practitioner. Learning to counsel in applied sport psychology blends art, science, and practice, so be patient, compassionate, and accepting of yourself as you set off on this long and winding road (Tod, 2007).

It is daunting, though, isn't it, to be confronted with so much to learn? How to start? Where to start? Well, let's just start here. Let us imagine you are setting off down a road you have not travelled before. You are not precisely sure where or when you shall arrive at your destination or whom you shall meet along the way, but you are excited all the same. You cannot complete the journey in one giant leap, so let's enjoy a most serene and civilised way of travelling – one step at a time.

As you begin your quest, you shall need at least one guide or map, which you are reading right now! Our sole purpose in this book is to concentrate your mind on learning the basic counselling skills to serve you when you meet people (e.g., athletes, coaches) along the road. A first step on this journey is to gather your knowledge of basic counselling concepts and theories before you learn on the job. We help you read the map and on you go. You will realise that a map is not the territory; however, as Korzybski (1933/1958, p. 58) explained, "A map is not the territory it represents, but, if correct, it has a similar structure to the territory, which accounts for its usefulness".

The map we sketched takes you on a logical journey of learning. We hope you can dip in and out of this resource, as you might check a map as your journey unfolds. We feel that we have outlined enough information without overloading you at this stage of your personal and professional development to make sound, informed judgements about how to use your skills and services to suit, which models fit, and which do not. At its heart are the values that sustain good practice: empathy, congruence, unconditional positive regard, and warmth.

We wish for our clients to feel safe in our care, so we need to find the right balance between 'being' and 'being there' because sport, in all its forms, seems alluring and enthralling – and while 'giving more' fits the performance narrative, you might find you have no more left to give. In short, you need to care and soothe yourself to be in a place to meet the needs of your clients. Sound practice supervision will see you right because safeguarding the client and you – the practitioner – remains the central goal.

A basic assumption in our work with clients is that we help them move towards their own solutions rather than us providing solutions for them. In sport settings, where most personnel (coaches, trainers, health professionals) tell athletes what to do and how to handle challenges, the principles of choice and self-responsibility feel disquieting initially, but facilitating their choices and the outcomes they seek pays dividends. To achieve this objective, however, we need to work with the client's preferences for service delivery and seek a balance between 'head' and 'heart' theories and practices. We temper the head aspects of judgement, analysis, and calculation with the heart aspects of warmth, simplicity, and defencelessness. Knowing that our biases pull us towards the head or the heart means we can slow our pace, find a resting place, and – perhaps with the succour of others (e.g., peers, supervisors) – make sense of where we are in our helping approach (Feltham & Dryden, 2006).

A fulfilling yet challenging and testing journey lies ahead, so let us take heart from the Latin proverb: *Initium est dimidium facti* (the beginning is half of the deed) and get started.

How is this book organised?

Once we began writing this book, we realised quickly that this book might go on forever, so exhaustive is the list of key concepts and skills for counselling in applied sport psychology, from getting started with a new client, paraphrasing and reflecting feelings, questioning, Socratic questioning, immediacy, structuring and monitoring the helping relationship, homework, giving and receiving feedback, and so much more. We decided this book would serve its readers best if it were introductory rather than exhaustive.

We organised this book into ten chapters and an appendix to help you get a broad understanding of basic counselling skills in applied sport psychology. You might read this book chapter by chapter to get a general understanding of how you could counsel a client-athlete. Or you might use this book like a manual to help you out and guide you as you begin your journey as a trainee sport psychology practitioner. For instance, you might wonder, "How do I establish a contract with a client-athlete?" or "What are useful opening statements when I meet a client-athlete for the first time?" or "What could I include in my case notes?"

We organised the book with several topics that are central to learning to counsel in applied sport psychology and several topics that are peripheral – yet necessary – to your practice. The overarching themes of working with clients are orienting the client to service delivery, assessing the client's concerns, starting change, encouraging change through homework, and working through middles and endings of service delivery. It might seem like the head trumps the heart in working with clients – especially with assessment, evaluation, evidence, and critical thinking running through university training programmes – yet this view misses the heart aspects of compassion, tenderness, warmth, simplicity, defencelessness, and love (Feltham & Dryden, 2006). Sometimes the client-athlete needs a peaceful space, where the pace of life slows to make sense of their problems in living or problems in performance or plan for new horizons. If the head holds judgement, analysis, and rationality, then the heart holds calmness, compassion, and empathy. Together, they are a blend we can trust to speed or slow our pace, to remain open to feeling, and to weigh evidence so that we do not swing so far from the heart or so far from the head.

We focused this book on the verbal and non-verbal skills related to listening and encouraging a client to explore practical and emotional problems in living and performance. We also use these verbal and non-verbal skills to excel in living and performance. Your journey as a sport psychology practitioner begins with understanding psychological principles, training to use your knowledge and skills for the benefit of clients to make their lives better. You travel with your clients, who are experts on themselves with the agency to choose how to change. Good helpers know how valuable it is for the client to engage actively in the helping process, to know themselves better and to choose what actions feel right for them. Good helpers help their clients to identify their thoughts, feelings, physical reactions, and behaviours and put their hands on the best answers to their presenting problems. Before a client walks through our clinic doors, they need to be aware of their situation, their feelings, and the problems or challenges facing them. They also need these elements to be greater than the perceived physical (e.g., time, money) or emotional (e.g., embarrassed, stigma) barriers to seeking help. Clients might legitimately feel that "No one could possibly understand my situation" or "The psychologist will blame me for my actions" or "People will see me as a weak person for seeking help". We, as practitioners, can bear witness to the benefits (e.g., emotional support, guidance to cope) that outweigh the costs (e.g., perceived stigma).

In summary, good helpers develop thorough self-awareness and a facilitative attitude, and they use helping skills well (Hill, 2020). All these skills take time to practise and assimilate into your work with clients, so aim for patience and compassion along the way. It is the interaction of these three parts – self-awareness, attitude, and helping skills – that makes us good practitioners rather than any of the tripartite on its own.

A synopsis of counselling skills

If you have been through your undergraduate studies or postgraduate studies in applied sport psychology, it is likely that you have gathered much knowledge and understanding about personality, motivation, emotion, and several other constructs besides. Practising to be a sport psychology practitioner, however, demands another set of skills and standards about counselling theories, assessments, helping skills, change interventions, ethical and legal guidelines, group dynamics, lifespan development, research, and much more. Our hope for this book is to help you take your first steps towards good counselling in applied sport psychology. With this hope in mind, we focus on cognitive performance skills, cognitive counselling skills, self-awareness, and professional behaviours (Bernard, 1979, 1997; Borders & Brown, 2022).

The counselling performance skills used by a sport psychology practitioner in a therapeutic session with a client-athlete include basic and advanced helping skills (e.g., empathic responding, confrontation, immediacy), theoretical techniques (e.g., reframing, two-chair exercise), and procedural skills (e.g., opening and closing a session and issue-specific skills (e.g., performance evaluation). Cognitive counselling skills refer to how the sport psychology practitioner thinks before, during, and after a session. These skills include case conceptualisation or formulation, which amounts to a comprehensive explanation of the client and the client's issues, which might include themes and patterns. These skills also include the moment-to-moment thoughts and actions of the practitioner in the session – by illustration, what is happening in the session, how to respond to the client, and how to intervene then evaluate one's actions. Self-awareness means capturing one's personal issues, beliefs, and motivations that might influence the in-session behaviour and case conceptualisation. Without self-awareness, it remains frightfully challenging to judge whether the case conceptualisation reflects the true nature of what the client presents. A sport psychology practitioner, based on their personal background, might establish an overly positive or negative view of the client or identify strongly with the presenting issues and feel stuck about how to help the client. Professional behaviours include recognising and adhering to ethical, legal, and professional guidelines and typical behaviours relating to protocols for referrals, writing case notes, and having safety plans for emergencies with clients.

This combination of cognitive performance skills, cognitive counselling skills, self-awareness, and professional behaviours we address within this book reflect one learning modality (i.e., reading); however, you will combine this reading with other learning modalities, such as hearing descriptions from your lecturers and supervisors and experiential learning activities in counselling skills classes. This triptych of reading, hearing, and doing strengthens learning (Borders & Brown, 2022). Not only will you learn how to be a good practitioner, you will learn a lot about yourself and it is this learning about oneself that carries the greatest treasure – personal growth and self-development – for your working life. Remember that most trainees beginning this journey hold only a little awareness of themselves, their strengths and weaknesses, and their motivations. They lack confidence in their skills and feel anxious about their work. This beginning stage gives way to intermediate and advanced stages of personal and professional development, so if you are feeling anxious and diffident just now, you know you are on the right road.

1 Exploring counselling skills in applied sport psychology

Introduction

Being a sport psychology practitioner means learning about yourself, and it also means learning about other people. Each of these challenges counsels us to prepare ourselves so the helping process benefits both parties – the sport psychology practitioner and especially the client. Developing skills to practise as an applied sport psychology practitioner means you begin on the helping journey years before the first client walks through your door and takes a seat in your clinic or stands beside you on a training pitch. Many trainees fear this prospect of a first client; however, taking time and care in the learning process means you will be better prepared for this first session and all those that follow it.

It is natural to feel anxious about this whole process, so we present this book as a guide for you to prepare for your first client. We also hope you have been able to participate in simulated skills sessions with a skilled helper to review your practice and support you. For example, you might train now within triads in your doctoral training programme at university. Whatever your training programme (university-led or self-directed), the more practice we engage with, the easier it feels to begin this work with a first client. But of course, the practice sessions (i.e., triads) with your fellow trainees also foster anxiety, especially learning new skills while another person watches you. The more you practise in this setting, the more comfortable you will become learning about yourself, others, and the counselling skills process. After a while, you will be comfortable with others watching, others' feedback, and being recorded for formative and summative assessments.

Though this situation seems contrived and daunting, remember you bring years of experience talking and listening to others, your interest in people, your caring nature, and a fondness for sport and physical activity, too. What you have already (all these resources) sets you up to learn an additional skill set (basic counselling skills). In the doctoral programme I (Paul) run, students are most concerned about managing their anxiety and being competent. These are typical responses in the early development of a sport psychology practitioner and luckily, these two parts – being anxious and

DOI: 10.4324/9781003453857-1

wishing to be competent – help each other. The more we learn to address our concerns about ourselves, the more we help our client and the less anxious we feel. Working well to work well with others continually pays off because we gather confidence in our abilities, and this confidence acts as a buffer for our anxieties.

With all good challenges in our lives, we need to offer ourselves patience, understanding, and acceptance. These three ingredients (among others) help us be patient with our development and others' development, to understand we develop at our own pace, and to accept all the slips and falls along the way. It has been and remains a privilege to be invited into the life of another person in a therapeutic relationship doing all we can to help benefit the client and ourselves.

The problems presented

Many of the problems presented to a sport psychology practitioner mean working with a client on change at three levels: internal, relational, and developmental. The context within which each of these unfolds helps us to understand the process of change. At an internal level, we have thoughts and feelings; at a relational level, we have relationship issues; and at a developmental level, we have life stage issues.

Here is an example. If an athlete injures himself competing in his sport (context) and will be out of training and competition for six months, there will be other effects on relationships and life stages. The injured athlete might not have the physical capacity to help at home with the usual responsibilities (e.g., childcare), straining his relationship with his partner (relational issues). Because of this long-term injury, his income and associated career might be adversely affected (developmental issues). Together, this load affects one's life and coping through thoughts and feelings (internal issues) (Ballantyne Dykes et al., 2017).

But before we dive into the issues presented, we need to address whether the problem is practical or emotional. In sport, we have a fair share of each, but some problems are best addressed by another professional. A practical problem might mean an athlete lacks the fitness to secure a starting position on a team. The client will want a practical-focused solution to this practical problem (e.g., a tailored fitness regime). For an emotional problem such as anger, anxiety, or guilt, then, these emotions are likely to influence the athlete's life. Here, we will seek an emotion-focused solution to the problem to help the athlete manage their feelings so they do not inadvertently interfere in their sporting life.

In sport, we might have an emotional problem with our practical problem. To illustrate, you might have a contracted tennis coach in your life you would rather not have (i.e., practical problem). You are angry about his lack of understanding and compassion (emotional problem) in training sessions. From a sport psychology practitioner's perspective, it would be best to deal with your anger first before handling the practical problem; otherwise, you might act while angry and make the situation worse.

The clues about whether our problems are emotional or practical usually lie at the heart of a few indicators. First, you experience feelings that hurt and present a sense of stuckness in your life. The emotional problems emerge from emotional pain and stuckness. Second, when we look deeper, we might see self-defeating behaviours leading to greater stuckness. These self-defeating behaviours might be: (1) handling the problem in ways that prolong or exacerbate rather than resolve it, or (2) avoiding opportunities to face the problem. Finally, after the self-defeating feelings and behaviours, we have thoughts and attitudes. These thoughts and attitudes bind self-defeating emotions and unhelpful actions, stalling the emotional problem-solving process. We have just described the emotions/behaviours/thoughts-attitudes schema here (Dryden, 2020) as a mechanism to understand whether we have an emotional problem. Sometimes, a well-meaning friend, coach, or teammate raises the possibility of an emotional problem. You may entertain their suggestion or dismiss it. If you entertain the possibility of an emotional problem, you can use the emotions/behaviours/thoughts-attitudes schema to decide where you stand. You might dismiss their suggestion because you feel they are mistaken or because you would feel ashamed if you admitted you have a problem. It is this feeling of shame that strengthens your resolve to deny this problem.

Regardless of the problems presented – emotional or practical – sport psychology practitioners work to solve problems with clients rather than solve problems **for** clients. One way of solving problems alongside our clients is through good counselling skills. Different professions (e.g., psychologists, nurses, sports coaches) refer to counselling skills as communication skills, helping skills, support skills, and so forth. Good counselling skills support the skills and competencies above them related to their primary role (e.g., nurse) like the foundations of a house (Postings, 2022). A physician with specialist medical knowledge, for instance, shares that knowledge with patients through effective and empathic communication. Though imparting the medical information seems most critical, attending to the listener's emotional expression helps the listener better recall the shared information (Jansen et al., 2010). Being in applied sport psychology, working with teams and backroom teams, means being vigilant for signs that someone needs emotional support in these informal settings. People hide and share information about their emotions, thoughts, behaviour, physical appearance, and physical health – but if you do not know what you are seeing, then these cues and clues go unnoticed. Can you spot signs of worry, stress, tiredness, and irritability? Can you hear negative, pessimistic, and hopeless attributions? Is it possible for you to recognise signs of alcohol or substance misuse? Perhaps you can spot a lack of motivation, avoidance behaviours, and withdrawal. Do you recognise when someone takes less care of their physical appearance and personal hygiene? Would you notice weight loss or weight gain? Is it possible to attend to issues of sleep hygiene?

Noticing these signs means someone might need support, but again, they might not. We need to proceed carefully and sensitively to enquire whether someone needs support (e.g., emotional, medical). If you have been building supportive relationships before this point, it is likely you can identify a need for help and, with trust, the people in your care might choose to help themselves. A sensible and sensitive response to those in our care means offering a private, safe space, with boundaries for them to talk. At this critical moment, we need to listen and respond, offer empathic understanding, and lean on the qualities, values, and skills we learned to create a wholesome and effective helping session (Postings, 2022).

Standards and ethics

Doing good work as a sport psychology practitioner depends on clients being able to trust the sport psychology practitioner. The meaning of this trust for the client might include sharing vulnerabilities, exploring ways to handle problems in living, and/or seeking ways to manage problems in performance. Sport psychology practitioners can use their knowledge and skills to help the client. A qualified sport psychology practitioner helps a client within the limits of standards and ethics set by their professional body (e.g., American Psychological Association [APA], British Psychological Society [BPS], Health and Care Professions Council [HCPC]) to act in the best interests of their clients. These foundations – standards and ethics – keep us as practitioners travelling safely in our profession to serve clients.

The standards (i.e., our competencies) are the safeguards and expertise to offer clients a safe and effective service. During training and after acquiring qualifications, we abide by the competencies and good conduct charted by a professional body. For instance, they set our training standards alongside continuing professional development, supervision, and insurance to practise safely and effectively, so we are fit to practise. Our standards represent the assurance to clients of the competencies we uphold and our accountability in service delivery. When we consider standards, we consider professional knowledge and skills that are measurable or observable so we can evaluate them to ensure they meet the required standards. Our registrations or regulatory bodies for our profession (e.g., HCPC) establish standards of education, training, and competencies to keep clients and practitioners safe.

Ethics is that branch of philosophy which is concerned with human character and conduct. Some people consider ethics and morals as the same thing – what is, or how to distinguish, good from bad? If you think about your morals, you might consider their genesis and development in the culture in which you grew up and the social background particular to you. The distinction between ethics and morals for us as sport psychology practitioners relates to professional ethics. Professional ethics are specific to roles and contexts within a profession. In an everyday sense, we might help our friends make sense of a problem extemporaneously. Yet, professional help fits within boundaries (i.e., terms and conditions), usually in a written contract signed by the client and practitioner. This contract stresses respect, competence, responsibility, and integrity. Without this ethical basis, sport psychology service delivery ceases to defend any worthwhile purpose. When you think critically about sport psychology service delivery, you recognise that a client-athlete, for example, seeks support for problems in living or problems in performance. These issues are their primary concern and they seek reassurance that these issues are also the primary concern of the practitioner, rather than service delivery serving some other purpose. Service delivery, therefore, succeeds only as an ethical relationship (Reeves & Bond, 2021). We shall explore ethical practice in applied psychology, morals, and ethical dilemmas in Chapter 9.

Why are counselling skills important?

This question seems reasonable to ask as you begin your journey of training and working as a sport psychology practitioner. Many people's experiences in sport convince them that a sport psychology practitioner represents another form of coaching – perhaps mental coaching. This assumption seems reasonable because if we have crooked ways of thinking, unhelpful ways of feeling, and awkward ways of behaving, then advice to set you straight must be the right way to proceed. After all, that is what we experience in sports coaching principally. Here, we encounter the first challenge because giving advice "violates the autonomy of the personality" (May, 1993, p. 117). But if athletes seek our advice, why not give the athletes the advice they seek? This ostensibly innocuous transaction happens every day across the world in sport, education, work, family life, friendships, and so forth, so why not in our work? One reason we encourage athletes to help themselves rather than expecting a psychologist to offer advice is that this need for directions and solutions ought to be explored. It is likely that in the therapeutic relationship, the athlete will reveal ways of thinking, feeling, and behaving that reflect their relations with other significant people in their lives. For instance, when we invite others or expect their control over us and agree to the strong views of others, what remains hidden are our skills, abilities, and resources. When the athlete learns more about why he feels secure behaving in this way and insecure trusting his capabilities, a new way of being in the world arises. Recognising an emotional (e.g., worry) or behavioural (e.g., lack of assertiveness) problem, and its origins and its effects, presents clients with a chance to direct their own lives where the opinions and suggestions of others hold no greater or lesser import than their own in their decision-making.

Not only do people in our lives advise, they also might blame, criticise, direct, judge, lecture, moralise, preach, question, teach, threaten, and warn us. Occasionally, we benefit from some of these responses (e.g., advising, teaching, questioning) but, as clients, we often feel at a loss, especially with the power differential emerging in such a relationship with the rise of the expert who knows best. In short, these responses emphasise the power of the other rather than the resourcefulness of the client. When others question, preach, moralise, criticise, or threaten us, we might feel less sure of our autonomy and more certain of our dependency, less certain of our strengths and more certain of our inadequacy and strengthen our resistance to change rather than weaken it. If you think for a moment of those times when you are told that you "must" or "should" think, feel, or do something, how do you feel? Do you feel inferior, guilty, angry, or accepting? Do you feel more or less likely to do as you are told? In a therapeutic alliance with a skilled helper, you are not going through this well-worn format; rather, you experience empathy, genuineness, acceptance, understanding, congruence, and warmth. You will hear examples of reflecting, paraphrasing, and summarising, for example, rather than criticising, blaming, and teaching. This therapeutic alliance aims to restore your sense of self, your strengths, and your capacities and resourcefulness to help yourself and others in your life.

In the next section, we explore what service delivery in applied sport psychology might be like for the client and the sport psychology practitioner. These general stages of beginnings, middles, and endings offer a perspective of what it might be like to be in the 'client's shoes' or the 'sport psychology practitioner's shoes' at each of these stages.

In the client's shoes

Every client attending a therapeutic encounter presents different issues, holds different agendas, and comes with a unique social and cultural history. Before attending, however, the client decides whom to see and if they should see someone to begin a therapeutic alliance. Choosing to seek help for the first time means some level of anxiety and fear, such as worries about what will happen, how the practitioner will receive them, and fears about one's vulnerability. Choosing to see a sport psychology practitioner, for example, also means reasoning about whether now is the right time and which practitioner best fits one's needs. For many athletes, however, their organisation presents the sport psychology practitioner without a choice on the athlete's part, which might or might not suit the athlete's needs and preferences (Cooper & Norcross, 2016). Added to this rigidity lies the typical reinforcement by authority figures (e.g., parents, coaches, physicians, trainers) about how to handle challenges and adversity (i.e., being told what to do), and these demands mean many client-athletes turn up at our door expecting a similar dynamic (Grange, 2010). When a client-athlete receives choice, they also might feel unsure what to do with it in this setting and seek more rescuing (i.e., "Please just tell me what to do").

When a client takes these first steps, it is also likely that they are unsure about the process of the service, the progress being made, and their role in the therapeutic process. It seems plausible to look at service delivery from the perspective of the sport psychology practitioner rather than the client because it might seem like the sport psychology practitioner does the work; however, this assumption misses the point and several other points besides. In short, we need to know whether service delivery meets the needs of the client; we need to know their experiences and what works or does not work. For years in applied sport psychology research, a focus lay on the approaches and actions of the practitioner. Although this work is necessary, researchers now gather evidence from the other chair – the clients' perspectives. The more we understand and appreciate the journey of the client, the better we can be as sport psychology practitioners understanding how it feels to work with us, the commitments to the process, and their reflections when it finishes.

Beginnings

The clients a sport psychology practitioner supports in sport and exercise contexts know much about the emotional and psychological challenges of a life in sport. Some of these challenges, however, might fall into a practical basket while others fall into an emotional basket. With sport psychology practitioners now working with many sports organisations, it is likely that athletes, coaches, and teams recognise sport psychology practitioners as options for support. Sometimes a coach recommends sport psychology support to an athlete and sometimes the athlete attends sport psychology support of their own choice. These autonomous decisions to attend treatment appear to benefit the client more than doing so in response to another's advice (Zuroff et al., 2007). The coach, parent, or colleague advising to see a sport psychology practitioner might well have the best interests of their athletes at heart, while others might exercise control and manipulate the athlete.

One challenge a client experiences symbolises the influence of choice – or lack of choice – in assessing which therapeutic approach and which practitioner suits best. Although most practitioners document their credentials, experience, and approach so a prospective client chooses what is right for them, some organisations present the sport psychology practitioner whom they employed. Choice about gender, age, experience, and so forth often remain out of bounds, with little choice to choose another practitioner because of an ill-fitting relationship. Not only does this forced choice influence the experience of service delivery, the client might well be unaware and unclear of expectations of therapy. Some guidance read online might present a particular picture of service delivery, but the experience of service delivery might not match their image or expectations. Another issue at the beginning of service delivery concerns the client's preference for service delivery. When clients' preferences match the service received, they report greater benefits at the end of therapy (McLeod, 2019; Walls et al., 2016).

Getting started with a practitioner means opening with a contracting phase to understand what the client wants from therapy with an outline of time, length, frequency, and location of sessions, along with confidentiality, payment, payment for missed session, issues of harm to self or others, and so forth. Many practitioners present this information online for the prospective client to read; however, altogether, these challenges running alongside the shame or embarrassment of asking another person for help means some prospective clients never begin working with a sport psychology practitioner. For others, though, this effort reflects a step in the right direction and heartens them because they are taking care of themselves positively (McLeod, 2019).

The content of one's communication (what one communicates) and the process of one's communication (how one communicates) form central pillars in the helping process. To do our work as practitioners, we begin by establishing a relationship, constructing a way of working together, discovering ways to understand the issues presented, supporting how client's structure and implement interventions, and challenging unexpected events. Counselling skills form a bedrock in any caring role. The sport psychology practitioner, for example, sits in a privileged position, listening to how others experience their lives. When support begins, the client, for example, sits in company with a professional, develops a professional relationship, meets regularly, and keeps their time and space free from interruptions and focuses intently on the client's story. The client's story – for example, the problems and difficulties bringing them to seek support – is one which they will judge by the progress made in alleviating their difficulties or moving towards their performance goals. Together, the structural elements of a specified time each week, with a trained professional, weaves with the experience and progress made with the presenting issue.

The professional sitting in the chair opposite the client presents as a source of support to whom the client tells their story. The practitioner might see the client playing a competitive game or training with a squad, for instance. There might be third-party information about them from the coach or a member of the backroom team. On the client's side, there remains a curiosity about this professional, especially who they are and what life they live. This somewhat imbalanced working relationship means the practitioner knows much about the client but the client knows little about the practitioner apart from what they can glean through accent, clothing, perhaps a wedding ring and other little bits of information.

The working relationship, therefore, depends on the connection felt and interpreted by the client. This connection is in the room each week (or at a training ground) and at the moment through the working alliance. Through this connection, the client asks and answers questions such as: "Am I being listened to?" or "Am I being heard?" or "Am I being understood?" or "Am I being respected?" The challenge here means that the client and the practitioner freely and willingly enter this association, but the connection between them then matters. In sport settings, the client might seek a practitioner because of their reputation or association with successful outcomes for other athletes. For example, there might be media coverage of a sport psychology practitioner working with a professional golfer who wins a major championship (e.g., the Open). This association and instant impression can affect much of what happens thereafter, especially the sense of connection between the client and the practitioner. Ethnicity, gender, social class, and race also influence this connection; though beneath it lays the question: "Can I trust this person?" One's competence and skilfulness matters to connect; however, factors such as kindness, dress, and non-verbal, physical presence matter as much, if not more (McLeod, 2019; Pearson & Bulsara, 2016). Through all the research on the qualities of therapists, the deep connection emerges from an authentic, genuine person who is an ally through the change in one's life over the practitioner performing a professional role.

Middles

The middle part of the therapeutic alliance means doing the work – being present in sessions, actively putting what they have learned into action between sessions – but this work challenges most clients because painful emotions (e.g., shame, fear) arrive with exploration. Allied to this exploration means to select and adapt what one learns about oneself to interventions in their lives. This sense-making of one's situation harbours the possibility of behaviour change and such changes also influence others in their lives. The athlete might have a team of support staff, with the sport psychology practitioner being just one. When change happens or does not happen, there will be reactions to manage from the backroom team, family, and friends. A period of slow – or no – change for the athlete among the sporting milieu means someone is getting something wrong and it might well be the sport psychology practitioner. Sport psychology practitioners might pursue unhelpful strategies with a client or forget key information, or be unavailable at critical moments (Richards & Bedi, 2015).

The work on the client's behalf might mean addressing a problem they have avoided for years. Many sports require physical, technical, and tactical expertise to play and perform well, so clients might convince themselves – or be convinced by others – that there is not a psychological basis for their presenting issue. If the client seeks support from a sport psychology practitioner, the commitment to change and the fulfilment of that change might incur time, effort, and engagement far beyond what the client expected initially. Moving from what one learns in therapy to real life presents a myriad of challenges. Change takes time and remains filled with uncertainty, twists and turns, before arriving at a new level of self-awareness, self-knowledge and self-acceptance. Even with the support of a sport psychology practitioner, efforts to change aspects of one's life might relapse and so they need more work to understand, accept, and manage the effects of misfortunes in one's life.

Endings

The end of support from a sport psychology practitioner means quite a difference to the client compared with the sport psychology practitioner. The sport psychology practitioner might not know how the client proceeds once the regular meetings stopped, though they might see their performance outcomes in the media as one possibility. For clients, they now sail away alone without their trusted support, someone who worked with them to overcome their problems. The end of service delivery for clients, therefore, means different things. Some clients hold mixed feelings about the end of therapy (Olivera et al., 2013) because when therapy has gone well, moving on seems manageable. But also, one loses a meaningful relationship. For others, ending a relationship means worry about coping on one's own or perhaps therapy ended before the client felt ready to go alone. The end, therefore, depends on the person and their meaning-making of their relationship.

Some therapeutic relationships follow the beginning, middle, and ending process in the way we have planned it at the outset. But sometimes the client feels as if the practitioner planned an ending without the client's whole input (Råbu & Haavind, 2018). On the other side, many clients stop attending of their own accord. In a broad sense, we know that those who end therapy on their terms are displeased with the service (Marshall et al., 2016), yet, some people stop attending therapy because they feel that they have what they need and they do not need to tell their therapist of their intentions.

Part of the ending of treatment involves evaluating what happened. The client reflects on what it meant and what they gained, while the practitioner explores what happened in sessions and whether the client improved. What practitioners ought to remember most is that service delivery forms part of the support in the client's life that might sit alongside other activities and engagements with other people. Service in the company of a sport psychology practitioner might end, but the client might leave with skills, insights, and support that lives long in memory.

Not all service delivery goes according to plan. Some clients leave the service disappointed. Perhaps the first place to open this event is the issues being addressed at the outset. With physical, technical, tactical, lifestyle, and social support influencing performance and well-being of athletes, the psychological dimension presented to the practitioner might unduly influence one – or a combination – of these factors. It might not be possible to address the psychological challenges without addressing other elements in the jigsaw of performance excellence. Some clients will feel disappointed that emotional issues at the heart of their problems remained unaddressed while an emphasis circled around psychological skills.

In the sport psychology practitioner's shoes

Most athletes, coaches, teams, parents and others seek the support of a sport psychology practitioner because some issues developed and perhaps seemed insurmountable to address alone. The presenting issue might be acute or chronic, occurring idiosyncratically in each case because the levels of support differ and the resources to cope might wax or wane. Though some people aim to help themselves (e.g., self-help books, podcasts), others benefit most from the guidance of a sport psychology practitioner to unpack their difficulties, develop a plan to address them, and work together to implement that plan. The context within which sport psychology practitioners work differs from private practice to professional clubs to national organisations, but their goals remain the same: helping others. What sport psychology practitioners do and how they do what they do gathers more pages in the applied sport psychology literature than how or what their clients do. Most clients (e.g., athlete, coach) seeking the support of a sport psychology practitioner need to: (1) resolve an issue, (2) learn skills and strategies to make their lives better, or (3) contribute to the well-being of others (e.g., coaching). In short, most people walking through the door to see a practitioner know they are 'stuck' and need to 'move on' (McLeod, 2019).

Beginnings

When an athlete, for example, contacts a sport psychology practitioner for support, they might be unaware of how a sport psychology practitioner works with a client. To begin, a sport psychology practitioner aims to offer a safe space for the client – a therapeutic space – within which to work. The sport psychology practitioner also offers a way of being that is like other helping professionals and yet different. This way of being captures a reassuring relationship to work with a client to make sense of their presenting issues while ensuring that the client is safe. The safe space a sport psychology practitioner offers a client to talk seems a basic offering, yet many clients do not have this resource in their lives. Talking and sharing one's thoughts and feelings helps clients to learn, change, and develop; yet, we might take this experience for granted because many clients feel there is no one to tell their story to, or they feel worried or ashamed about what they have been thinking and feeling. Telling one's story to a helping professional, therefore, means hearing one's own story, creating distance to reflect upon it, and creating space for understanding and planning one's next steps. Being a caring, helping professional, creating the right conditions for the client to tell their story, means further understanding of thoughts, feelings, and behaviours. The monologue in the client's head now becomes a dialogue, creating a reality beyond one's self. One's story, how one tells it, and the words used combine to offer a new landscape of perspective for the client.

For this work to happen safely, most practitioners offer a'50-minute' hour in an office each week. Sometimes this work continues online or at training arenas and competitions, too. The basic principle here creates a space for a therapeutic conversation with the privacy and confidentiality to share one's innermost thoughts and feelings – however painful, shameful, or embarrassing they might feel to the client. Let's say the client and sport psychology practitioner meet each week for 12 weeks on a Monday at 4 pm. This time and space becomes an oasis of calm in an otherwise hectic life. What emerges in each session might be a source of encouragement to think, feel, and act in ways that reduce one's problems in living or performance. The challenge for the practitioner to create this safe, therapeutic space means handling issues outside the clinic door (e.g., free from noise and interruptions).

Within this therapeutic space, the unfamiliar practitioner becomes familiar. Their interpersonal style resembles other helping professionals – yet, there are differences. The warmth experienced by the client reflects the non-judgemental stance and acceptance of the client. This acceptance emerges through the beliefs one holds, such as the client's resourcefulness, valuing the person, and a sense that things can improve. The client leads the way, while the practitioner follows. This following comprises reflecting, paraphrasing, and summarising. There are pauses that allow a space for reflection; perhaps asking fewer questions, offering more silence, a slower pace of work, and a softer voice. All this time, the practitioner attends, observes, and listens. Though such behaviour seems strange initially, it becomes familiar. Somehow, the practitioner's view and reflections might differ from the clients. The sport psychology practitioner's way of being also requires much of what athletes possess: courage and persistence. The pain, sadness, or despondency which we might readily limit or avoid in our own lives needs to be tolerated in the therapeutic encounter, with the persistence to return to these issues which the client might wish to mitigate or avoid.

The way of being of the therapist presents a model to the client about how to think about their issues with patience, understanding, and respect. The calm, understanding, and tranquil space in the clinic might also offer the space for reflection in the client's life. As the sessions pass by, the professional relationship excavates a personal dimension unlike any other professional relationship because what unfolds affects the professional, too. While a coach, physiotherapist, or performance manager, among others, spends time with an athlete, this deeply personal relationship with the sport psychology practitioner focuses on making the relationship work. This good relationship offers a model for repairing one's relationship with oneself or others; however, there will be challenges along the way because the client needs to build trust and feel whether the practitioner genuinely cares for them. Most clients bring with them their understanding and experience of relationships (e.g., family, friends, squad members, coaches), which means understanding this helping relationship in these other relationships.

Middles

From the layperson's perspective on the outside looking in, it might seem that the practitioner fixes the problems of the client – and many trainees enter training with a similar view. Instead, the client explores their problems to make sense of them and figure a way out in a supportive relationship with the sport psychology practitioner. But most clients enter the helping relationship with a sense of 'stuckness' in which they do not know what to do next. Through training, experience, and supervision, the sport psychology practitioner learns about how people think, feel, and act with a toolbox to make sense of troubling emotions, unhelpful thinking, and problematic behaviours and relationships. This toolbox of concepts, models, and theories from sport psychology and related fields aligned with therapeutic modalities (e.g., cognitive-behavioural therapy [CBT]) helps in the helping process, but it is their judicious use that helps the client make sense of their problems and ending the helping relationship with an intelligible perspective on their lives.

Achieving these goals, however, means adhering to sound ethical principles and practice. Although a commitment to place the client first might be challenged occasionally, practitioners work to avoid doing harm to clients by developing competence in therapeutic techniques, monitoring, and seeking feedback from clients, supervisors, and peers, updating skills as they progress through their careers.

Sport psychology practitioners learn specific practices in training and hone them over years of practice, reflection, and supervision. Practitioners wish to know how to practise best and offer the best service to a client. Much of the practitioner's work lies in micro-skills, interventions, and techniques, which we explore later. When we think about the work a sport psychology practitioner does with a client, we think about micro-skills – brief sequences of interaction between them. These micro-skills form the basis of competence and allow service delivery to flow. Attending, observing, and listening represent skills one develops as basic counselling skills. Listening, for example, means attending to the client's verbal and non-verbal content, noting how the client speaks and what implicit meaning might lie behind their communication. When we attend, we lean forward, showing curiosity in the client's story, while attending to our own awareness as a listener. When we listen, we do so intently, following the client's story and clarifying what we hear through reflecting, restating, paraphrasing, and summarising. These micro-skills allow us to reassure the speaker that we are following them. We tentatively reflect on what we hear, leaving space for the client to correct or refine the summary. The pace and tone of interaction reflect the issues the client presents. Sometimes the practitioner allows silences to develop to stay with a feeling or process an aspect of an issue. In everyday conversation, silence might feel awkward and unsettling – and so, too, in the therapeutic work practitioners can guide the client through. The informal nature of sport psychology within an organisation means that while there is one-to-one work in formal times, the sport psychology practitioner will see their clients informally at lunch, travelling, at the training arena, and other places. There is an informal self-disclosure here because the client sees the sport psychology practitioner going about their working life. They can see what they eat, with whom they socialise, the car they drive, perhaps a child seat in the car, and so on. In formal self-disclosure, a sport psychology practitioner might tell a story about themselves that resonates with the client.

Perhaps the most difficult process for a practitioner is challenging or confronting a client because it rubs against the supportive role they hold with the usual encouraging responses. Challenging an athlete about particular behaviours or attitudes puts the therapeutic relationship at risk, yet it is the practitioner's judgement here about what feels right. One danger in sport settings is the norms of attitude and behaviour which might suggest commitment at all times, positivity, resilience, and so on, which become the values of the sport psychology practitioner – and yet, the client might not be ready for this perspective. At other times, the client needs and wants this challenge, confrontation, and feedback as a perspective on how they are handling a problem in living. The high-stakes nature of confronting and challenging a client means sensibly and sensitively presenting the information and perhaps the discrepancies between what the client wishes for and what the client is doing (McLeod, 2019).

Endings

It might seem from the outside that the sport psychology practitioner dips into a bag of interventions and techniques, pulls one out, and applies it to the athlete or team. If it works well, then that is the end of their work with the client; however, the reality presents so differently. In this view, the power lies with the sport psychology practitioner rather than the client, engendering dependence rather than independence. The sport psychology practitioner aims to empower the client so that the client and the sport psychology practitioner can judge the most suitable ending to their relationship (i.e., when the goals for service delivery are met). Through their work with the sport psychology practitioner, clients learn to help themselves, solve their problems, seek support where necessary, and lead independent lives. Choosing to end a relationship works best when both parties – client and practitioner – feel ready to end the therapeutic relationship because they completed the tasks to meet their goals.

Different working alliances have different conclusions. Nelson-Jones (2016) presented the following endings: fixed, open, faded, and booster sessions (see Chapter 8). In sport and exercise settings, sport psychology practitioners encounter a range of endings that ought to be explored to understand more about the service delivery and the needs and preferences of the client. The endings also present an opportunity to reflect on process success and outcome success or some variation of each (see Chapter 8). Maybe the sport psychology practitioner achieved process success in helping the golfer, for example, to manage their worries on the course; however, the golfer performed better but did not win the tournament (i.e., outcome success).

Maybe the sport psychologist could not play her role because other members of the multidisciplinary team held authority. Although a multidisciplinary team, like the Knights of the Round Table, assumes equal roles, they may afford unequal space to their musings. A golfer in a slump might seek solace in a new backswing take-away or forearm rotation, but it is not always easy to discriminate sharply between technical difficulties and emotional ones. Has the practical problem of an unsuitable club path led to an emotional instability about one's ability to strike the ball well and compete competently under the strain of competition? The challenge for any multidisciplinary team is to decide where to drop anchor – in the waters of emotion or technique. Often a tug-of-war ensues between the two perspectives: one towards procedure, mechanics, and technology; the other towards attitude and processes.

Under the floorboards of one's mind lies the theoretical complexity that guides the practical simplicity of formulations and interventions with athletes. We make explicit this implicit knowledge so the athlete can judge the accuracy and fit of the proposed intervention. Yoking an athlete to a course of action that does not sit well seems a regrettable footing from which to begin a journey towards change. A danger at this stage is the stream of information that might overwhelm rather than coalesce and raise the confidence in perpetuity. The golfer's tragedy is that he cannot play for himself and enjoy the game for its own sake; his efforts gush through the storm drain of perfecting his mechanics. There is a rhythm to practice and performance that swings from magnificent to mediocre with neither rhyme nor reason, so we sit forlornly searching for acceptable answers. A misfortune in the mailbox or inbox of most sport psychology practitioners is the case that has papered over the cracks and someone hands the problem to the sport psychology practitioner.

Summary

In this chapter, we have explored counselling skills in applied sport psychology. First, we defined the problems presented to a sport psychology practitioner and the challenges of being in the field, such as adhering to the standards and ethics required by our professional bodies and working to meet clients' needs. We then drew attention to the importance of basic counselling skills and presented an overview of the beginnings, middles, and endings for a client and a sport psychology practitioner. Our next task is to explore more about you, the trainee, with a focus upon personal development, self-awareness, self-knowledge, and self-acceptance.

2 Understanding your self

Introduction

According to legend, carved into stone at the entrance to Apollo's temple at Delphi in Greece is the inscription: "Know thyself". This injunction, rather than question, encouraged people to search for self-knowledge and self-understanding. A quest for self-understanding still has cachet today – 2,300 years later – especially in helping others, because by developing our self-awareness, we can monitor and possibly understand what goes on within. Without knowing ourselves and accepting ourselves, we impede our ability to help others. Self-awareness is a continuous and rolling process to get to know who we are by monitoring thoughts, feelings, intuitions, attitudes, beliefs, and sensations, and how these manifest themselves in our behaviour. When we pretend or avoid knowing ourselves, we leave parts of us hidden in darkness. Opening ourselves up to self-understanding allows the light to reach those dark, untended corners within us, generating empathy and genuineness which helps us to understand what makes other people tick (Sutton & Stewart, 2017).

Helping ourselves to become well adjusted, productive, and fully functioning, people often depend on compassion, forgiveness, hope, love, and selflessness. In a world where the voice in our heads undermines our well-being, we need to focus on ourselves and stride along with such human flourishing and harness the mental apparatus in our head. If we jump back thousands of years before civilisation in Ancient Greece, to our prehistoric hunters, gatherers, and scavengers, for the first time people could think about themselves and their lives to plan, act, and solve problems more skilfully than any other creature on earth. The self refers to the mental machinery that allows people to think consciously about themselves (Leary, 2004). In this chapter, we explore more about self-awareness and how it leads to self-knowledge and self-understanding – critical foundations for a safe, ethical, and professional practitioner in applied sport psychology.

Knowing me, knowing you

When we work with another person, we bring with us all our life experiences, thoughts, feelings, memories, attitudes, values, and beliefs to the helping

DOI: 10.4324/9781003453857-2

relationship. What we bring influences the relationship in helpful and less help-ful ways. Being a sport psychology practitioner means learning about yourself. If you do not wish to learn about yourself, being a sport psychology prac-titioner is not the right job for you. Why, as sport psychology practitioners, do we need to know ourselves? To begin, when we work with an athlete, for example, the athlete shares the troubles in their life, so we work together for a more satisfactory change of direction. Because we are involved in this process as a sport psychology practitioner, their issues mean something to us, too, as a person and as a professional. Many of these 'problems in living' or 'problems in performance' involve anger, anxiety, fear, and other painful emotions often aris-ing out of difficulties in relationships or traumatic life events (e.g., losing one's professional contract). To manage any of these 'problems in living' or 'prob-lems in performance', we need to trust another person to provide a safe and supportive relationship to solve the issue at hand. This relationship, however, does not happen by accident and depends upon the person and their qualities as a helper. If we think about these circumstances, we see the practitioner needs to look at themselves and how others experience them. In short, the practitioner maximises those qualities that help and minimises those tendencies that hurt. But how do we know which of those we bring to the relationship?

We need to be aware of ourselves and commit to changing through personal learning, leading to personal growth. This self that learns and grows helps the helping relationship along. We refer to this work as personal development. Each person will present a different agenda for learning – and within this agenda, we might cover values, how we think, how we feel, how we act, how we explain the events in our lives, and many more. The second part of this work involves other people because though we are learning about ourselves, we are learning about ourselves in relation to others. This 'development' continues for our lifetimes. The good sport psychology practitioner knows the value of personal develop-ment and so pursues it for personal gain and relational gain for those seeking support in their lives. This openness to explore ourselves and our relations with others, to reflect on our experiences, to make sense of life events – and to rec-ognise current themes and ongoing themes – is an unending process. This jour-ney of discovery, though personal, finds its way into the helping encounter, so our personal development has a fluid boundary with professional development. Professional development reflects knowledge and skills for one's line of work. In applied sport psychology, we, as practitioners, are the tools in the change process, so our personal development leads to our professional development; however, to distinguish one from the other, we shall begin with understanding personal development before tackling professional development.

What is personal development?

Personal development encompasses so many facets that an encompassing defi-nition can be difficult to locate, but we can begin with this opening definition. Personal development comprises long-term *learning* and *reflection* through life experience and professional practice, presenting new ways of understanding the self and others to benefit the self and the clients one supports (McLeod & McLeod, 2022). It seems a strange paradox to expect a client to learn about themselves and change but be unwilling to do so yourself, as a practitioner.

Personal development sits as a lifelong and career-long process, not an event. The centrality of the working alliance between client and practitioner for client outcomes means that the practitioner plays a crucial role by being present as herself or himself in the relationship. But being present as oneself is challenging because we bring with us many defences, assumptions, and biases to the relationship, and because encouraging growth in others presents interpersonal and intrapersonal challenges. Through personal and professional development, we develop self-awareness, self-knowledge, awareness of others, openness to others, and an openness to growth and self-acceptance.

Self-awareness, self-knowledge, and self-acceptance seem like sound building blocks for anyone helping another through a change process. With our 'self' as the principal tool or instrument of change, personal development seems inevitable. If personal development means awareness, knowledge, understanding, and acceptance of self and others, then it sits alongside our development through life – but it is a purposeful process, not aimless. Learning at university, for example, usually comprises awareness, skills, and knowledge (which creates the acronym ASK) but we spend most time and effort on knowledge (e.g., theory, concepts), less on skills (e.g., counselling skills), and little if any attention to awareness (e.g., self, other) (Johns, 2012). For our work as lecturers and supervisors with applied sport psychology practitioners in training, we need to begin with specifics to explain self, development, and growth.

Self-awareness

Self-awareness means knowing and understanding yourself. Being aware of our emotional, mental, moral, physical, social, and spiritual qualities makes us who we are now as we develop towards our potential (Sutton & Stewart, 2017). In these terms, self-awareness seems straightforward, but have you ever wondered why you do what you do? It is likely you have reflected deeply on different parts of your life (e.g., a relationship) and yet other parts (e.g., the sports you play) remain squashed into the darker corners of our mind. One golf professional likened self-awareness to investigating every pocket in her tour bag (which had lots of pockets!). Some people think about self-awareness as exploring every room in their house, acknowledging what needs to be tidied, repaired, removed, and modernised (Ballantyne Dykes et al., 2017). Like most families, we use some rooms more than others. We might notice how tired, dimly lit, and uninviting a room might appear. Perhaps there are parts of ourselves that resonate with that room. We need to draw back the curtains, let the daylight fill the room, and figure what needs to change. I (Paul) grew up in an old farmhouse with lots of rooms, and one room remained shut. I was always curious to know what treasures or horrors I might find inside it. Perhaps you know of sealed rooms that represent hurt, loss, failures, and painful feelings you wish to keep out of sight and out of mind; however, part of our self-awareness and personal development means opening these rooms, cellars, or secret passages to be tended and restored. We need not undertake this exploration and refurbishment alone. We can request help. Those rooms you are frightened to open because you cannot be certain what you might find when you turn the handle on the door; you can open in a safe, respectful, and empathic relationship with a psychotherapist, supervisor, or encounter group.

One way to develop self-aware sport psychology practitioners is through reflective practice. Anderson et al. (2004) outlined personal journal writing, supervision, and professional sharing through conferences and peer-reviewed journals as the main mechanisms for steering reflective practice. They acknowledged that one limit to reflective practice conducted alone is that the sport psychology practitioner's self-knowledge limits the practitioner, so what they need is the resource of another trusted, well-intentioned, and skilled practitioner to challenge and support their development (Winstone & Gervis, 2006).

Several researchers and practitioners acknowledged the centrality of self-awareness in practitioner–athlete relationships to deliver sport psychology support successfully (Danish, 1985; Giges, 1998; Orlick & Partington, 1987; Petitpas et al., 1999). Two related issues often arise in practitioner–athlete relationships: transference and countertransference. Transference occurs when the person, situation, or relationship trigger thoughts and feelings from a previous relationship. Countertransference occurs when the client triggers thoughts and feelings in the sport psychology practitioner (Winstone & Gervis, 2006). Countertransference features because we are human and our quotidian experiences and relationships prompt unresolved emotional conflicts (Hayes, 2004). If we learn from our past interactions, we tend to apply this learning to other interpersonal encounters. Learning to be compliant or defiant in relationships with authority figures means we are likely to continue this process of interaction with a sport psychology practitioner. Knowing this information means that we, as sport psychology practitioners, should sensitively appreciate what might be happening in the therapeutic alliance with the client (Giges, 1998; Petitpas et al., 1999). With countertransference, we need to be self-aware to recognise how we react to clients during interactions with them. Recognising our thoughts and feelings helps us to corral what is ours and what is theirs (i.e., the client's) so we can focus on their goals rather than ours.

It is challenging to separate the person from the process of service delivery because sport psychology practitioners are the instruments of service delivery (McEwan et al., 2019; Tod et al., 2017; Wadsworth et al., 2021). This weaving of the personal and professional means we need to develop self-awareness and reflective practice as one way to do so. According to Knowles et al. (2014, p. 10), reflective practice is:

A purposeful and complex process that facilitates the examination of experience by questioning the whole self and our agency within the context of practice. This examination transforms experience into learning, which helps us to access, make sense of, and develop our knowledge-in-action to better understand and/or improve practice and the situation in which it occurs.

This definition focuses on the whole self to understand who we are and how we influence service delivery in sport psychology. One's whole self reflects personal and professional identities, core values, and beliefs which influence one's choice of philosophy and theoretical paradigm for practice (Wadsworth et al., 2021).

Exercise 2.1: Mapping your life to develop self-awareness

Reflective practice has been, and remains, a foundational component of learning and practising as a sport psychology practitioner. Supervision and personal therapy support the reflective practice process throughout our careers. Whether you are beginning your journey or at some juncture through your journey, mapping your life journey or 'life chart' (Adolf Meyer, 1866–1950) to date can enlighten and inspire (Meyer, 1935). You can begin from your birth date and chart your life to the present day. Some trainees enjoy drawing and colouring their life events on a large sheet of paper with the timeline showing 'highs' and 'lows' in chronological order. Remember, this exercise will take some time and it might suit you best to spread it over several sessions.

Here are some suggestions for mapping the time points in your life journey:

- When were you born? What was the make-up of your family? Where did you come in the family? Do you remember to whom you were closest? What did if feel like being a child in your family?
- What can you remember about your childhood? For example, any significant events, successes, failures, illnesses, grief and loss, changes in your family, your school days, and so on. You can repeat this step by thinking about other stages in your life (e.g., young adulthood) as you move along your timeline.
- Try to consider 'now' and 'then'. Can you recall the thoughts, feelings, and behaviours associated with these events (e.g., a birthday, arrival of a new sibling) at the time, and how you feel about them now?
- Some people like to speak with family and friends to fill in the gaps or details when memories might be blurred. This life chart is yours, so you can choose with whom you wish to share it.

Trainees also like to include specifics that relate to arriving at their training programme. Following are some questions to guide you.

- When did you first become interested in applied sport psychology?
- Which life events influenced your interest in applied sport psychology?
- Did you ever meet or work with a sport psychology practitioner?
- Which people or events influenced your choice to study psychology?
- Which relationships played a role in your training to become a sport psychology practitioner?

This timeline of personal events will be significant to you and perhaps differ considerably from fellow trainees. McCarthy and Jones (2013) invited sport psychology practitioners from around the world to share their life journey of becoming sport psychology practitioners. Their stories share similarities and differences, but the collage of stories reaffirms to us that the journey to becoming a sport psychology practitioner almost always emerges through a passion to help others.

But when we scratch the surface of motives to be a helper – a person who eases the suffering of others, comforts the wounded, and empowers those who wish to excel in a public arena – we see a patchwork of motives admirable and contemptible, conscious and unconscious. In short, their motives are many and intertwined. The conscious, socially desirable, and professionally acceptable reasons for becoming a sport psychology practitioner obfuscate the completeness of this picture. The altruistic motive of 'wanting to help people' seems incomplete (Norcross & Farber, 2005). No doubt, there lies a deep motive to heal and grow the self. To paraphrase the findings from other fields of helping, there is a sport psychology practitioner in the client and a client in the sport psychology practitioner (Rippere & Williams, 1985). Our struggles and the struggles of our clients enter the frame together; however, it is mostly the client in the foreground and the sport psychology practitioner in the background. Sport psychology practitioners heal and grow in their work – and if they do, they benefit and so also do their clients.

Through personal development, we – as sport psychology practitioners – enhance our self-awareness. This awareness helps us recognise when our agendas, beliefs, attitudes, and opinions encroach on working with others. While our self-defeating behaviours and patterns of relating are identified, our helpful personal attributes are, too (Postings, 2022), and we realise how we can separate our needs from the needs of the client. For whatever reasons, you have found yourself training or practising as a sport psychology practitioner. Some of the wounds from the past were inflicted upon us, some we inflicted upon ourselves responding to trauma, core shame, and damaged self-esteem. This wounded nature presents healing, too. But we ought to know how, when, where, and why we were wounded to prevent it from leaking onto others (e.g., rescuing). The echo from a client who has been deselected from a football academy might resonate with our pain of deselection in a similar setting and perhaps the ensuing loss of a professional career. To defend and protect ourselves, we might slip past the issue, advise, criticise, placate, or dismiss the feelings. Our old ways of coping rush in to save us; however, we can learn and grow through self-awareness. Knowing our behaviours that self-heal and those that self-harm or self-defeat works well for our helping work, relationships, and widening gyre of our lives. Norcross and Farber (2005) cautioned us to remember how much chance plays in our lives and career choices. Chance shapes the course of our lives and our professional careers, as the contributors in McCarthy and Jones (2013) illustrated. Perhaps the chance encounters nudge us down the road we wished to travel. In our experience, echoing the words of Robert Frost, we took the road less travelled by, and that has made all the difference.

Case study: Jessica

Jessica swam internationally since she was 15 years old. Now aged 20, she struggled with performance and well-being issues. One of our early homework exercises was to create a life chart. Jessica felt that this homework exercise would be straightforward because she had kept a training diary since the age of 10. When she returned, she had drawn an elaborate and detailed life map with a key to find an account of the events in her journal. What seemed most perplexing was the lack of feelings in her journal. She had described significant life events in a matter-of-fact way (moving home, moving schools, illness in the family, an alcoholic mother, a troubled older brother). When I reflected I could not gather how she felt 'now' or 'then' from reading her life map or journal, Jessica said, "You know, I didn't even ask myself how I felt. It was as if I conveniently forgot to share how I felt now and then. Let me try that exercise again".

When Jessica returned the following week, she had completed the exercise. She explained how upsetting and unsettling, yet relieving, the whole experience had been for her.

> I started on Sunday morning and it took me most of the day. I know you said how unsettling this activity might be for me and to take my time and perhaps do it in stages, but once I started, I couldn't stop. And I couldn't stop crying either. Look, the pages are all smudged and the ink too.

Writing about her early childhood and her older brother, she wrote,

> John always seemed in trouble. He was six years older than me and he couldn't do anything right in my parents' eyes. I didn't like the shouting in my house, so I just tried to be good all the time so I wouldn't cause any shouting. I'm not sure I was ever a child – a carefree child. I was always looking after people. I felt afraid then, and I feel angry now.

Jessica reflected, saying that she did not need other people, but they seemed to need her a lot, especially her mother.

The next significant event was when Jessica was aged 9 when they moved house and schools for her father's job. She recalled her father always seemed anxious or angry, but not at the swimming pool. He always seemed to enjoy the swimming pool. She realised how much strain he was under with his job and providing for the family.

> You know, writing this piece now, I can see why I started swimming. It kept Dad happy and out of the house, and somehow I made that happen.

I could control things. Dad kept everything together in our house and in our family, so I felt I had to keep him together.

Keeping her father happy meant her father could manage better with the strain of work and his marriage.

He ran a successful business and showered Mum with gifts and holidays to keep her happy, but it never lasted long. She went through good times and bad times. The good times were when she was drinking and the bad times were when she was drinking. She kept herself and our house immaculate. Dad's friends used to rag him saying that it must have been his money, not his looks, that won her over.

Jessica wondered: "Is this why I am so vigilant of others, reading their moods, trying to keep them happy?".

Another significant incident was at the height of her eating disorder, for which she was receiving ongoing treatment from a clinical psychologist. She recalled it was a bleak time emotionally.

I was in control and I loved it. And then I wasn't in control. And I would swing between the two all the time. I trained like a robot and swam my best times. I was in control in the pool and I didn't want to leave. One day I collapsed at the training centre and I woke up in the hospital. I was destroying myself and I thought I was being such a good girl.

Jessica's life chart brought a clarity and insight she had not realised. This self-awareness exercise helped her to separate the tangled strands of her life and recognise how emotional, mental, moral, physical, social, and spiritual qualities intertwine, and how they need her care and compassion.

Seeing what we cannot see

Reflective practice helps us to see our strengths and limitations as developing professionals. Some of us can only see our limitations and dismiss or disregard our strengths and need the support of others to rebalance that pictures. Strengths and limitations known to us and known to others raise the question: are there aspects of ourselves that others know but we do not? Others know our habits, perhaps a little better than we do. Our friends and family see our facial expressions, our leaning towards things we prefer and away from things we fear. These 'blind spots' of ours have much to tell us about ourselves. Joseph Luft (Jo) and Harrington Ingham (Hari) (1955) developed a model – the Johari window – to illustrate what we know and do not know about ourselves in relation to others. In this model (see Table 2.1), there are four quadrants. In the 'open' quadrant, there are aspects of ourselves known to us and known to others, while the 'hidden'

Table 2.1 Your Johari Window

	Known to Self	Not Known to Self
Known to Others	Open	Blind
Not Known to Others	Hidden	Unknown

Table 2.2 Jordan's Johari Window

	Known to Jordan	Not Known to Jordan
Known to Jordan's Teammates	'Open' quadrant Confident Outgoing Cheerful Intense	'Blind spot' Easily distracted Dominates the conversation Assertive Respected by others
Not Known to Jordan's Teammates	'Hidden' quadrant Tense Uncertain Need to be liked	'Unknown'

quadrant holds those aspects we keep hidden from others. There might well be things unknown to us and others (e.g., underlying medical condition) as well as the 'blind spots' which others know about us but we do not know about ourselves.

Case study: Jordan

Jordan, the team captain at a professional football club, exhibited a confident, outgoing, and cheerful demeanour around the training ground. What they also know, Jordan and his teammates, is that he is intense, especially on the training pitch, and there seems little balance to this intensity. What his teammates noticed, but Jordan remained unaware of, is that opposing players distracted him easily and he took too much notice of them. Jordan talked much more than he listened, and it felt like he could not hear suggestions or instructions on the pitch from others. They admired his assertiveness on and off the pitch, especially improving conditions for the players, which earned their respect; these qualities Jordan did not recognise in himself – he felt that he was "just doing his job". What his teammates did not know about Jordan was how tense he felt in his role and how uncertain he felt about the job he was doing as captain and how much he needed others to like him.

The information gathered in a Johari window extends a choice point to you. The information in these quadrants changes over time; however, we have a choice to stretch ourselves and to grow in ways we might have been less willing to address in the past. As trainee sport psychology practitioners, you study, reflect, and practise, intending to meet course requirements and assessments.

In a similar vein, you widen and deepen your skill set as a practitioner, much like the athletes we support. We need to work deliberately to improve our skill set, to improve ourselves, and to improve our service delivery (Stafford & Bond, 2020).

How we protect ourselves

Many of us are unlikely to process our thoughts, feelings, physical reactions, and behaviours. Instead, we choose ways to defend or protect ourselves because we sense a threat and feel a sense of foreboding. Protecting ourselves from pain is atavistic. When we hide from danger, we feel better, at least momentarily. If a savage dog threatened us, we might seek a safe place. This behaviour is clear and visible; however, sometimes we are unaware of our defence mechanisms – ways to protect ourselves from ourselves (and others). After a loss, we might shrug it off and say it did not matter that much to us. This denial helps in the short term to ease the pain of loss, but it might hurt us much more than we will show, and other problems arise because of how we protected ourselves. Our 'defence mechanisms' and 'safety-seeking behaviours' might obfuscate what we need to see to change our lives. Let us address some of these defences next and read some examples.

1. Denial – refusing to accept reality about you, others, and the world. You might deny that you are upset about being dropped from a squad. This denial protects you from the sadness and worry that truly is there.
2. Displacement – redirecting thoughts, feelings, and behaviours from the person to whom they are inappropriate towards another person, animal, or object to whom or which they are inappropriate.
3. Projection – attributing our feelings and motivations to others. When we have failed to live up to a standard, we blame others for the difficulties we experience. For example, a player might believe that he scores the goals and does not need to track back and help his team – they do the work and he takes the spoils. When he finds himself sidelined because of poor form, he blames his team and the manager, claiming they do not help him in his hour of need. He projected his lack of helpfulness onto others to protect himself from taking any responsibility for his current circumstances.
4. Rationalisation – giving socially acceptable reasons for our behaviour that are false. The genuine reasons seem too upsetting, so we present what is socially acceptable. If a friend were to ask whether to join her at the gym, she might decline citing "a lack of time" or "too many things on right now" when in fact, she cannot afford the fees but it would be too upsetting to admit this circumstance.
5. Reaction formation – behaving in a way different from how one usually behaves. These actions protect one from accepting oneself as they are.
6. Repression – preventing our thoughts or feelings from entering our consciousness that might upset us.

7. Splitting – viewing the world in black and white. We protect ourselves by categorising people and events as good or bad, right or wrong, and so on. Life and people and events present complexities, but we protect ourselves from the emotional challenges of, for instance, loving someone even though they behave in ways we do not favour.

Safety-seeking behaviours and avoidance

Safety-seeking behaviours (also called safety behaviours) and avoidance, similar to our 'defence mechanisms', are ways to protect ourselves from the feared catastrophe from happening. Many athletes avoid, escape, or try so hard to stop a catastrophe that much of what they can learn about themselves and the situation remains hidden. For instance, the event you fear might not happen. If it happens, you will cope. Finally, the feared event might be a hassle, feel uncomfortable, or unpleasant – but seldom is it unbearable.

When someone is completely avoiding a situation, we can spot it easily; however, safety-seeking behaviours are usually less obvious because they are often subtle or outside our awareness. To recognise safety-seeking behaviours, we need to observe ourselves. One simple way to achieve this goal is to take part in a situation you fear and note how you keep yourself safe. We can also imagine ourselves in a situation and note how we see ourselves behaving. Jess, a basketball player, struggled to approach her coach about changes to the starting line-up that affected her confidence each week. She imagined herself in her coach's office, avoiding eye contact, apologising before she made her point, and speaking softly and hesitantly, hoping to get out of her office quickly.

Here are some examples. You might use self-protective moves to hide your 'weaknesses'. Or, you might aim to please everyone to gain their approval, or try to do everything 'right'. Another way to protect yourself is to keep yourself to yourself. You might hide your anger because you feel you need to accommodate what others expect of you, and displaying anger might not be expected or accepted.

Biased thinking

We all think in a biased way from time to time. Sometimes, however, our biased or crooked thinking means we fall into our own thinking traps, which affect our lives to different degrees. Sometimes these faulty ways of thinking mean we inadvertently fall into a bad mood. Here is the list of faulty thinking biases in alphabetical order.

- Black and white thinking. Like splitting we wrote about earlier, there are two sides, either black or white: things are good or bad, right or wrong. Yet, the realities of life mean there are many more shades here. Here are a few examples: "If I can't score the conversions, I might as well not play at all" or "The mistake early in the game ruined the whole game for me" or "If I make a mistake, the game is over".

- Catastrophising. This faulty thinking is predicting the worst outcome. For instance, "If I make one wrong move, the coach will never play me again".
- Discounting the positive. This means filtering all the positive things as if they held no value. "He said I played well to make me feel better" or "I could figure nothing out on my own" or "I was lucky today, the ball fell to me, and anyone could score from there".
- Exaggerating. Here, we highlight the negative and give them prime attention, regardless of their importance. "I'll never recover from that mistake – there's no way back" or "Getting selected means nothing; it's all about not making mistakes".
- Emotional reasoning. In this reasoning, we mix up feelings with facts. "I'm so nervous, I'm going to have an awful game" or "I haven't heard from the coach yet so I'm definitely dropped".
- Fortune telling. Here we try to predict. "I'll never cope on my own" or "That trial run was so bad, I know they will not ask me back" or "I'll never defend properly".
- Mind reading. Here, we believe we know what others are thinking. "She doesn't like me" or "He knows how useless I am" or "They all think I'm hopeless as captain".
- Name calling. Calling ourselves names that are unfair. "I'm a fool" or "I'm useless" or "I'm cold and heartless".
- Overgeneralising. Thinking that if something occurred once, it will always occur. "I always mess up" or "I just can't seem to get my point across ever" or "I never get things right".
- Personalising. Here we take things personally. For instance, "They're laughing at me" or "She always ignores me".
- Taking the blame. In this faulty thinking example, we accept responsibility readily when it is not ours to take. For example, "He would have won the race if I had trained him better" or "If only I had worked harder, the team would not have made any mistakes".
- Scare mongering. "What if she gets injured?" or "What if the equipment breaks?" or "Some athletes just freeze and don't perform".
- Wishful thinking. Thinking things would be better if they were different. "If I were thinner, everyone would value me" or "If only I were smarter, my life would be so much better".

This list of faulty thinking errors is common to us all. What we need to do is watch out for them in our lives so we can choose to change them. Sometimes, words we use seem so natural and acceptable that we do not explore their meaning and effect on our feelings. Words like 'should', 'must', 'ought to', 'have to', 'always', and 'never' influence us by putting unnecessary and unfair pressure on us. These words and phrases abound in sport with the intention to 'motivate' ourselves or others, but these demands often overwhelm and the motivation intended fades away with strong feelings of guilt because we didn't live up to the 'standard'. If you listen carefully, you will hear these statements in training and competition. For instance, a defender might say to a midfielder, "You always leave me exposed at the back" or "You never listen to my instructions" or "Nobody sees the effort I put into making tackles".

All of what we have presented helps us to identify our thoughts, and these are thoughts, not truths or facts – just thoughts. Even if we think we are stupid, it does not mean we are stupid. And because our thoughts are just thoughts, we need to assess them, evaluate them, and make sense of them. We need to judge their value, accuracy, and meaning. These thinking foibles might slacken your motivation towards change and the possibilities of a different way of living and a stirring attitude to live with vitality. What is happening here is your assumptions mean you take no further action. You might think "What's the point? . . . people never change. I can't change, either. Nobody cares about me". What you will learn in this book is how to change your thinking, but also how changing your actions can change your thoughts and your assumptions.

Case study: Henry

Henry, a professional rugby player, played all his rugby at scrum half through his school years and transition into a professional rugby team. He played internationally, but not yet at a senior international level. He trained diligently, always working a little more than everyone else, always doing extra repetitions in the gym or the training pitch, always giving his level best. But his efforts never seemed to amount to a change in the starting 15 players each week and occasionally he played the last 10–15 minutes of a game if the coach felt the game was secure. Henry assumed his coach had no faith in him and did not see a future for him as scrum half in the team. Rather than speaking with the coach, Henry became disillusioned with the situation and felt his confidence drain. One of the senior members of the squad could see what was happening to Henry and suggested he speak to the coach because he felt the coach had long-term plans for Henry but he was not the type of coach to discuss his plans unless you asked him directly. Though Henry felt unsure of himself meeting the coach and discovering his fate, he met with him. Contrary to what Henry thought, the coach valued Henry highly and felt that he needed to protect him in his first season at senior club level. The coach witnessed all his efforts and his supreme example to others in the club. Henry's actions – speaking to the coach – meant he now had evidence to contradict his faulty thinking and renew his confidence. If Henry had not acted, it is likely his confidence, effort, and commitment would continue to drain, leaving him with few assets to train and compete for his place at the club.

Getting to know you

In the last section, we introduced the many ways we protect ourselves or think in crooked ways. We reveal ourselves to ourselves using these methods of acting and thinking, but often it feels so uncomfortable to acknowledge our feelings, thoughts, and actions that we prefer to continue as we are rather than change our lives. But getting to know ourselves helps us to enjoy a freedom unknown to us before; we put the pieces of the jigsaw together that make us who and what we are without judgement. One of the first places to begin is with our psychological needs. Our psychological needs help us understand how we make our way in the world and how critical it is to meet our psychological needs along the way.

A hierarchy of needs

Clients in professional practice present various issues to the sport psychology practitioner. Though they might not recognise it, they try to meet their needs as best they can; however, the ways (i.e., their solutions) in which they meet their needs often create problems. For example, rather than meeting a need for safety and security healthily, the client acquires this need unhealthily by controlling or dominating others or its opposite (e.g., remaining passive). Acquired needs reflect the solution we arrived at, which is a problem. Another example might be a need for self-acceptance. When we cannot meet our need for self-acceptance healthily, we acquire the need by criticising, judging, and disapproving of ourselves or others.

These needs are inner psychological experiences and are basic to our growth, stretching through our lifetime. Though we might know them (e.g., a need to quench a thirst or stay warm), our needs are not typically in our everyday awareness. Abraham Maslow proposed each person has a hierarchy of human needs that one must satisfy to reach self-actualisation. In Maslow's theory, as we meet or satisfy each need, we are motivated to reach for the next higher level. One's higher needs cannot be met without meeting those needs below them. Though Maslow's hierarchy of needs is often presented in a pyramid for explanatory and illustrative purposes, but rather than climbing upwards from one need to another, it is best to consider that needs at all levels are being met to some degree. A client-athlete high on self-actualisation today, performing flawlessly on the pitch, arrives home to find someone had burgled his home, thrusting him back into satisfying his basic needs for safety.

In Maslow's (1943) hierarchy of needs, we begin with our basic needs before progressing to safety needs, belongingness needs, esteem needs, and – finally – to self-actualisation. Our basic needs include biological, physiological, and survival needs such as air, clothing, shelter, and sex. Next, we have our safety needs such as orderliness, rules to protect and avoid risk, and security ' which we meet by earning a salary, insurance policies, and a system of law and order. Then we have our belongingness and love needs we meet through family, friends, and work colleagues. Within this step, one has a need for relationships with others to be appreciated, approved, and accepted. Above these needs lie esteem needs. With a group, for example, we attain status and a desire to excel – the ego status needs motivate people to display competence to gain social and professional rewards; however, these needs require others (e.g., willingness to support you). Finally, we reach self-actualisation – the capacity to grow and develop towards maturity (i.e., emotional and psychological) and self-fulfilment. A sports person demanding greater achievement might display self-actualising behaviours, such as taking risks, acting freely and autonomously to reach a goal. Personal growth at this level might involve striving to win a championship or rowing across the Atlantic Ocean (Maslow, 2013; Sutton & Stewart, 2017).

Exercise 2.2: Developing self-awareness using Maslow's hierarchy of needs

1. Where do you feel you are now on the needs hierarchy?
2. For each level of the hierarchy, which needs are being met and which are unmet?
3. For each level of the hierarchy, what could you do to meet or nourish these needs?
4. For each level of the hierarchy, what needs are being met in an unhealthy way?
5. Which gifts and talents could you develop over the next few months?

The limits of self-awareness

Self-awareness, like all processes, has its limits. Gathering one's awareness about oneself means seeking to know who we are, our strengths and weaknesses, and our vices and virtues. Being self-aware means we know what we know now about ourselves, and this knowledge will change with time and experience. We might have worked through some problems, but it does not mean we have solved all our issues; rather, we are in a better place to understand and recognise how these parts of us influence our thoughts, feelings, and actions. We might have addressed some fears and haunting memories while shining a light on cherished memories. Rummaging around in the basement of our personal selves scares people enough to keep the door locked, yet there is much to be gleaned from understanding yourself and your world to allow you to enter and understand the world of others.

Dealing with feedback

The process of self-awareness brings feedback in various guises. Some feedback feels gratifying, accurate, and uplifting, yet other feedback feels frustrating, inaccurate, and undermining. Sometimes you give feedback, sometimes you receive feedback. On our learning journey, feedback helps us and others to learn, so it is a valuable resource. But like all skills, practice and pointers fortify the learning odyssey. Giving and receiving feedback often feels risky because of how the listener receives the feedback from the sender or how the sender sends the feedback to the receiver. Will I offend him? Will I upset her? Will she humiliate me? These concerns for ourselves and others persuade us that the feedback route ought to have values in action and a structure. For instance, when giving feedback, we might begin with our values of mutual respect, care, and support for the receiver. When we activate these values, we think about where, when, and how to give feedback. Perhaps you need a private space and time to discuss what you share. In this way, you respect the receiver's need for privacy and a right to respond, so we learn collaboratively. Your value of support means you aim to be specific, sending your message supportively and constructively. This specificity means your point is clear rather than a series of points that overwhelm the receiver. Finally, the information you share might be experiential (e.g., your experience of the person) or factual (e.g., how they performed in a race), so we need to be clear how we present this feedback.

Trainees and qualified sport psychology practitioners receive feedback from clients, employers, supervisors, colleagues, and so on. Similar to giving feedback, our values help us receive feedback. For instance, we might also hold values of curiosity and openness. In this curiosity and openness, we might hold a non-defensive stance to develop as a practitioner and learn about yourself. We might notice how we feel about the feedback, like feeling belittled, excited, uplifted, or embarrassed. These feelings might mean we cannot hear any more from the sender and we might need to share how we are feeling. Our curiosity means those parts of ourselves we do not see, but others see bring us closer to knowing ourselves. Our mutual respect means we try to know more about what the sender is sharing with us by asking questions and clarifying our understanding. In a supervisory relationship, reflecting and acting on feedback when necessary show that you are open to learning, changing, and improving. These experiences with feedback, for example, lead us to the chest of challenges we face and the common personal development problems arising in our work as sport psychology practitioners.

Ballantyne Dykes et al. (2017) positioned feedback as an affirmation to build one's confidence and presented a used acronym to remember that feedback ought to be a BOOST.

B – Balanced
O – Observed
O – Objective
S – Specific
T – Timely

Balanced: When feedback captures one's strengths and areas for improvement, it recognises what the person has achieved and what they can improve next. These points for reflection and change deserve a sensitive and respectful passage.

Observed: We need to attend to what happened precisely. Our feedback, without knowing, might have generalities rather than specificities within it. Here is an example: "The client looked like they lost all contact with you in the session" rather than "I noticed you found it unsettling to take notes and make eye contact with your client at the outset of your session".

In the opening example, the supervisor levels a judgement at the trainee rather than an invitation to explore. In the second example, the supervisor invites the trainee to explore what she noticed at the beginning of the session.

Objective: Useful and instructive feedback helps us to grow personally and professionally. General subjective feedback that does not focus on the skills and techniques used in the session and how one can change and improve these skills and techniques does not allow the trainee to move forward. Honest feedback, presented empathically, helps the trainee to remember what is helpful and work towards improvements.

Specific: When feedback is specific, it helps the listener to attend to a precise behaviour. For instance, a general piece of information might develop from "You jumped around a lot" to "I noticed how unsettled you appeared when the client mentioned her loss of form over the past few weeks. You seemed to hesitate and fiddle with your pad and pen. Perhaps we could explore what you were thinking and feeling."

Timely: Feedback works best when it fits closely after the behaviour. Though it might not always be possible to offer such timely feedback while trainees are on practicum placement, audio and video recordings shared with supervisors for feedback mean the supervisor can prepare a section to explore with the trainee. The good supervisor focuses on the specific content and skills in the session, uses adverbs to describe rather than adjectives to judge, and weights options with the trainee to develop skills.

Sharing feedback sensitively and gingerly means we find a balance in what we choose to share and acknowledge how our thoughts and feelings at the time might influence our feedback. When we assemble feedback as a BOOST, the listener feels acknowledged, included, and sure about the next steps to flourish.

Experiential learning and feedback

Experiential learning forms a central pillar of one's training to become a sport psychology practitioner. Part of the experiential learning process means receiving feedback from fellow trainees (i.e., peers) and facilitators (e.g., tutors, lecturers). The learning group, or personal and professional development group, help us learn from our experiences relating with others. Receiving feedback in an encounter group or skills triad with others watching and listening, for example, strains many new trainees because the new experience feels uncomfortable. In the usual learning experience, we learn after doing or experiencing something (e.g., skills practice). Next, we reflect personally or receive feedback from the group. Our reflections and the feedback from the group point us towards what we can change for next time. Finally, we test our skills in novel situations and take our learnings with us. In summary, there is experiencing (i.e., doing) and feedback. In the skills triad work, taking on the role of helper, for example, means receiving feedback from the observer, client, and tutor. Some feedback feels threatening, piercing, and unfair until we process it in the way others share it.

Case study: Martin

Martin lectured in sport and exercise psychology after completing his doctoral studies and progressed up the professional ladder quickly. He held a strong desire to practise as a sport psychology practitioner, so he received long-study support from his department to pursue his ambition. Part of Martin's training programme involved counselling skills in applied sport psychology. Martin knew volumes about theory and research in applied sport psychology, but could not understand the feedback from his peers in triads each week. The feedback acknowledged his strengths (e.g., reflecting, paraphrasing, summarising) but the clients in the triads seemed to share the same feedback. It went along the lines, "You follow the processes well and I understand the flow of the work; however, it's almost like you're not there or I feel you do not feel my feelings". What frustrated Martin the most was that he was doing what he was supposed to do: reflecting, paraphrasing, and summarising; yet he was not receiving positive feedback. The tutor recognised this familiar issue of the divide between head and heart, especially among those training alongside each other in health psychology, counselling psychology, and sport and exercise psychology. The content of sessions (i.e., what the client brings) trumps the process (i.e., what is happening between the client and the practitioner) so it feels like the practitioner 'hears' the story but does not 'feel' the story – so the client feels unheard. It was as if Martin, like some others in the sport and exercise cohort, could not 'open' himself to 'feel' what the client felt while sharing their stories. It just did not feel like it had a place in sport and exercise.

With this feedback, it was as if someone had pierced his armour and Martin realised the emotional desolation others complained about in his personal life. This experience brought waves of strong and destabilising feelings that Martin could not hold down any more. For Martin, there were painful connections to his childhood, his relationship with his parents, and his current relationship with his fiancé. Somehow, it all seemed to make sense to him. He had been stifling his relating skills – such as 'sensitivity', 'understanding', and 'kindness' – because they seemed unwanted and unwarranted in sport. And his mother trampled on these same qualities throughout his childhood: "You're too soft. There you go again: you can't handle anything". Martin realised the weaknesses he tried to hide were the strengths he needed working with others, especially as a sport psychology practitioner. The feedback from his peers captured the change in Martin: "You're doing the same things like paraphrasing and summarising, but you sound different – you seem different – you seem at ease". His tutor noticed the difference too and spoke with Martin after the skills class. Martin said,

> I never thought being open, sensitive, and caring would be exactly what I needed to work well as a sport psychology practitioner. It's almost like it never occurred to me. How could I not see it? I know that sounds strange given my role as a lecturer and researcher in the field, but it's almost like it I couldn't parse "soft skills" with being a sport psychologist. But I get it now, I truly do. And I feel so much better in myself – I don't need to pretend anymore. I can stop pretending I don't exist anymore.

Martin's experience highlighted a common misunderstanding in service delivery that our vulnerability and humility presents as a weakness in the performance-driven arena of sport. What Martin learned was that he could, through his own personal development, learn how to be with a client, fully present, with openness, trust, and empathy moving forward collaboratively allowing the client to lead to where the client felt it were best to go. In the next section, we explore common personal development issues, like Martin's experiences early in his training programme.

Common personal development issues

McLeod and McLeod (2014) presented several practical issues that arise for helpers such as sport psychology practitioners in their everyday work: avoidance of specific areas of experience, one's needs taking priority, crippling self-doubt and unenviable comparison, sense of superiority, boundary issues, selective acceptance, depersonalisation, and being a rescuer. Let's explore each personal development issue in the sport context.

Avoidance of specific areas of experience: many areas of experience feel uncomfortable or unversed to us as sport psychology practitioners, and we would rather avoid than explore them with a client. For example, conflict, emotions (e.g., anger, sadness), finance, sexuality, and religion can feel uncomfortable because of our lived experience, cultural norms, or the training we undertake. Our feelings about these issues may consciously or unconsciously steer us away towards more palatable issues.

One's own needs taking priority: our needs (psychological, interpersonal) as sport psychology practitioners' figure in how we relate to a client, but we might not notice them only through personal therapy or supervision, for instance. At one end of the scale, a sport psychology practitioner who needs to be liked might not confront pertinent issues with a client, while at the other end of the scale, a sport psychology practitioner might gratify personal needs by keeping a client in therapy to generate income. Through supervision, a trainee can explore their motives for becoming a sport psychology practitioner and how those motives might figure in our relations with clients.

Crippling self-doubt and unenviable comparison: doubting our skills and abilities as well as comparing ourselves unfavourably with others seems a normal part of our everyday lives; however, it is challenging to see such doubt and biased comparison undermine your practice as a sport psychology practitioner. Such trials mean with often lose sight of the strength of the therapeutic models (e.g., CBT) we use and only see our weaknesses personally in our professional work.

Sense of superiority: on the other side of crippling self-doubt lies grandiosity and narcissism. Some sport psychology practitioners feel overwhelmingly confident in their abilities, and so feedback from clients or supervisors falls on deaf ears. Although clients value the sense of confidence and competence in a sport psychology practitioner, a sport psychology practitioner might adopt the persona of superiority to hide the self-doubt underneath.

Boundary issues: We remind trainees about boundaries from their first day of training with such topics as confidentiality, privacy, and time within a therapy room or at a training ground. But in the world of sport, working at a training arena, standing on the sidelines, we often use our implicit boundary rules influenced by experience, culture, and social norms. But how do such norms fit into therapeutic settings? What level of disclosure is acceptable? What level of physical touch is permissible when we celebrate a victory? We bring these questions to our personal development groups to establish and maintain boundaries so we may respond to violations of our boundaries.

Selective acceptance: this happens when we accept some categories but not others in our work with clients. A sport you dislike might trigger psychological barriers and judgements when you work with an athlete. For instance, you might have difficulties working with perceived 'masculine' or 'feminine' sports because of how others might label you.

Depersonalisation: this is a failure by the sport psychology practitioner to respond to the client as a person. The practitioner might treat the person as a 'case' because of a fear of one's own response to others or the challenges in caring, handling heavy emotional labour from over working. Some sport psychology practitioners reveal the effects of a heavy workload on their ability to care for other athletes.

Being a rescuer: lots of people enter the profession of sport psychology to help athletes, coaches, and teams. This well-intended motive becomes tangled when the sport psychology practitioner believes and behaves as if they can sort their client's problems on their behalf – this is the rescuer. When the sport psychology practitioner reassures and/or advises a client, or colludes with a client to avoid specific topics (e.g., over-training), then a rescue mission is operating. Our lives are replete with examples, in family relations and friendships, whereby we rescue – and while it might be necessary occasionally, it also undermines the ability of the client to face their troubles, learn to tolerate their discomfort, and work to help themselves.

Being a rescuer is one role of three we often adopt in our relationships and interactions with others. The other roles are victim and persecutor. Stephen Karpman (1976) described a drama triangle with these three roles. The rescuer does more than expected without being asked and works to a rule of what they believe others need rather than asking what someone needs. In short, they are assuming responsibility for others rather than themselves. Working in this way and trying to be indispensable makes the rescuer feel needed. This role, however, puts the rescuer on a slippery slope towards the victim or the persecutor roles. The rescuer finishes feeling the victim because their efforts go unrewarded and feel aggrieved about what happened. The victim, however, feels unable to take responsibility for themselves, feeling helpless and inadequate. Unable to cope, they blame others for their situation, and in this role, they might seek a rescuer to help, who might overwhelm them or let them down. The persecutor seeks to meet their needs through control and coercion. Feeling a sense of self-righteousness issues power over others, but not an authentic power; it is, rather, a destructive power (Ballantyne Dykes et al., 2017). Regaining a sense of responsibility helps each of these roles to adjust and recover. The rescuer, by taking responsibility for themselves, acknowledges their troubling feelings and vulnerability. The victim, by taking responsibility for themselves, witnesses their legitimate power and exercises it rather than awaiting others to help them. Finally, the persecutor, by taking responsibility for themselves and meeting their needs, healthily breeds a healthy power to use rather than abuse.

These examples are personal development challenges for all practitioners in sport psychology because these themes recur in their lives, prompted and triggered by personal and professional circumstances. These examples pop up in personal therapy, supervision, personal development groups, reflective practice journals, and peer supervision groups. We can address these issues, but they are not always apparent to us, so we might need to check in now and then about how we relate to our range of clients. The clue to the puzzle, as McLeod and McLeod suggested, is when a therapist's response to a client seems peculiar.

Case study: Coach Hayley

When Haley arrived at my office, she fell into her chair. "I'm exhausted, utterly exhausted". Hayley's career on tour lasted a few years when an injury forced her to retire. Upon retiring, she qualified as a golf teacher. She worked the most out of all the teaching professionals in the academy, listened to all their problems, offered advice, and could always guarantee she would answer her mobile when called. Not only did she give freely to the other staff members, she also gave freely to the touring professionals she coached. She bent over backwards to meet their needs, and nothing was ever too much trouble. Exploring the roles of rescuer, victim, and persecutor, Hayley lamented,

> I can see myself now – I'm the rescuer, aren't I? All the giving, all the rescuing, all the time. No wonder I feel so tired and recently, I've been feeling so frustrated with it all. And yet, I cannot say "No". My husband gets the brunt of it and he doesn't deserve it. I can see myself falling into the victim role recently and I seem to get the blame for doing everything I can for the players. I'm blaming everyone and everything, but I can see I am not blameless or helpless. I know what I have created. Being wanted by the players on tour was something I loved. Somehow, I mattered when I mattered to them. I thought the more I gave, the more I helped.

Using the Johari window helped Hayley to see all the hats she wore, or the masks she carried with all the people she coached and worked alongside.

Philosophical assumptions

The philosophical foundations of applied sport psychology might not be the most attractive topic to study; however, it holds the key to all elements of the service delivery process. The aims, content, and practice orientations of a sport psychology practitioner influence the entire delivery service. For example, aims (e.g. to address performance issues, to promote physical well-being), content (e.g., presenting issues, measurement, observation, analysis), and practice orientation (e.g., how we work with a client) differ among many sport psychology practitioners – yet they all offer services to clients. How can sport psychology practitioners all purport to offer service delivery with such differences? The answer to this question lies within one's philosophical stance, and knowing your philosophical stance helps you to offer an effective service built upon sound ethical, theoretical, and evidence-based practices.

The world of sport, like many other parts of one's life, cultivates little certainty. And with little certainty, we need to proceed using assumptions. Assumptions are those things we accept without proof as true or likely to happen. Acquiring an awareness and understanding of our assumptions serves us well throughout our career. As sport psychology practitioners, we might hold basic assumptions about people, how they ought to be helped, and how they achieve personal change, which reflect the way we work, the frameworks we choose, and the interventions we use. If you tell clients what to do, your actions could reflect your belief that others cannot help themselves without help or without your help. Our guiding values, once they are clear and open, allow us to examine, challenge, and change them. Culley and Bond (2011) presented some examples of assumptions helping professions might hold.

Based on your training and specialising in one or a few therapeutic modalities, these assumptions might resonate for you.

1. People are capable of change: though clients might have learned ways of behaving that do not help them, they can also develop ways of behaving that help them. In a supportive environment with a low risk of rejection or ridicule, they will find ways of behaving that suit them better.
2. People are experts on themselves: only the client knows how they think, feel, and act. The way the world makes sense is unique to them. From their experiences, they know the joy of success and the pain of defeat. They know their hopes and dreams, and their fears and worries. They may have lost their 'inner voice' because others feel they know what is best for them. Given the right help and support, they can find the answers that are right for them.
3. People deserve acceptance and understanding as human beings: here you distinguish between the client and the client's behaviour. You valuing the person does not mean you value or agree with their actions.
4. People work to achieve their chosen values and goals: personal values and goals drive intention, so helping clients to choose their way forward pays dividends for the individual.

On a more holistic level, Tod and Lafferty (2020) wrote about how sport psychology practitioners could develop an integrated service delivery system. Tod and Lafferty explored how we can integrate theoretical orientations and the obstacles to integration. Integration means when practitioners combine multiple theoretical models and ways of operating to increase the efficacy, effectiveness, efficiency, and ethical standing of their services to clients (Castonguay et al., 2015; Fernández-Álvarez et al., 2016; Tod & Lafferty, 2020; Zarbo et al., 2016). Please see Tod and Lafferty (2020) for an exploration of integration and the reasons practitioners integrate models from technical eclecticism to theoretical integration.

Summary

Two themes emerged from this chapter: first, the centrality of developing one's self-awareness, leading to an understanding of our inner worlds – our attitudes, values, and beliefs; and second, recognising that our past helps us to cultivate self-understanding and self-acceptance to know, like, and value ourselves as people and practitioners as we begin our journey to help others raise their self-awareness. Learning to see what we could not see before, noticing our defences, understanding our needs, and recognising common personal development issues help us to become better practitioners and allow us to recognise and understand the philosophical assumptions we make and develop as sport psychology practitioners. The next step is to understand people from a psychological perspective.

3 Understanding people from a psychological perspective

Introduction

When we try to understand people from a psychological perspective, we do so accepting that common personal problems and goals do not exist within a vacuum. Anyone reading this book comes with their unique blend of culture, education, economic and socio-political influence, social groups, and biological and personality attributes within their family of origin. Your family of origin, biology, and personality seem most relevant because they are local to you – and as dependents, we grow up reliant on others (e.g., parents, guardians) to survive and learn much about ourselves, others, and the world from our mix of biology, personality, and the habits, roles, and actions of those upon whom we depend.

We learn much about our worth (or worthlessness), lovability (or unlovability), and usefulness (or helplessness) through our interactions with ourselves, others, and the world. Parents, caregivers, siblings and our experiences in school, sport, and other engagements profoundly shape our capacity to manage the trials and tribulations which life brings. Some challenges we handle in helpful ways, and some challenges we handle in less helpful ways. In sport settings, we meet athletes, coaches, parents, backroom staff, and others who seek our help because, while they often have healthy coping strategies, occasionally they cannot locate the resources they need to cope. Our line of work in sport, therefore, means exploring the uniqueness of the client before us. We need to look at ourselves (i.e., personal development) before we can work well with others (i.e., professional development) because of the role of power and social influence in the helping process. Many of those training to become sport psychology practitioners will have gathered a social perspective from their undergraduate studies about the influence of society on opinions, attitudes, values, and beliefs.

We briefly explore topics such as attachment, lifespan development, and family systems as guiding structures for your work with clients. Although the past may be less relevant to your chosen therapeutic modality (e.g., CBT; rational emotive behaviour therapy [REBT]), the past connects to the present and the future. To add a bit of verisimilitude, it is helpful to see the story of the person in the detail you might expect.

DOI: 10.4324/9781003453857-3

In Chapter 2, we explored why someone might become a sport psychology practitioner. Most practitioners might give reasons such as "to help others" or "to contribute positively to those in sport and exercise settings" or "to increase participation in sport and physical activity". But behind these quotidian responses lie one's hidden or shadow motives. Aligned with these hidden motivations lies power and social influence in our helping profession we might not obviously recognise. As practitioners, we are guests in the sporting milieu, invited to work with those working in sport, so we might not step back to understand and realise how power (e.g., access to education, health services, economic security) pervades sport and society. Occasionally, we might read in the media or hear on a podcast stories about those advantaged or disadvantaged (e.g., marginalised groups) in the journey from playground to podium. Part of the personal and professional journey of a sport psychology practitioner lies in critiquing power, authority, prejudice, discrimination, oppression, and marginalisation in our clients' lives and our own. In each chair, whether client or practitioner, we bring with us an assortment of experiences, so we need to appreciate each other's journey and unique story so we commit to anti-oppressive practice. Not only do we make sense of the helping relationship, we also explore the environments in which we work and in which the client plays and performs. It can be most alluring to see ourselves as compassionate persons riding in to save the day (e.g., knight in shining armour), but to do misses so much of the client's story regarding seeking help, personal authority, and working with others (perhaps having experienced prejudice, discrimination and oppression).

When we lift the veil on power, prejudice, discrimination, harassment, and oppression in sport and society, we see a view of social difference (e.g., ethnic and cultural backgrounds), stereotypes, and discriminatory attitudes and behaviours which we might not have pondered previously. For example, as practitioners, we work with athletes with physical and mental disabilities. As practitioners, we might present with our own physical and mental disabilities and experience inequality, ableism, and ageism. Over the decades, athletes have shared their stories of verbal, emotional, physical, and sexual abuse as children, adolescents, and adults.

Some relationships in sport harbour emotionally abusive behaviour, yet we might not recognise the signs because of what seems acceptable behaviour in that setting – an assumption that we accept all behaviour while pursuing success, that the end justifies the means. We might witness displays of superiority (e.g., blame and ridicule), extreme expectations (e.g., nothing is ever good enough), undermining one's experiences (e.g., distorting your reality), creating disarray (e.g., dramatic mood changes), manipulating one's feelings (e.g., guilt trips), and isolation and control (e.g., of one's time and relations). Though there might not be visible signs of abuse, the invisible effects lie inside the helplessness, hopelessness, and worthlessness one feels. The pursuit of success means paying a price the athlete never intended to pay at the beginning, yet one might not see it – and as time passes, the verbal abuse creates an internal critic.

As a trainee or employee within an organisation, the demands of our employer often constrain the work we do with clients because the employer expects the client to return to the team or performance arena as soon as possible. Our beliefs about what is in the client's best interest may clash with the time, resources, and values of the organisation with which we work, and the power hierarchy might demand specifics of you. With these challenges and constraints, we need to rely on models, theories, and approaches to help us work best to meet the client's needs. There are hundreds of theories and approaches to counselling and psychotherapy that guide the work of psychologists and therapists working with clients and patients. To offer you an overview of each one is beyond the goals of this chapter and book; rather, we present a brief introduction to a few theories and approaches as an illustration of how an approach works. Most theories fall within five major categories: (1) psychodynamic, (2) cognitive-behavioural, (3) humanistic and existential, (4) constructivist, and (5) integrative and eclectic (Feltham et al., 2017). Those working in sport, exercise, and performance settings can choose which approach or blend of approaches fits their philosophical assumptions and ways of working. Each approach contains its own history; basic assumptions; view on the origin and maintenance of problems; theory of change, skills, and strategies; and research evidence underpinning it.

When you read through the research and practice literature on applied sport psychology, you will see a reflection of the variety and vibrancy of therapeutic approaches of sport psychology practitioners. This variety and vibrancy bring overlap among approaches, differences of opinions, challenges, and debates. The therapeutic landscape seems messy and uncoordinated to some, while for others, it reflects the complexity and needs humans present each day in practice. As we wrote previously, doing applied sport psychology work with athletes, coaches, teams, parents, and others means blending art and science. We are, as we shall see in this book, acknowledging the healthy relationship between research and practice while remembering research-informed does not mean research-driven or research-absent (Hanley et al., 2013).

Psychological and therapeutic perspectives

Understanding people from a psychological perspective means that practitioners apply theory or theories to understand the client's presenting issues. Sometimes clients wish to understand what went wrong; at other times, they wish to make things which are good even better. Practitioners then integrate theory and skills to work towards the client's goals. A good practitioner will explain what they are doing and why, using skills and techniques which mirror their model for understanding the client's presenting issue(s). For instance, the person-centred approach is based on the philosophical notion that clients find their own way and answers in life and in the therapeutic approach. A trainee who spent the past five years coaching athletes using structured training plans might find such an approach counterintuitive and worrying.

Though we opened the chapter with a statement about psychological perspectives to understand people, we also consider people from a social perspective. As a trainee or client, the influence of power in society, for instance, will have shaped each person's view of the helping relationship. Consider for a moment the society in which you live. Are services and opportunities such as schooling, recreation areas, healthcare, economic security, and choice about one's life equally distributed, or do some people win while others lose because of their neighbourhood, income, or social status? Is power distributed evenly? Power influences the practitioner and client variously, such that they may or may not see the influence of authority, prejudice, and oppression in their lives. The helping relationship could perpetuate oppression. In a helping relationship, listening, reflecting, clarifying, summarising, and some forms of question (e.g., open-ended) comprise the helping skills giving power to the client. Postings (2022) presented the acronym OARS to capture the skills conducive to change and change talk: open-ended questions, affirming, reflective listening, and summarising. Advising, prescribing a course of action (e.g., giving instructions, solutions), acting on behalf of the person, and some forms of questions, however, swing the power pendulum back to the helper because the responsibility, authority, and control slides back to the helper. In applied sport psychology settings, some psychoeducation lessons, for instance, you will feel you are advising, prescribing, lecturing, and so on. This balance between power and control depends on the role you play in the helping process. In a psychoeducation session, you might describe psychological skills to cope with stress and performance anxiety. You might feel your responsibility to this group means they learn, practise, and integrate the skills into their training and competition routines, as written in the contract for your work with them. In these settings, you can be clear about your role and responsibilities tied to the limitation of the role. We can arrange these boundaries in our contracts and job descriptions.

In sport settings, for example, we need to consider what happens outside and inside the helping relationship because our responsibility might mean shaping the environment we work in. We might find ourselves in a work environment to fulfil our own needs. For instance, we enjoy being needed by others and unconsciously meet that need by encouraging dependence in our working relationships, or we dredge gratification from other's feelings and actions. Though we as helpers might work on issues of performance and well-being in a therapeutic space, our client might experience prejudice and discrimination in the workplace from attendees at a sports event. Cases of physical, sexual, emotional, and verbal abuse run throughout sport as a recreational activity and workplace. Emotional abuse might include unrealistic expectations; invalidating your thoughts, feelings, and efforts; isolation and control; verbal abuse; behaving erratically and unpredictably; and emotional blackmail.

Case study: Faye

Faye, a professional golfer, came to see me (Paul) during a week's break from her tour schedule. She felt her season had stagnated, and she sought a fresh impetus. Though she had not seen a sport psychology practitioner before, she had read several books about the psychology of golf. Faye arrived with the impression that I would tell her or teach her how to improve her mental game. I explained the person-centred approach and how we work together. After our first session, Faye reflected,

> This is not what I expected at all – I mean, not at all! I know you explained what a person-centred approach means, but I've never been around anyone in golf who listens to me – you know, properly listens. Most people are doing something with me, or to me, but you don't. You seem to be just who you are, if you know what I mean. And another thing: you made no demands of me. But everyone makes demands of me! It's almost like you believe in me to recognise and understand what I need and find my own answers, which seems so strange yet wonderful!

When we meet an athlete in our clinic, we may not immediately consider who might sit before us. This athlete, shaped by nature (e.g., biological or genetic inheritance) and nurture (e.g., social and psychological upbringing, experience) shares with us a story of their lives. While our nature may be fixed, the influence of other people and the environment affects us incalculably. Exploring some of these earlier experiences and current challenges, alongside one's relationships and resources, assists us in the helping process.

The formative experiences of childhood and adolescence run into adulthood. In sport, however, many of our clients walk through our doors as children, adolescents, young adults, and older adults. Working with children and adolescents especially means several transitions psychologically, emotionally, socially, physically, and academically. One dominant feature of all stages of development is relationships. The development of our early relationships with parents, siblings, and caregivers influences our relationships later in life.

Approaches to therapeutic support

There are several approaches to working with client-athletes and hundreds of specific theories related to therapeutic work. To offer a framework for these many theories, we organised them into five sections (1) psychodynamic, (2) cognitive-behavioural, (3) humanistic and existential, (4) constructivist, and (5) integrative and eclectic. This sharp organisation suggests clean lines between approaches, but several arguments unravel when we discuss where one ends and another begins. Within this book, however, space permits only a brief acknowledgement of a few well-versed approaches in applied sport psychology. Each approach holds its own history, basic assumptions, view on the origin and maintenance of problems, theory of change, skills and strategies used by practitioners, and a background of research evidence for that way of working (Feltham et al., 2017). Like all theoretical perspectives, historical, theoretical, practical, and research developments vary, which offers us to an assortment of ways of working. How one sees this assortment depends on one's view of its complexity and the multitudinous needs of humans.

A person-centred approach

Originally developed by Carl Rogers and his colleagues from the late 1930s onwards, person-centred therapy or client-centred therapy represents a form of therapy about the whole person and being of the client. Today, this person-centred therapy represents one application of the person-centred approach (Embleton Tudor et al., 2004). Several basic assumptions underlie the person-centred approach. Tudor (2017) presented these assumptions under three core principles: (1) The human organism tends to actualise, (2) the practitioner embodies a non-directive approach and attitude to support growth and change, and (3) the practitioner and client co-create conditions to facilitate growth, challenge, and change.

1. Tending towards actualisation: the values of fluidity and creativity are implicit in the attitude to the person in the person-centred approach. The self-concept or self-structure presents a fluid but consistent pattern of perceptions of 'I', 'me', and 'we' as it relates to goals, ideals, personal and social values, and the environment. After the development of the self-concept, our self-actualising acts to maintain that concept. For example, if a part of one's self-concept is to please others, one might act to support that part of one's self-concept at the expense of one's organismic direction. An awareness of one's self – self-experience – when judged by others as more or less worthy of positive regard, a person's self-regard becomes vulnerable to such external judgements. In these situations, a person seeks or avoids self-experiences to gain or surrender self-regard, and acquires conditions of worth, which are the basis of person-centred theories of psychopathology.
2. The practitioner embodies a non-directive approach and attitude to support growth and change: based on the first assumption that an organism tends to actualise because of the inherent directionality within, it makes sense that the practitioner would support this orientation. This positive, constructive, and co-creative approach does not deny we could be negative, destructive, and anti-social; however, there is potential for positive, personal, and social change throughout one's life. Our environmental influences (e.g., a positive supportive relationship with a practitioner or a coach or its opposite) shapes our positive or negative self-concepts and our healthy or unhealthy functioning. Our behaviour reflects the drive of our needs (Rogers, 1951).
3. The practitioner and client co-create conditions to facilitate growth, challenge, and change: in person-centred psychology, a person is trustworthy, social, creative, congruent, or integrative within themselves. In relationships, a person is loving, understanding, receptive, and resourceful. Distortion and denial represent two defence mechanisms which prevent us admitting all experiencing into our awareness. When a client shares power

and control with a practitioner, the client can rediscover their organismic valuing process and direction in a facilitative climate of psychological attitudes and conditions.

Problems originate and maintain whenever there is an antagonism between a person's tendency to actualise lying in one direction and their self-actualisation lying in another. We know this divergence of these two tendencies as incongruence. At the beginning of one's life, a person is fully congruent. There is no denial or distortion of awareness. The social challenges of life – such as disapproval, disruption, threat, and rejection – mean the person becomes anxious in their need for positive regard from significant others. These experiences affect a person's self-concept and their conditions of worth become internalised while the person seeks to protect themself from further negative experiences. One's conditioned self-concept – conditioned by these experiences – becomes so strongly reinforced that the person is a stranger to themselves and their organismic direction. This alienation from oneself means one's self-concept and one's experiencing diverge, disturbing one's psychological functioning. This alienation or disturbance is maintained by a person relying on others' evaluations for their sense of self-worth. A person will feel anxious, threatened, and confused when one's experience and one's self-concept (with internalised conditions of worth) diverge. In this anxiety, a person will default to their defences (denial or distortion of experiencing).

The work with a practitioner depends on the attitudes, values, and conditions of the practitioner, which the client receives, perceives, or engages with how the client receives or perceives these – or not. There are conditions on the side of the practitioner and client. On the practitioner's side, Rogers' (1959) seminal paper drafted a theory of therapy, personality, and interpersonal relationships within the client-centred framework, he described the following (p. 213).

> For therapy to occur it is necessary that these conditions exist. (1) That two persons are in contact. (2) That the first person . . . the client, is in a state of incongruence, being vulnerable, or anxious. (3) That the second person . . . the therapist, is congruent in the relationship. (4) That the therapist is experiencing unconditional positive regard toward the client. (5) That the therapist is experiencing an empathic understanding of the client's internal frame of reference. (6) That the client perceives, at least to a minimal degree, conditions 4 and 5.

For therapy to occur, the client has to fulfil three conditions: (1) that they are in (psychological) contact, (2) that they are in some state of incongruence, and (3) that they experience/perceive being received.

Because person-centred therapy (PCT) is non-directive, the practitioner has no goals for the client. The practitioner attends to a non-judgemental acceptance and understanding of the client's experience. The qualities of the practitioner and the relationship are of congruence, acceptance, and under-standing. In the therapeutic relationship, change for the client occurs through experiences of self-acceptance and integration owned as part of oneself and integrated into one's self-structure without distortion or denial. The good practitioner communicates empathy, congruence, and unconditional positive regard in ways in which the client perceives them as non-threatening. With no threats or demands, the client feels free to share experience without a need to deny or distort perceptions.

Psychodynamic psychotherapy

Psychodynamic psychotherapy is based on the premise that in a one-to-one relationship with a reliable, concerned other, the client is 'held', allowing a safety and freedom to share aspects of the self which were predominantly hidden. This relationship with a practitioner who attends to the emotional exchange between the practitioner and client helps to change (or reduce) the anxieties emerging from unconscious phantasies about the world (Segal, 2017).

The work of Sigismund (later abbreviated to "Sigmund") Freud and col-leagues, developed by many others (e.g., Melanie Klein), explored how the mind worked and how therapy might relieve distress. Sigmund Freud, for example, presented the relationship with a therapist as a tool to understand a patient's problems and used techniques of free association to interpret uncon-scious drives, motivations, and emotions. Many examples of Freudian concepts (e.g., id, ego, superego) can be found in Nietzsche's work, and Nietzsche's work substantially influenced Freud and other psychodynamic theorists and practitioners (e.g., Carl Jung, Alfred Adler). Freud profoundly changed our understanding of ourselves, highlighting our irrationality as human beings and our behaviour emerging from internal conflicts, unconscious desires, and childhood biographies inaccessible to conscious access (Hanrahan & Andersen, 2010). His language and concepts secured themselves in our language, and we use these concepts to talk about ourselves every day such as slips of the tongue (parapraxes), libido, regression, denial, projection, and so on.

The unconscious lies at the heart of psychodynamic theories. This uncon-scious houses early childhood memories, conflicts, unacceptable sexual and aggressive desires, and anything else one finds difficult to endure. These inter-nal conflicts influence our lives in maladaptive ways, so psychodynamic psy-chotherapy attempts to unveil what is unconscious and decrease their power. This emotional understanding available in a psychotherapeutic relationship allows the client to think, feel, and understand themselves and others better. The client works through their feared reality, feelings, and phantasies, as well as grieving for real losses. Anxiety maintains illusions and defences which sus-tain anxiety. The emotions we store in our unconscious need to be explored to bring a fresh understanding of ourselves in relation to others. The past is present. What we mean here is that difficulties in relationships with caregivers (e.g., parents) underlie problems in the past and in the present. The relationship we have with ourselves and with others harbours these difficulties. To face these difficulties and disturbances (unpleasant, destructive, and shameful feelings) alone feels overwhelming and unmanageable; however, with the help of a practitioner, the task feels more wieldy. It may also be destabilising to face deeply loving feelings in ourselves. What is true for the client may well be true for the practitioner, so the capacity to face these pleasant and unpleasant feelings is as much as a result of the practitioner and their training, supervision, and ongoing personal and professional development (Segal, 1985).

Like all relationships, an inherent imbalance lies within despite efforts to reduce the power between the practitioner and client. After all, the client attends sessions to receive something (e.g., self-understanding, reduction of distress) which the client might believe the practitioner holds. So, the relationship throws up emotions like hope, envy, fear, anger, and so forth. In therapy, these feelings can be explored, and the associated attitudes, beliefs, and behaviours mined. The relationship in the room with the practitioner helps to re-evaluate the client's feelings and behaviour in relation with others who cared for them in the past.

The origins of problems can be understood in how we understand the world and ourselves within it. Our 'phantasies' – or pictures or models to understand the world and us within it – are dynamic, changing with the changing world and the relations with others. These phantasies are unconscious. We do not see how we created these phantasies from our experiences. Feeling happy brings happy phantasies and feeling sad or mad brings frightening or disturbing phantasies. Growing up, we develop a more realistic picture of the world around us which differs from that of our childhood; however, sometimes we do not mature emotionally or psychologically. We may hold onto phantasies created under painful circumstances (e.g., loss of a loved one), and fear the pain will return.

Conflicts in our lives bring about problems, too, because we manipulate phantasies and emotions in relation to such conflicts (e.g., conflict with a parent). Splitting good feelings (e.g., happy, capable) from bad feelings (e.g., angry, jealous) might mean we behave in ways to be all the good things only; however, this splitting sets an impossible standard to achieve and a likely collapse without someone to turn to in our time of need. To cope with the world as we experience it, we might deny, idealise, or denigrate to rid ourselves of the jealousy or envy we might feel towards another.

We try to project into others the unbearable feelings we might feel (i.e., projective identification) or rid ourselves of something that feels bad (e.g., 'let off steam'). An infant may cry to rid themselves of painful emotions, which alerts the parent (i.e., the parent now feels distressed) and tries to do something about it (e.g., feed the baby). This process of projection between a parent and child seems normal and features in most other relationships, as well. As children grow, they usually develop a capacity to handle their experiences, and what was once unbearable now seems tolerable.

A coach might be worn down with media duties, training, travel, and a run of poor results, and the irritability shows, for instance, in snapping at someone for seemingly inconsequential things. Feeling miserable, the coach makes those around feel the same (without consciously intending to do so). While the coach's behaviour might rid the feeling for a while, guilty feelings often follow. Sporting organisations in which the power lies with one or a few people often project their feeling into those beneath them in the hierarchy. Perhaps at an unconscious level, the power broker hopes someone will recognise their call for support and help them.

Change within psychodynamic psychotherapy depends on altering the phantasies we hold about the world and use to navigate it. Each day presents opportunities to learn, change, and grow. These opportunities (e.g., a relationship) stir our emotions and challenge how we see ourselves and others (i.e., awareness, assumptions, attitudes, beliefs) – but emotions might be painful and straining, which encourages us to fear or avoid change. The work with a psychodynamic practitioner means bringing to consciousness parts of the relationship between the practitioner and clients. One phenomenon to bring about change is transference. In transference, the client transfers – or projects onto the therapist – those thoughts and feelings with which they responded to caregivers or fantasised others previously. Our ways of responding in current relationships find their origins in our early lives. The transference in the room with the therapist helps the client to see their attachments to others, whether adaptive or maladaptive. A client might not see an issue with lateness or missed sessions, yet they all have meaning for the client and the relationship with the therapist allows them to uncover and address them. This seeing and understanding of relationships with others through the work with the therapist acts as a model and practice ground to develop healthy human relations (Hanrahan & Andersen, 2010). Countertransference represents what the therapist transfers from past relationships onto the client. Positive and negative responses to the client ought to be examined because they offer increase self-awareness for the therapist.

This mutual reflection on the therapist and client, and their relationship, means the client's emotional states can be felt, tolerated, recognised, and understood in a new way. With the support of a good therapist, those parts that were hidden – painful, humiliating thoughts and feelings – gain awareness and become tolerated, understood, and accepted and better possibilities for coping with conflict emerge. The psychodynamic practitioner offering insight does so skilfully because of the implications for their relationship. An overt meaning might also contain a covert meaning. What we hide, we do so for good reasons, and when another raises what we have hidden; it raises strong feelings.

A cognitive-behavioural therapy approach

CBT represents a collection of therapies sharing philosophical and theoretical assumptions and techniques (e.g., cognitive therapy, rational-emotive behaviour therapy, acceptance and commitment therapy). In the 1960s and 1970s, Aaron Beck developed a psychotherapy he originally named "cognitive therapy" – a term often used synonymously with "cognitive-behavioural therapy". This structured, short-term, and present-oriented psychotherapy for depression has been adapted for many other disorders and problems. In CBT, our problems in living emerge from faulty thinking. In the next section, we shall explore cognitive therapy – an evidence-based, relatively short form of therapy for a range of issues (e.g., psychological, psychosocial, emotional).

In the 1960s, two renowned American psychologists, Albert Ellis and Aaron Beck, dissatisfied with the psychoanalytic approach in which they were trained, developed new therapeutic approaches for working with people and their presenting issues. Albert Ellis developed rational-emotive behaviour therapy, while Aaron Beck developed cognitive therapy. A key feature of each approach is that our thinking about ourselves, the world, and our future plays a critical role in what we feel and what we do (Beck, 1976).

In Beck's research with depressed clients, he noticed a negative bias in their thinking, which he termed the Negative Cognitive Triad, which comprised a negative view of: (1) themselves, (2) the world, and (3) the future. This research shifted 'thinking' to the centre of our understanding of distress. Cognitive therapy, therefore, focused on teaching clients to identify and change unhelpful thought patterns (Beck et al., 1979). Over the years, this evidence-based intervention to understand and treat psychological difficulties grew into a most influential psychotherapeutic model in the treatment of psychological (e.g., depression) and body-based (e.g., chronic fatigue syndrome) problems.

With 'thinking' or 'cognition' at the centre of our psychosocial and emotional well-being, we can understand our feelings, actions, and reactions to events in our lives (e.g., losing a relationship, finishing a career) depend not only on the event but our interpretation and meaning we give to that event. In short, this understanding explains why people can response differently to the same event. For instance, two rugby players who played their roles equally well for 60 minutes before being substituted might leave the pitch with vastly different interpretations of the event. One player reflects,

> It's disappointing to be taken off after 60 minutes because I was playing well. The coach wants the team to finish strongly, and that's why he uses substitutions. I have done what they asked me to do. I will keep working on my tackling and fitness for the next international game.

In contrast, the other player reflects a much different meaning to the event:

> Being taken off while I'm playing well just shows that the coach doesn't rate me as a player. I know he thinks I'm useless in this position. The whole crowd can see I am not up to it. I'm sick of putting in the effort because what is the point?

This invented example shows how two people place a different meaning in the same event, which influences their emotional and behavioural responses. People are free to choose how they respond emotionally and behaviourally to events in their lives; however, to change these responses, we need to address the negativity bias and distorted thinking.

Thoughts, feelings, physiology, behaviour, and life experiences (environment) combine in a reciprocal interaction, so an event perceived as threating brings a cascade of reactions. For instance, a golfer waiting on the first tee perceives the situation as threatening because she wishes to launch the ball down the fairway but fears hitting the ball out of bounds. Along with these thoughts comes a physiological reaction (e.g., increased heart rate, increased muscular tension). These thoughts and physiological responses prompt greater performance anxiety (i.e., emotion) so the golfer wishes to get the shot over and done with as quickly as possible ('fight-flight-free-fawn–type' behaviour) and so rushes her shot without preparing properly and following her routine (i.e., behaviour).

One might ask: where do these issues begin, and what maintains these problems? In Beck's cognitive model, distorted and negatively biased thinking lies at the root of psychological disturbance. Trapped by such thinking, one cannot choose the right course of action to manage these challenging events in their lives. Negative automatic thoughts (NATs) comprise those thoughts in our mind laden with errors. For example, black and white thinking, in which the person thinks in extremes: "I always miss the fairway with my first tee shot and I will never hit a fairway today". Or catastrophising, assuming a negative outcome and a chain of worst-case scenarios. For instance, "If I get any more nervous on this tee, I cannot hit a ball and my chances of winning the Open will be gone forever and I'll probably lose my playing rights by the end of the season and my life as a golfer will be over" (for a complete list of cognitive distortions, please see McCarthy et al., 2023).

Throughout early childhood and beyond, individuals learn core beliefs about the self, others, and the world. These schemas (i.e., core beliefs) comprise memories, emotions, and bodily sensations, and they are the templates through which they filter information. Healthy and adaptive schemas support a person in living. Unhealthy and maladaptive schemas tend to be rigid, absolute, and negative. In this context, holding a core belief "I am worthless" means any incoming information sifts through this schema, distorting the information to match the underlying belief: "The coach gave me a chance to play today because he was all out of options". In a stressful situation, perhaps performing in front of a hostile crowd might activate an unhealthy schema, meaning, for example, an anxious athlete is susceptible to NATs such as "I can't cope with this hostility"; these negative thoughts activate matching emotions (e.g., worry) and behavioural responses (e.g., avoidance and withdrawal).

To reduce or ease these emotional and behavioural problems means targeting how we think and respond to our environment. We target cognitions while acknowledging the emotional, behavioural, and physiological components.

The change process begins with psychoeducation about the cognitive model. The cognitive model explains that the client's way of thinking influences the client's emotions and behaviours. Specifically, the practitioner and client collaborate to relieve symptoms at the beginning and then work to set goals and challenge cognitive distortions, NATs and schemas (i.e., core beliefs) and identify strategies for behavioural change. Together, the client and practitioner work to help the client manage themselves.

They establish part of this process through formulation or case conceptualisation. In this process, the practitioner and client build an understanding of the client's presenting problems. A formulation is a hypothesis about the origins (i.e., predisposing factors) and maintenance (i.e., precipitating, perpetuating factors) of the client's difficulties, alongside their positives (i.e., protective factors). For example, predisposing factors might be past traumatic events, adverse childhood experiences, and personality factors. Precipitating factors (i.e., current stressors) might relate to work, family, loss, illness, injury, and so on. Knowing this information means the client can intervene meaningfully with personal strategies, practical and psychological skills to help the client gain a sense of agency to progress towards change. As the client and practitioner gather more information about the client's presenting issues, this information and understanding can be added to the formulation (Mytton & Sequeira, 2017).

The centrality of a healthy therapeutic relationship remains fundamental to the process of change. The joint efforts of the client and practitioner (i.e., collaborative empiricism) encourages the client to contribute to their therapeutic journey and build self-efficacy and agency along the way. For example, cognitive strategies help the client identify, examine, challenge, and change automatic negative thoughts, errors in schemas, and information processing. One example of a cognitive strategy is Socratic questioning, in which a person's monologue is challenged using systematic questioning and inductive reasoning. Another example might be reality testing, which means searching for evidence for and against distorted thoughts. The practitioner introduces these cognitive skills and strategies in sessions so that the client can practise them at home and in the 'real world' setting so the client masters the strategies and gains control over the challenges of the past. In sport, for example, a practitioner might introduce emotion regulation strategies such as distraction, labelling, and reappraisal, which the athlete might use while on the tennis court or golf course.

The roots of the therapeutic modalities we use (e.g., CBT, REBT, PCT) ought to be explored for ethical and effective practice to allow the practitioner – along with the client – to choose interventions which facilitate change depending on the formulation created between them. Ethical and effective practice depends on integrating theory, research, and practice in an informed and considerate fashion. Juggling roles such as researcher and practitioner means we have many scientist-practitioners working in applied sport psychology. In this way, there is research in applied practice and applied practice in research

(Belar & Perry, 1992). In the world of sport, perhaps pursuing a research-informed over a research-driven or research-absent approach seems sensible to meet the needs of clients in dynamic and fluid terms (Hanley & Amos, 2017). Perhaps there is much more art than science to applying sport psychology; however, much also depends on several contributing factors, such as education, training, therapeutic orientation, and place of work.

Attachment

We are a social, relational, and bonding species living our lives with, and around, other people (Johnson, 2018). The basic tenets of modern attachment theory developed from the early work of John Bowlby (1969, 1973, 1979, 1988) and developed further by social psychologists (Mikulincer & Shaver, 2016). John Bowlby, through his work observing children in orphanages and mother-child interactions in his clinical practice, documented how children thrive among consistent and caring adults. He understood attachment schemas grow through all the experiences with caretakers that become unconscious reflexive predictions of the behaviour of others, and these schemas activate in relationships with others to seek or avoid proximity. Under stress, we readily witness attachment schemas because of their primary role in regulating our feelings. Schemas contour our conscious experience of others by triggering rapid and automatic appraisals hundreds of milliseconds before our perception of others reaches consciousness (Cozolino, 2014). Our attachment to our earliest caregivers formed a bond that shaped our brain and nervous system development, our emotions, and assembled plans about relationships to make sense of others and the world.

Attachment schemas are implicit memories known without being thought. Johnson (2018) offered three general facts about attachment theory. First, bonding with others confers an intrinsic survival strategy for human beings. Second, this theory focuses on emotion and its regulation with a particular focus upon fear, not just in everyday worries but also at a survival level regarding isolation, loneliness, loss, and death. Third, because it is a development theory, it focuses on growth and adaptation and those factors preventing it.

Though our social brain learns throughout life, stable patterns of attachment are obvious by the end of the first year of life (Ainsworth et al., 1978). Attachment researchers observed four categories of behaviour reflecting a child's implicit prediction about a mother's capacity to soothe and serve as a shelter: (1) secure, (2) avoidant, (3) anxious-ambivalent, and (4) insecure-disorganised. These four categories reflect the child's reunion behaviour – the child's reaction to the mother on returning following a brief absence. This 'strange situation' (Ainsworth et al., 1978) was an experimental design to examine an infant's innate tendency to move towards exploring new things; however, by moving away from the primary caregiver (e.g., mother), the infant may be scared because the primary caregiver is the infant's secure base. Our attachment style shapes our relationships later in life. Yet, we need to remember the interplay among culture, biological and physiological factors, genetic endowment, patterns of neural activation, and environmental processes (Sasaki & Kim, 2017) rather than focus solely on early attachment styles.

As an adult, for example, a secure attachment means you are likely to feel safe and relaxed around others, and safe to share your emotional experiences and soothe yourself. In a relationship, you feel worthy of the love and support of others. Secure attachment offers resilience under stress, optimism, high self-esteem, a sense of belonging, and the ability to self-disclose and be assertive, and to regulate difficult emotions. More anxiously attached people can become preoccupied with managing their own distress while avoidant individuals dismiss their own and others' needs, express less empathy and reciprocal support, turning away from vulnerability in themselves and others. In short, a secure attachment positively influences our ability to regulate emotion, social change, and mental health.

Researchers associate anxious and fearful avoidant attachment with vulnerability to depression, and various stress and anxiety disorders (e.g., obsessive-compulsive disorder). With depression, anxious attachment appears to relate to more interpersonal forms of depression categorised by a sense of loss, loneliness, abandonment, and helplessness. Researchers associate avoidant attachment with achievement-oriented forms of depression characterised by perfectionism, self-criticism, and compulsive self-reliance (Johnson, 2018; Mikulincer & Shaver, 2016). These achievement-oriented forms of depression seem commonplace in sport and performance settings. Anxious- and avoidant-attached people often hold a controlling stance towards others. Anxious-attached people struggle to assert themselves but use much criticism and complaint, whereas avoidant-attached people adopt a more dominant stance. Some people, however, learned that adults were unreliable and inconsistent, suggesting that relationships with others might be dangerous and an emotional upheaval. With an insecure-avoidant attachment style, one might feel anxious or fearful the other might reject or dismiss them. We can foster secure attachments by attending to children being seen, safe, soothed, and secure.

When faced with threat, our attachment system becomes activated, and we seek proximity and protection from our attachment figures. Caregivers who offer a safe base to reduce anxiety and promote security encourage the child to explore and engage confidently and rewardingly with others. Unavailable and unresponsive attachment figures or those ineffective in soothing mean children feel insecure and worry about whether they can trust others, handle feelings, or feel worthy of care. With an unpredictable caregiver as an attachment figure, the child tries even harder to get a response from the caregiver. Without an appropriate response, the child learns not to rely on others for help when threatened. With repeated experience, the child creates internal working models or mental representations of self, others, and relationships. These internal working models allow people to predict what to expect from others, how others will respond, and whether the world is a safe place – but change continues throughout the lifecycle, so change for the better or worse is possible (Bowlby, 1988).

Attachment in sport and therapy

Attachment is an interdisciplinary theory of social development (Bowlby, 1969, 1982). In this theoretical view, early relationships with caregivers are central to how individuals learn to regulate attention under attachment-related stress (Fonagy & Target, 2002; Forrest, 2008; Main, 2000; Hesse & Main, 2000). Few researchers in sport psychology have examined the links between early attachment experiences of stress (e.g., abuse, loss of a loved one, neglect, rejection, pressure to achieve, trauma) and how an athlete responds to competitive stress; however, an attachment-based self-regulatory perspective suggests these types of attachment experiences may underlie individual differences in athletes' attentional flexibility under competitive stress (Forrest, 2008).

In sport settings, we might search for markers to distinguish between attachment styles. One avenue of support comes from research on emotion-focused therapy, which distinguishes between stories and differences in vocal quality. Angus and Greenberg (2011) described differences in the structure of stories, and Watson and Greenberg (2000) described differences in vocal quality, based on research by Rice and Kerr (1986). For example, with a secure attachment, the personal narrative unfolds over a linear timeframe from the beginning to the middle to the end. With an avoidant attachment style, however, the client often tells 'empty stories' without the expected emotional content and focusing on external details as if told by a disinterested bystander (Baljon & Pool, 2013).

Adult attachment styles

We can study the adult attachment style in several ways. For example, the Adult Attachment Interview accesses a person's state of mind regarding attachment. It is a clinical interview focused on mental representations of parent–child relationships (Hesse, 1999). Bifulco et al. (2002) developed the Attachment Style Interview – a semi-structured interview based on the ability to make and maintain supportive relationships with attitudes on areas such as anger, constraint on closeness, desire for company, fear of rejection, fear of separation, mistrust, and self-reliance. Fonagy (2001) presented attachment styles in a two-factor structure: a secure-fearful axis and a dismissive-preoccupied axis. Security represents an experience of safety in closeness, while fearfulness represents a disorganisation of attachment. The dismissive attachment style protects the self through isolation, while in the enmeshed preoccupation style, one protects oneself by amplifying the other while negating or subjugating the self. An adult with a disorganised attachment style learned as a child that the parent or guardian is unpredictable so they remain hyper-vigilant to the state of others but pay little attention to their inner experience because they find it difficult to focus on their own thoughts, feelings, and sensations. They avoid focusing on the self because self-awareness arouses fear.

Lifespan development

Lifespan development explores how biological, cognitive, psychological, and environmental forces influence an individual's development across their lifetime. Every client has a unique journey that led them to walk into your office. By understanding this journey, we can tailor our support accurately to the client's needs. Lifespan development models provide a framework for doing this, exploring where the client has been and where they may be going. Proposing theoretical and practical principles about human development, lifespan development models highlight what a practitioner might expect to see with clients at different points in their life – and how to respond. We might hear the importance of this in conversations with coaches and other sports professionals, to make training or interventions 'age and stage' appropriate. So, where should we start?

Several lifespan development models have been presented by researchers working in developmental psychology, sports development, and sport psychology. We will cover a few of these. A common feature across models is the acknowledgement of normative and non-normative influences alongside non-events (Baltes & Smith, 2004). Normative changes refer to influences that affect everyone in a population or sub-group. Normative changes can either be age-graded, in that they have a strong correlation with chronological age – for example, transitioning between junior and senior age categories, or experiencing puberty – **or** they can be historically graded, in that they are linked to socio-cultural features of the time – for example, the COVID-19 pandemic or Russian doping scandal. Normative changes can normally be accounted for easily in a lifespan model. Non-normative influences are unpredictable events or experiences that not everyone will experience and/or experience concurrently; for example, athlete injury or parental divorce. Non-events are the transitions which individuals hope for or expect but that do not happen, for example Commonwealth Games selection. When these contextual factors are considered, a broader understanding of a client's development can be gathered.

Developmental psychology models

Lifespan development models originated in developmental psychology, with development considered a lifelong, multi-directional process, including periods of growth and loss. In 1963, Erik Erikson presented the psychosocial development theory, which identifies eight developmental stages that a healthily developing individual moves through from infancy to late adulthood. Each stage is characterised by a 'psychological crises', or tension, between a person's individual needs (psycho) and/or the demands of society (social). By successfully resolving these crises, individuals develop certain 'virtues or presentations'. For example, during stage two, if children are provided autonomy and encouraged to be independent, develop at their own pace, and be self-reliant, they are likely to present as wilful, or secure and confident in their ability to decide; however, if children in this stage are overly criticised, controlled, or instructed, they may develop experiences of shame around their ability to make their own decisions, lacking self-esteem and depending on others. Researchers identified that while useful, developmental models such as Erikson's fail to account for the nuances and complexities of life in a sporting context (Henriksen et al., 2010).

Sports development model

Clients often mention that their sport "is [their] life". While this is not always useful rhetoric, researchers have recognised that athletes' careers represent and warrant consideration as a miniature lifespan (Stambulova et al., 2020). Sport development models often come from a talent development or career transition perspective (Schinke et al., 2017), the most prominent of which is the Developmental Model of Sport Participation (Cote et al., 2007; Bruner et al., 2010). The DMSP proposes athletes transition through four stages across their athletic lifetime: (1) sampling, (2) specialising, (3) investment, and

Table 3.1 Stages and Key Tensions in Erikson's (1963) Psychosocial Development Theory

Stage/Age	Psychosocial Crisis	Existential Questions	Resultant Virtue
Stage 1 Infancy (<18 months)	Trust vs. mistrust	Can I trust the world?	Hope
Stage 2 Toddlerhood (1–3 years)	Autonomy vs. shame	Am I allowed to be myself?	Will
Stage 3 Early childhood (3–5 years)	Initiative vs. guilt	Can I do, explore, and play?	Purpose
Stage 4 Late childhood (5–12 years)	Industry vs. inferiority	Can I succeed?	Competence
Stage 5 Adolescence (12–18 years)	Identity vs. role confusion	Who am I? What can I become?	Fidelity
Stage 6 Early adulthood (18–40 years)	Intimacy vs. isolation	Can I be close with another?	Love
Stage 7 Middle adulthood (40–65 years)	Generativity vs. stagnation	Has my life been meaningful?	Care
Stage 8 Late adulthood (65+)	Ego Integrity vs. despair	Was it okay to be me?	Wisdom

(4) discontinuation. As clients shift through the stages, changes in the time spent engaging in deliberate play vs. deliberate practice, time spent engaging in one vs. multiple sports, and focuses for participation (e.g., enjoyment vs. performance outcome) shift. These stages are investment-based and not age-based, with transition points often dictated by sport and family circumstance. For example, two 7-year-olds may enter your office seeking support to increase their sports confidence. However, if one athlete is from an early specialisation sport (e.g., gymnastics) and the other is still in a sampling stage (e.g., playing football, hockey, and netball) their investment in and time spent playing sport may differ significantly.

Holistic athletic career model

The holistic athletic career model (Wylleman & Lavallee, 2004) offers a concise solution for sport psychologists. The comprehensive framework – incorporating both developmental psychology and sports development models – enables us to consider development of clients as athletes, and as people, too. The model presents four concurrent layers of lifespan development: (1) athletic, (2) psychological, (3) psychosocial, and (4) academic/vocational (Wylleman, 2019). The top layer, athletic development, accounts for athletes' transitions through sport investment and skill development. The second layer, psychological development, accounts for a variety of different developmental frameworks (e.g., Erikson, 1963) to consider the cognitive and psychological changes that occur during childhood, adolescence, and adulthood. The psychosocial layer reflects the influence of socialisation (e.g., cultural competence) and how the prioritisation of social sources changes over time. Finally, the academic/vocational layer explores a client's pursuits outside sport, for example through education and/or into work. These nested systems are constantly interacting, leading to the developmental outcomes our clients experience.

Using lifespan models in applied practice

Why are these models important, and how might we use them in applied practice? For you to use lifespan perspectives in your practice, you need to consider how you collect lifespan information as part of your intake/assessment process. Some of this information might be self-explanatory, for example, a client's age and education/employment status. Other aspects may take longer to ascertain and come out discretely during your intake or as you build a therapeutic relationship with your client. Psychologists have demonstrated that lifespan models influence the way they work in several ways (e.g., Davies, 2018; Moffat et al., 2023). Four examples include: (1) assisting the explanation of presenting difficulties, (2) identifying and developing appropriate interventions, (3) preparation and awareness for clients, and (4) self-discovery for practitioners.

Lifespan perspectives can be helpful for explaining a client's presenting difficulties. Several client presentations can be linked back to previous experiences and/or developmental stages. For example, in a sporting context, difficulties with athletic identity, athlete burnout, and low motivation have been associated with experiences of specialisation (Cote et al., 2020). Meanwhile, from a developmental perspective, transitions are stressful. Each of Erikson's (1963) stages is linked with an increase in anxiety. Maybe if your client is going through a developmental transition (e.g., puberty), their negative thoughts, feelings, and appraisals are magnified. When working with a client, we might then ask ourselves how lifespan markers might be creating, influencing, or perpetuating the client's difficulties.

Developmental features should be continuously considered when making therapeutic decisions, with content tailored appropriately to the client's stage (Kipp, 2018). Environments often teach us to follow directions, with the world of work/education and sport being no different. Adolescents might enter an office filled with self-doubt, confusion, and frustration as they navigate the challenges they face. Here, practitioners might consider the importance of providing autonomy. Autonomy provision is always important in sport psychology practice, linked to various positive outcomes (e.g., Deci & Ryan, 2002); however, for adolescents, it might be increasingly important with healthy autonomy development and increased self-confidence attached to the ability to decide. Using lifespan perspectives may also highlight the need to take a step back with a client, resolving underlying tensions or difficulties.

Using lifespan perspectives may also enable the focus of practice to not just be on 'what is happening now' but on preparing for 'what might be about to happen'. If applied psychologists are aware of developmental transitions that may be upcoming for a client, they may help them prepare proactively, as opposed to responding reactively as/when they occur (Danish et al., 1993). This might include developing relevant psychological skills (e.g., breathing techniques for managing anxiety, or goal setting for establishing expectations and managing or directing motivation). In most cases, the amount of influence lifespan perspectives have on psychologist decision-making will be dictated by the time available to the psychologist with the client. For example, a psychologist practising full-time in an academy context may have more contact time to prioritise lifespan changes than say, a psychologist working in private practice where a client approaches for a short-term (e.g., six-session) service.

Equity, diversity, discrimination, and inclusion

The work we do as practitioners with others brings the obvious observations that the clients we see differ from us in several ways. Some of these differences are visible (e.g., age, race, language, accent, physical appearance, disability [which we can see]), and some are invisible (e.g., disability [which we cannot see], sexuality, religion, values, upbringing). It is easy to make assumptions about others only to realise later how inaccurate and insensitive we were in making these assumptions. Our relationship with difference and diversity ought to be explored and understood to help us appreciate how we judge, discriminate, exclude, and cause harm through fear, ignorance, prejudice, and so forth (Postings, 2022).

The importance of diversity and difference in our work relates to legal requirements (e.g., The Equality Act, 2010) and to ethical and professional responsibilities which we can find in the ethical guidance documentation of the HCPC (2016) and BPS (2018). On a wider scale, issues of power, privilege, and oppression pervade society so we ought to consider issues of social justice. Social justice is "both a goal of action and the process of action itself, which involves an emphasis on equity or equality for individuals in society in terms of access to a number of different resources and opportunities, the right to self-determination or autonomy and participation in decision-making, freedom from oppression, and a balancing of power across society" (Cutts, 2013, pp. 9–10).

This social justice perspective draws in the social and political contexts within which we aim to understand people we support in service delivery. Working with a client on a tennis court or on a running track highlights the many individual psychological factors influence the person and their performances, yet at the same time, we might be blinded to the numerous social factors triggering distress (Feltham et al., 2017).

Sport, like many other walks of life, witnesses inequality on micro- (individual), meso- (team, squad) and macro- (political and societal) levels (Winter & Collins, 2016). If, however, we do not hold a socio-cultural perspective in applied sport psychology, we will not see the issues of inequality, power, and oppression.

Assumptions

The nature of sport, especially elite and professional sport, means there is a divide between us (i.e., public) and them (i.e., elite performers, coaches, backroom staff). Many practitioners work with these elite performers, coaches, and backroom staff but may be unaware of their strongly held assumptions entering these organisations. To assume means to make undue claims without proof. We might assume how a professional golfer lives her life or an Olympic swimmer lives his life. With our firmly held assumptions, what do we wish to know and understand about our client? Perhaps little if we cannot see how our assumptions limit our curiosity and understanding. We need to challenge our assumptions to work effectively with others. We might assume the following.

- She has millions in the bank, so she has no worries.
- Being an Olympian must be amazing.
- This slump will end soon.
- Professional footballers have the perfect life.
- Things can only get better.

If we are unaware of our assumptions, we cannot see how much they influence our work with clients. We might gamble with their life's work rather than assessing for accuracy. We need to separate fact from fiction.

Culturally informed applied sport psychology

No matter which topic we meet in applied sport psychology, the element of cultures lies within and around it. We encounter age, community, disability, sport level, sexual orientation, and so forth. In short, every human interaction contains cultures (Hanrahan, 2010). To be a culturally competent practitioner, therefore, means understanding norms, beliefs, values, and behaviours which are much more than nationality or race. Cultural competence means understanding other cultures and being aware of one's own cultural assumptions (Quartiroli et al., 2020). Wells (2000) published a synthesis model of cultural development suggesting cultural awareness, sensitivity, and competence do not meet the level of cultural development necessary to meet the health care needs of a diverse population. Wells (2000) presented six stages, from cultural incompetence to cultural proficiency. The first three stages represent the cognitive phase and comprise cultural incompetence, cultural knowledge, and cultural awareness. The final three stages form the affective phase and comprise cultural sensitivity, cultural competence, and cultural proficiency. This final phase focuses on changes in attitudes and behaviours because of the knowledge gathered in the cognitive phase. A critical component of the final stage is working with individuals from other cultures to progress through the affective stages. The culturally competent practitioner ought to work within a culturally competent organisation; however, maybe the work one undertakes in a sports club or organisation is to develop a culturally proficient organisation by providing information about culture(s) in the cognitive phase of development and discussions, interactions, and experience in the affective phase of development (Hanrahan, 2010).

Quartiroli et al. (2020) explored the perceived cultural competence of sport psychology practitioners using an online survey of 203 respondents. Though most participants reported receiving formal training in cultural competence, it appeared to be only moderately effective – it had a limited ability to predict the reported level of sport psychology practitioners' perceived cultural competence. The authors suggested that one reason for these results could be the lack of support for sport psychology practitioners engaging in culturally centred self-reflective practice and the narrow role of these factors in training programmes. To address these issues, training programmes and curricula could integrate cultural competencies following the International Society of Sport Psychology (ISSP) "Position Stand on Cultural Competence" (Ryba et al., 2013). Beyond this contribution from training programmes and professional bodies, the responsibility and accountability of fostering cultural competence lies with the sport psychology practitioner. A proactive approach to cultivate and ripen one's cultural competence fosters scholarly, applied professional practice and supervision so that trainees may understand other cultures and be aware of their own cultural assumptions.

The performance narrative and identity foreclosure

A foundation of the performance narrative is that the only way to be success-ful in elite sport is to fix sport performance at the centre of one's life story (Douglas & Carless, 2006). Extricating oneself from culturally available nar-rative scripts challenges most athletes, coaches, parents, and teams because "Even when a teller is recounting a unique set of individual, personal events, he or she can only do so by drawing upon story structures and genres drawn from the narrative resources of a culture" (McLeod, 1997, p. 94). Yet, we find other narratives to challenge this specific performance narrative (Carless & Douglas, 2013). These other narratives offer a point of resistance to the domi-nant performance narrative, such as the relational narrative and the discovery narrative. The relational narrative proposes that relationships with others are as significant or more significant than training or performance outcomes. In the discovery narrative, self-worth is unrelated to sporting achievement. The need to explore and discover a rich and fulfilling life takes primacy over the need to perform in sport, regardless of others' expectations (Douglas & Car-less, 2006). It is precisely this tension among narratives which might persuade us to ignore or silence some narratives to champion the culturally preferred narrative.

This line of research argues that alternative narratives can liberate those who feel ensnared in the performance narrative because they can re-story or reappraise their own lives and futures owing to these narratives. Perhaps a balance among narratives (e.g., performance, relational, discovery) fits the balance of one's day, from family commitments (e.g., relational narrative) to training and performance (e.g., performance narrative) to rest and recovery (e.g., discovery narrative). Each of these roles might involve one or a few of these available narratives, but choice remains at its core (Sparkes, 2004). The potential alternatives to the performance narrative mean more space for well-being alongside performance.

One challenge of the performance narrative, especially for those who live the part of the athlete, is that they chronicle their lives and behave in ways that conform to the culturally dominant narrative, foreclosing their identity, sac-rificing relationships to pursue success, and threatening long-term well-being (Carless & Douglas, 2013). Carless and Douglas (2013) illustrated alternative narratives and multidimensional stories from 'living the part of the athlete' to those who 'resist the part of the athlete' and those who 'play the part of the athlete'. Those who resist the part of the athlete present alternative narrative types and a multidimensional story, whereas those who play the part of the athlete change their story and actions according to the socio-cultural context and present the performance story when required to do so.

A critical life task and process of late adolescence is to establish a sense of personal identity (Erikson, 1959). Extending Erikson's theoretical proposi-tions, Marcia (1966) operationalised four identity statuses: identify achieve-ment, identity diffusion, identity moratorium, and identity foreclosure. Identity achievement involves a stable commitment to occupation and ideology that follows actively exploring alternatives, whereas identity diffusion means neither exploring nor obligating to any stable career or ideological commitments. Identity moratorium means actively exploring career and ideological options, while yet to make a firm commitment. Identity foreclosure represents those who make steady commitments to career and ideology without exploring alternatives. The idea of identity foreclosure seems clear in sport, especially when parents, siblings, friends, coaches, and teachers socialise children and adolescents into sport and the young athlete then receives rewards and recognition for competing and investing countless hours in their sport. Considering alternatives to their occupational identity might not amount to much because their time, energy, and interest lean towards being an athlete (Brewer et al., 2021; Linnemeyer & Brown, 2010; Petitpas & France, 2010). Brewer et al. (2021) developed a sport-specific, self-report measure of identity foreclosure with the potential as an assessment tool for research and practice with athletes.

The caprices of sport mean one's early and exclusive commitment of time, effort, and energy to sport does not guarantee one's place in sport, in either the short or long term. For example, an injury that ends one's career or deselection might mean a fractured career for an athlete just getting started in their career. For other athletes, their skills and abilities feel tightly wound around being an athlete without ever exploring how to cope and challenge themselves in other ways outside the sport setting. Tying up one's competence and confidence in a specific line of work (e.g., running, golf, tennis) bestows security on one level but reduces one's exploratory behaviour or an awareness of one's other skills, abilities, and needs. Some athletes see nothing wrong with confining themselves to their work to avoid any feelings of self-doubt which might arise in other aspects of their lives (e.g., relationships, raising a family) (Petitpas & France, 2010).

For athletes facing retirement after a long career, a personal identity crisis might unfold as the threat to the individual's sport identity makes way to establish a new identity. Life skills such as time management, job searching strategies, interviewing skills, and creating a curriculum vitae hold value; however, they might not meet the psychological needs and concerns of the athlete facing the prospect of retirement. We need to tread carefully here to allow the foreclosed athlete to choose a way forward that addresses shared and hidden motives.

Keeping pace with theory, research, and practice

Most trainees who read this book will cover a range of core components (e.g., research and research methods, applied sport psychology in practice) and specialist components (e.g., cognitive processes, developmental processes, social processes, individual differences, psychological skills training) at undergraduate and postgraduate levels. Trainees might read about research and research methods, personality, motivation, self-confidence, concentration, arousal, stress, anxiety, group processes, psychological skills training, practising sport psychology, and skill acquisition across several modules. This core and specialist knowledge base helps to set the stage for specialist training in a taught doctoral programme, for example. Within a taught doctoral programme, a trainee might begin with basic counselling skills (e.g., developing rapport, mutual respect) before addressing specifics related to how one could practise, such as assessment (e.g., intakes, observation), theoretical and therapeutic approaches (PCT, CBT), individual issues (e.g., referrals, career termination), team-related issues (e.g., managing conflict, shared identity), working with specific populations (e.g., children, athletes with physical disabilities), and mental skills (e.g., imagery, self-talk). Within each of these themes, subthemes of success, failure, desires, abuse, loss, and trauma find a home. When collated in this manner, the knowledge and skills to be an effective practitioner seem overwhelming; however, we need to remember a few core principles.

First, sport psychology practitioners work with people. To work with people, we need to develop our basic counselling and therapeutic skills, which are skills we develop continuously throughout our working lives. Second, we rely on and trust our therapeutic models to guide our work with clients, so it helps to appreciate that we can let the models take the strain rather than us, the practitioners. Third, the presenting issues among our clients might mean reading a current peer-reviewed article or two as part of our continuous professional development to help our clients and ourselves. Reading two peer-reviewed articles each week adds up to about 100 peer-reviewed articles across the year. After all, our clients present complex and multifaceted issues that require our attention and effort. Fourth, you are not alone. There are peer groups, supervisors, special-interest groups, and many more who are keen to support you at each stage of your career. Fifth, through these groups, you can contribute to our knowledge, understanding, and practice within applied sport psychology by contributing your applied research and reflections to peer-reviewed journals for the betterment of the field. Finally, the profession of sport and exercise psychology thrives on the excitement and passion of its members, so reading books and articles, connecting with others, sharing knowledge and experience at workshops and conferences, and supporting peers creates a buzz about the work we do with experience, knowledge, courage, and empathy. Sport and exercise psychology endlessly fascinates us – perhaps it fascinates you, too.

Summary

In this chapter, we have presented some approaches to therapeutic support to set the scene for working with a client from a person-centred approach. Next, we presented a general background to some theoretical perspective that is helpful when working with athletes across the lifespan, such as attachment theory and adult attachment style. Lifespan development and developmental psychology models add to our work with athletes. Finally, we consider equity, diversity, discrimination, and inclusion in our practice before we work with clients. In the next chapter, we explore the therapeutic relationship and the essential qualities of an effective sport psychology practitioner.

4 The therapeutic relationship and working contexts

Introduction

In the late 1990s, Poczwardowski et al. (1998) suggested that the field of sport psychology would benefit from a crossing with counselling psychology in theoretical frameworks, delivery models, service delivery, and supervision. This argument made sense then, and makes sense now, because to establish credibility with other disciplines and the public, we need dependable standards of service delivery. We need to make a case for how and why sport psychology services benefit the client. But before we outline the case, we need to survey the terrain of the sporting milieu. Although a clinical model of diagnosing illness, prescribing a course of action, and fulfilling the treatment might be appropriate occasionally, a counselling approach resonates profoundly. For example, a counselling approach might open with a client feeling dissatisfied or ambitious to reach a goal. Through setting goals and developing skills, the client achieves a goal or set of goals. This distinction between a clinical approach and a counselling approach works well for sport psychology practitioners and athletes because historically, the delivery of sport psychology emerged from physical education and sports science (motor learning and control, skill acquisition), meaning sport psychology practitioners may more closely resemble coaches than clinicians or counsellors (Andersen et al., 2001).

If we, like coaches and counselling psychologists, aim to work well with athletes, teams, and coaches, then good working relations seem sensible. From research nearly 90 years ago (e.g., Rosenzweig, 1936) to recent meta-analyses on the practitioner–client relationships in various treatments, what influences client outcomes might appear to be factors specific to treatment models (e.g., PCT, CBT), but it is the common factors across different treatments that account for a substantial amount of variance in outcome (Schore, 2014; Tryon & Tryon, 2011), and the most frequently researched common factor is the quality of the therapeutic alliance (Ivarsson & Andersen, 2016). Again, many studies and meta-analyses have shown that the relationship accounts for as much – if not more – variance in outcome as the treatment itself (Ardito & Rabellino, 2011; Norcross & Lambert, 2011; Sexton & Whiston, 1994).

DOI: 10.4324/9781003453857-4

Getting our relationships right matters because without it, when the client does not feel understood and/or when the helper seems lacking in concern and competence, client adherence falls. The client's adherence will also fall when interventions are too complex, too effortful, and heaved upon the client without the client's input. What we know is that the client needs to be ready – we need to adhere to the client's 'needs' and 'wants' (Meichenbaum & Turk, 1987; Petitpas et al., 1999). Orlick and Partington (1987) conducted one of the first studies to evaluate sport psychology delivery. In this study, the researchers explored the characteristics of effective consultants by interviewing 75 Canadian athletes who had participated in the 1984 Olympic Games and had employed consultant services. The best consultants were good listeners, built rapport, and cared for their athletes. They were knowledgeable, with something helpful to offer bespoke to the client. In contrast, the worst consultants had poor interpersonal skills, lacked sensitivity to individual needs, and spent little time one-to-one with the client.

Developing one's skills, experiences, and interpersonal skills to develop rapport and a positive working environment takes time. This work normally begins in doctoral training programmes and continues throughout one's career; however, an emphasis on self-awareness, self-knowledge, and adaptability means the good psychologist can get off to a great start.

The essential qualities of an applied sport psychology practitioner

The developing profession of applied sport psychology means we are researching more about the essential qualities of an applied sport psychology practitioner. Although on the surface, such a question might seem obvious, we need to understand what works for whom when seeking the support of a sport psychology practitioner. Stakeholders such as coaches, athletes, and physicians, among others, want sport psychology practitioners to have psychological, sport-specific, and contextual knowledge to help their clients. Alongside this knowledge, however, effective practitioners are empathetic, likeable, open, and trustworthy – so interpersonal skills rank highly, as well. The help a sport psychology practitioner brings to a therapeutic encounter also needs to be client-centred, so that formulations and interventions remain practical and meaningful to the client. The sporting milieu demands knowledge, skills, and – critically – psychosocial characteristics to work effectively with all clients. These psychosocial characteristics (e.g., courage, flexibility, integrity, self-awareness, self-acceptance) influence interactions with clients and relations with the wider team and community. Without self-awareness, self-knowledge, and self-understanding, practitioners would not – consciously or unconsciously – know how they are behaving. Lack of awareness of one's attitudes and beliefs might lead a practitioner to behave in line with homophobic, racist, sexist, or other oppressive stereotypes in a workplace. In summary, research and practice tells us we define effective practitioners by what they know, what they do, and how they present as individuals (Tod et al., 2017).

For most practitioners, however, arriving with confidence about knowing, doing, and presenting oneself takes time. This time spent in training, supervision, peer supervision, and reflection operates in stages. For example, neophyte practitioners might assume an expert problem-solving perspective, fitting clients to their interventions. One can understand this rigidity because of countertransference issues trying to show one's competence to the client, employer, or supervisor. Through experience, the developing practitioner recognises, values, and accepts the role of the client in the therapeutic alliance and collaborates rather than leads the problem-solving process to harness their resources and moulding interventions to suit the client (Owton et al., 2014; Tod et al., 2009, 2011).

The relationship between the practitioner and client drives effective outcomes in service delivery in applied sport psychology, but this relationship may not seem so obvious in a sport setting where the hierarchy of power pervades, with owners, managers, and coaches steering strategy and operations. Witnessing service delivery as a collaborative process means cherishing the client, shrinking the self as the change agent, and heightening the co-operative fortitude when two people work together towards the tasks and goals of service delivery (Tod & Bond, 2010).

The effective practitioner delivering effective services relies on several factors, such as relationships and goals, presenting cues, client needs, situational context, professional knowledge, and theoretical orientation. Among these factors, one weight-bearing pillar among all helping professions is analytical thinking (Martindale & Collins, 2013). Expertise develops with experience, reflection, meta-reflection on experience, and feedback. What begins as variable, inconsistent, and awkward (e.g., establishing a working alliance with a client) becomes stable, consistent, and relaxed. The efficiency of judgements and decisions integrates several areas for work combining to an overall strategy rather than handling variables in isolation. Martindale and Collins (2013) offered the example of a one-off incident of aggression which we witness in sport regularly. The skilled helper acknowledges the isolated variable but perceives complex patterns of behaviour. Where the beginning practitioner needed support and reassurance from a supervisor, they now rely upon themselves more to generate suitable strategies and discuss their choices in supervision afterwards.

Though we have some research to explain what works with whom and why in applied sport psychology, we have some way to travel before definitive answers abound. Martindale and Collins (2010) argued that when we explore why a process or intervention worked with a client-athlete, we can understand the decision-making process, what information we consider and ignore, and which ensuing direction one travels with one's client. Framing or setting the boundaries of our attention helps to cohere the situation (i.e., framing the context) and we can peek behind the curtains to understand how professionals think in action (Schön, 1991). Such thinking in action helps novice and experienced practitioners and clients ultimately gain the most because, together, practitioners develop competence and gain a broader conceptualisation of their practice, interpersonal and relational issues, and presentation to the public (Hays, 2006).

The research exploring the qualities and characteristics of practitioners for delivery effective services continues to grow. Researchers gathered perspectives from each side of the therapeutic dyad: athletes and sport psychology consultants (e.g., Anderson et al., 2004; Lubker et al., 2008; Orlick & Partington, 1987; Sharp & Hodge, 2011, 2013; Sharp et al., 2015). For example, Sharp and Hodge (2011) recounted that effective sport psychology consultants could show confidence in building a professional, respectful relationship with their clients but also sustain a collaborative relationship to meet their clients' needs. This strong, balanced, and collaborative relationship ties itself to a positive therapeutic process, which supports interventions to improve performance. Sound, ethical practice such as establishing and clarifying boundaries of confidentiality built trust with coaches (Sharp & Hodge, 2013).

Keeping your head – the mindful sport psychology practitioner

Being involved in sport at all levels challenges the most experienced sport psychology practitioners to manage anxieties, expectations, frustrations, and pressures that might be personal, social, political, or economic. The greater one's exposure to supporting athletes and teams at Olympic and Paralympic Games, for example, the greater the scrutiny. Williams and Andersen (2012, pp. 140) neatly captured the stance for a sport psychology practitioner in the lines from Rudyard Kipling's poem, "If", to "keep your head when all about you are losing theirs" and to "meet with triumph and disaster and treat those two impostors just the same". Being mindful and present in precarious settings means preparing oneself personally and professionally – it is a way of being (Andersen & Mannion, 2011; Zizzi & Andersen, 2010). These authors argued for mindfulness for the sport psychology practitioner to become attuned to themselves and their clients to hold a non-judgemental, empathic sense for others and raise the quality of client care.

We know from the accumulated research in clinical and counselling psychology how critical the working alliance – or therapeutic relationship – between a sport psychology practitioner and an athlete-client remains for positive outcomes (Lambert & Simon, 2008). For best practice in sport, exercise, and performance settings, knowing what connects or disconnects us from our clients remains paramount. If, as Williams and Andersen (2012) identified, professional identity (i.e., insecure professional identities), ego (i.e., fragile and defended egos), and boundaries (i.e., rigid adherence to professional boundaries) prevent us from working productively with our client, then we need greater understanding and correction for the context (McCann, 2000).

Identity – professional identity

Struggles with one's personal and professional identity are common phenomena in sport and exercise psychology for sport psychology practitioners in training and post-training (e.g., Tod, 2007; Tod et al., 2009, 2011;

Tod & Bond, 2010). To think there might be another view on identity seems far removed from the socio-cultural view of a sport psychology practitioner, yet Bruce Ogilvie, the father of modern applied sport psychology, advised that "The extent to which you can lose your ego as a consultant in this field is going to determine the extent to which you are truly a contributor in the lives of the athletes you seek to serve" (cited in Simons & Andersen, 1995, p. 467). But if one needs to lose one's ego, it is worth knowing what one means by 'ego' in the beginning. If we think of 'ego' as the 'I' or 'self' which is conscious and thinks, it seems wholly relevant to engage one's ego in service delivery; however, how one's ego contributes or interferes with service delivery ought to be understood from the sport psychology practitioner's own sense of 'self' and the defences wheeled in to protect that 'self'. Andersen (2020) argued that concepts about the self – like self-esteem, self-image, and self-worth – are illusory and misunderstood, hitching much suffering to the person. If we construct our egos or identities or selves, perhaps we can deconstruct them. In the Dalai Lama's lectures (1984), he talked about the nonexistence of a self:

> With regard to selflessness, it is necessary to know what "self" is—to identify the self that does not exist. Then one can understand its opposite, selflessness. Selflessness is not a case of something that existed in the past becoming non-existent; rather, this sort of "self" is something that never did exist. What is needed is to identify as non-existent something that always was non-existent, for due to not having made such identification, we are drawn into the afflictive emotions of desire and hatred as well as all the problems these bring.
>
> (pp. 51–52)

If we construct our self and identity (e.g., "I'm a talented sport psychology practitioner"), and prize this construction, then we are opening ourselves to the possibility that another's actions (e.g., someone discrediting our work) might harm or extinguish this identity. This false self (e.g., "I'm a talented sport psychology practitioner") creates much suffering and unhappiness.

How does one go about being 'no one' in applied sport psychology practice? Letting go of one's judgements about one's self begins this process of 'no-self'. Andersen and Mannion (2011) presented one example with an athlete called Sammy. Sammy, a baseball player, described his two selves, one who excelled in practice as "Baseball-Beast Sammy" and one who faltered on a game day as "Scared-Shitless Sammy". We too, as practitioners, can set off on this journey of self-discovery, or no-self-discovery, but our constructed self – being fragile and protected – needs a non-judgemental space, filled with compassion and understanding, to unshackle. Which voice shall we return to when we feel like we are 'no good' or 'not helping anyone' or 'not making any progress'? The voice that brings us back to the concept of no-self can be our own voice. Dropping the self and its attachments makes up a movement, not a move.

Feeling fraudulent

Most students and professionals travel through peculiar, confusing, and worrying places on their way to becoming competent practitioners in applied sport psychology. Though one might never arrive at a place of comfort, practitioners' growing competence, confidence, and familiarity with challenges makes the surrounding terrain traversable (Stevens & Andersen, 2007). Occasionally, all those on the practitioner continuum from trainee to senior professional feel fraudulent. Although this fraudulent feeling finds its strength among trainees, it lessens with growing experience working in the field. The observations and questions might include: "I don't know enough to do this job well" or "I don't have enough experience and there's so much I don't know" or "My problems overwhelm me. How can I help others?" or "I don't seem to make a difference to the athletes who see me". Such thoughts and feelings of fraudulence also serve as points of reflection to understand how and why we practise in the ways we do. Academia challenges students to learn about selected topics (e.g., therapeutic modalities, theories of motivation) and gain experience in clinical practice (e.g., practicum placement at a professional football club) while underscoring how much the student does not know and what remains to be learned. Rather than understanding this experience as becoming, many students feel that they need to know more, do more, and be more. This tug-of-war between what I know and what I need to know strains most students and one's self-image (e.g.," I am knowledgeable" or "I know what to do") because it remains opens to scrutiny and examination in assessments, triads, and placement experiences. Now one's defences come to one's aid such as denial (e.g., "I am not incompetent") and projection (i.e., "My supervisor is incompetent") (Stevens & Andersen, 2007). The difficulty here means that the student or trainee receives an opportunity to learn but cannot accept it because their defence prevents their learning – and the crooked thinking athlete-clients present, sport psychology practitioners present, too. The psychopathologies and worries shared by clients (e.g., anxiety, depression, pathogenic weight control) are ours, too. Our willingness to see and accept our maladaptive thoughts and actions helps us to be more congruent, empathic, and warm. Taking the heat out of our shame takes the heat out of the shame client-athletes feel, too. Being human means we are fallible, and as fallible human beings, our acts of charity and acceptance towards ourselves become examples to others, especially to trainees undertaking their training (Stevens & Andersen, 2007).

Boundary blurring adds to this sense of feeling fraudulent. Though most sport psychology training programmes dedicate much teaching and learning to professional ethics, especially for practicum placements, trainees and seasoned professionals often slip into grey areas of professional boundaries (Andersen et al., 2001). One example comes from Williams and Andersen (2012) where the first author, Dave, shared his experiences with the Australian Paralympic table tennis team when he travelled with them for a tour of Europe in the lead-up to the 2012 Games in London: "On this tour I found myself as a lifeguard (of sorts), a beautician, a luggage carrier, a stand-in pretend coach, a cameraman, and also a psychologist" (p. 148). These many 'hats' (i.e., fulfilling other duties) might give one a sense that one's core role as a psychologist does not afford the prominence of a physician or other member of staff whose role remains clearly defined. But when we view this experience through the lens of a team and everyone helping each other, the context makes more sense.

Gaining entry

Gaining entry to work with athletic teams sets in place a foundation upon which to deliver services in applied sport psychology. In 1988, Ravizza wrote about the notion of 'gaining entry' to work long-term with athletic clients after working extensively with elite athletes at intercollegiate, Olympic, and professional levels to enhance performance specifically through mental skills training. When Ravizza (1988) wrote about gaining entry to working with athletic teams on a long-term basis, he emphasised strategies for overcoming barriers to entry such as establishing respect and trust of key athletic personnel (e.g., head coach), clarifying services to be provided, presenting services to coaching staff and athletes, knowing the sport and the coach's orientation and team dynamics, and gaining support at all levels of the organisation (e.g., support staff, administration, medical staff). On the practitioner's side, clarifying one's role meant identifying one's own consulting needs from the team, maintaining confidentiality, communicating openly and honestly, and collecting research data.

Since the publication of Ravizza (1988), much has changed and yet much remains the same. As Ravizza explained, the world of sport did extremely well without sport psychology practitioners and continues to do so. In these circumstances, therefore, we need to proceed carefully, yet confidently, within our allotted roles. At each step of the process to gain entry, challenges lie ahead for the sport psychology practitioner: (1) initial meetings and interviews; (2) building relationships with athletes, coaches, and support staff; (3) understanding and respecting the specific sport and its personnel; and (4) preparing for an appraisal by the athletes and coaches of your approach and fit with the team (Fifer et al., 2008).

From these and other accounts, we know what to expect setting off to work with an athletic team; however, unless we plan and operationalise our knowledge for these trials (e.g., interviews, presentations), we are no further forward. We need to acknowledge the role played by location, luck, expertise, and serendipitous relations (i.e., who you know and what they think about you), yet not lose hope in pursuit of our goals. Each sport brings its own physical, emotional, and mental demands for each athlete. Open (e.g., rugby), closed (e.g., golf), subjective (e.g., gymnastics), and objective (e.g., 400-metre hurdles) sports need to be understood and our work tailored to their needs. Yet, we remain at a disadvantage because we do not know why the practices of experienced professionals work (Martindale & Collins, 2010)

To gain entry to work with athletics teams presents several challenges (e.g., barriers, preferences for the type of support, age, gender) for the sport psychology practitioner, yet it remains a vital professional ability (Mack et al., 2018; Poczwardowski et al., 2020). We think about 'gaining entry' as a therapeutic alliance built around goals, tasks, and bonds (Bordin, 1979), but it more likely comprises two parts: formal entry and psychological entry. Formal entry encompasses initial meeting and contracting, and psychological entry reflects being accepted by the clients, gaining their trust and cooperation (Brown et al., 2011). Applied sport psychology practitioners are beginning to sketch their exploration of 'gaining entry' (Poczwardowski et al., 2020).

To move along discussions, exploration, and research, Poczwardowski et al. (2020) organised a two-phase roundtable discussion with four consultants with extensive experience in sport psychology. The discussions confirmed Ravizza's (1988) original insights about gaining entry – but they also added new insights reflecting the social and generational changes since his original publication, such as the role of gender, preferences of modern athletes, interactive observation, and the advent of technology and teleconsulting in service delivery bringing opportunities and threats to the service delivery process. The swift changes in client demographics – and in sport and performance knowledge – means one's professional development remains ongoing to optimise gaining entry in sport and performance contexts.

Working in context with specific populations

Sport psychology practitioners work with individual issues (e.g., career termination), team-related issues (e.g., managing conflict), and with specific populations (e.g., children). These specific populations might include child athletes, professional athletes, masters athletes, athletes with disabilities, athletes with intellectual disabilities, and/or athletes who are blind/visually impaired or deaf/hard of hearing (Hanrahan & Andersen, 2010). We cannot prepare for the needs of all these athletes in a training programme; however, we can meet their needs at the point of entry with genuineness, empathy, unconditional positive regard, warmth, and presence. As we develop as practitioners, we can broaden and deepen our knowledge, skills, and competencies. We shall briefly consider working with the range of populations just described, and you can find further guidelines in other resources (e.g., de Bressy de Guast et al., 2013; Hanrahan, 2015; Hannan et al., 2010).

Hanrahan (2015), in an article about psychological skills training for athletes with disabilities, suggested that the greatest adaptations required when working with these athletes related to communication issues rather than the content of the skills being taught. Working with athletes with disabilities means working with patience and creativity to find the most appropriate communication. For example, working with athletes with hearing impairments might mean developing visual communication (e.g., video, text messaging, whiteboards) while working with athletes with visual impairments might require audio recordings and vivid descriptions).

Who is the client?

Though it may seem obvious to you that your client is the person with whom you work, the wider interconnectedness of one person means others play a role in the person's therapeutic experience. For instance, the client sitting in your private practice might have been encouraged, persuaded, or pressured to seek your support. We might assume the client's self-determined actions establishing an initial meeting and setting off for the experience of our services. For much of our work within the sporting milieu, we work with individual clients (individual therapy), but also sometimes a child will have a parent or parents present (family therapy). With child and adolescent athletes, the problems in living and performing in sport often intertwine with their experience of family life.

Working with families

A significant proportion of my (Paul) private practice involves working with child and adolescent athletes and their families. Understanding and engaging with systems like families and organisations presents old and new challenges to sport psychology practitioners. Something going wrong within the family as a system (e.g., broken boundaries) or the sports team as a system (e.g., ineffective communications between team members) means we need to explore the structural and systemic elements of that entity. In short, it is the relations between two, or among more than two, people which we explore. This broad perspective of the systemic dimensions of one's life means we can better understand presenting issues and the social, cultural, and organisational context in which they arise. While presenting issues might focus on the self, they also present the wider systemic context in which the client exists (e.g., school, sports team, family). All these interrelated parts of the system mean that change in one part affects the whole system. In a family system, we might have a mother, a father, and three children. If, for instance, a mother gains a promotion to chief executive officer (CEO) meaning more travel during the working week, the roles and tasks of everyday living change and tip the balance of relationships within the family. The stable conditions of family life change with this change within the system, and the feedback from the experience further changes the system. For instance, the mother, now earning more money, finds herself away from home, her husband, and her children. She does not pick up her daughter from gymnastics or her sons from rugby practice anymore, so she tries to make up for this disturbance on Saturdays and Sundays by attending competitions. Her roles as a 'mother' draw greater demands on her time alongside her role as a CEO. What was before is different now and each person within the system experiences these changes differently.

The family system – with its unwritten rules about parental roles and responsibilities, gender roles and responsibilities, and child roles and responsibilities – might function well in times of stability and any changes or disturbances within the system mean new rules, new roles, and new responsibilities for all. This family system flows through its own life cycle with predictable and unpredictable disruptions, transitions, periods of stabilisation, and periods of change in between.

Working with groups

Working with groups such as backroom teams and squads often means setting clear boundaries about one's roles and responsibilities in this system; however, without clearly appreciating the complexity of the system, it might be challenging to intervene effectively. Understanding how this system (e.g., football squad) works helps to understand problems or issues within the system and the failures of the system to adapt to change. It might mean making implicit rules explicit so that all members understand their roles and responsibilities and feel competent to undertake them. Perhaps parts of the system need to be overhauled to balance the demands of each part of the system or organising and clarifying the processes of communication and feedback.

Regardless of the trials, the universal skills of a practitioner – such as being open, warm, accepting, empathic, and non-judgemental – allow the practitioner to explore the presenting issues with all involved. The modelling of supportive, empathic responses and guiding the process of support (i.e., explaining how the process moves along) means that the group can move to active engagement to adjust the system for better functioning. Some key skills and strategies help the group make sense of something that happened or is currently happening, such as reframing how the issue or issues present, or Socratic questions to understand how people relate to each other in the group. From a CBT orientation, Socratic questions help the group witness the connections between beliefs, values, and behaviour of the group members.

This work with families and groups takes much time, practice, reflection, and supervision to plan, deliver, and review effective group work. We encourage trainees to work in small groups (e.g., in a classroom with a facilitator) to begin this work and to work with the feedback to improve the group work process before working in professional practice settings.

Getting started as a sport psychology practitioner

The first outings in one's career as a sport psychology practitioner appear filled with worry and self-doubt about one's competence (Tod & Bond, 2010), prompting practitioners to 'fix' all the problems their clients present (Owton et al., 2014; Tod & Bond, 2010). This 'fix it' approach resonating through the literature might be a legacy of the limited professional training routes and programmes for aspiring sport psychology practitioners, though this circumstance has undergone substantial changes. The glamour of sport – especially elite performance sport and elite sport performers – shines brightly in all forms of media, yet the dark side of sport – thoroughly apparent in the media also – sits in opposition to this allure. When undergraduate-, master's-, and doctoral-level students in sport and exercise psychology shared their hopes and dreams with whom they would most like to work, they mostly stated applied sport psychology working with college and other elite athletes (Fitzpatrick et al., 2016) or performance enhancement work with athletes in different contexts (Gnacinski et al., 2016). The notion of performance drew some respondents to suggest a transfer of skills learned in applied sport psychology to other domains, such as the military and the performing arts (Bucknell, 2015).

Although the desire to work in these settings seems clear, the possibility and probability of secure employment remains precarious because it is precarious. Over the past 30 years, while early career professionals held a similar desire to work with athletes, few reported making a living from this work (Andersen et al., 1997; Waite & Pettit, 1993; Williams & Scherzer, 2003). Great expectations from students within the field bump up against the reality of working in the field (Fitzpatrick et al., 2016). Taking responses from sport and exercise psychology master's and doctoral students, Fitzpatrick et al. (2016) presented the top five challenges to secure a job: limited job market, limited access to athletes/teams, limited financial support, and competing with licensed psychologists and untrained practitioners. These issues of scarcity, access, support, and competition emerge in all markets; however, we can achieve more by educating potential employers about the work and practice of sport and exercise psychologists, developing suitable internships and training, and showing the effectiveness of the work in the field. Another challenge for students entering the field of applied sport psychology is that few resources are available to manage the transition to the jobs market (Basevitch et al., 2016). Much depends on the psychological qualities of the practitioner, such as creativity, initiative, and self-motivation (Johnson & Andersen, 2019; Owton et al., 2014).

Sport psychology practitioners might work unpredictable hours, travel extensively, and operate in non-traditional settings (Andersen et al., 2001; Martin et al., 2021), which means they need to find ways of 'staying loose' yet work within ethical bounds. The challenges to one's work/life balance means constructive collaboration between the employer and employee because though there are losses (e.g., compassion fatigue) (Maslach & Leiter, 2008), there are also gains (e.g., compassion satisfaction) (Martin et al., 2021). Quartiroli et al. (2019a) reported that most sport psychology practitioners shared positive experiences in their professional work; however, several factors hindered their professional quality of life (Quartiroli et al. 2019c), such as the number of hours and location of their work, few career opportunities, and financial worries about sustaining a career in the field (Quartiroli et al., 2019b)

Summary

In this chapter, we introduced the therapeutic relationship and the essential qualities of an applied sport psychology practitioner. The centrality of the relationship means we attend to the processes of the relationship and address issues of professional identity and feeling fraudulent in the role. The challenge to work in context with specific populations means learning about what the client needs and wants from our service delivery. Whether we are working with a client-athlete, a family, or a group, we are continually developing knowledge and skills to meet the needs of the client(s) in that context.

5   A model for counselling skills

Introduction

A model or theoretical framework helps us to understand how skills fit together. When we can work from this place, we can reflect on practice, share understanding, and develop within supervision. Though there are several theories of counselling skills, we shall focus on three of them as options for you in training and supervision. These theoretical models help us learn and practise together because we can work from basic to advanced skills, learn the functions of each skill, and then decide which skill works best for that point in the helping process. Though there are several theories of therapy (e.g., client-centred, cognitive-behavioural, psychodynamic), trainees need a skills framework relevant to these theoretical orientations (McLeod & McLeod, 2022).

The micro-skills approach

The micro-skills model by Ivey et al. (2018) offers a complex multidimensional framework for practice with two underpinning principles: first, some core skills are essential to all helping circumstances; and second, particular interaction sequences can be useful for clients. Underpinning this approach lies the intentionality of the helper, who chooses the skill (e.g., listening over questioning) that best addresses the client's needs and preferences at that moment in time. Being aware of what one is doing means one can choose from a set of responses rather than assuming a fixed formula works for all clients. This flexibility to the client's needs and the varied approaches to helping means an inclusive approach for all seeking help.

A firm emphasis emerges in the micro-skills model on attending and a well-formed interview. For the skills of attending, Ivey et al. (2018) refers to the 'three Vs + B': visuals, vocals, verbals, and body language. When we relate these back to the helping process, we can imagine a sport psychology practitioner employing eye contact and a warm, interested tone of voice, following the client's story with orienting body language (e.g., leaning forward, encouraging gestures). If we think about a well-formed interview or counselling session, we see five parts: developing a relationship, story and strengths, goals,

DOI: 10.4324/9781003453857-5

re-storying, and action. Starting a session with structure and rapport helps to develop a relationship. Next, the client offers their story, issues and concerns, and strengths. Then, we identify what the client would like to happen – their goals. After that point, the client can re-story – think about alternatives, while checking for accuracy in the story. Finally, the client acts on the new stories and understandings before ending the session. This five-step sequence offers direction and hope that the client feels that they are progressing.

When there is an appropriate need to do so, the helper can use advanced influencing skills comprising recognising mixed messages and contradictions in the client's story, challenging the client supportively, clarifying issues, seeing the issue in various guises, reframing and reinterpreting the client's experience, and working with the 'here and now' of client responses (McLeod & McLeod, 2022). Moving from basic skills to advanced influencing skills and interventions, fit around and within the distinctive style, values, strengths, and contexts of the sport psychology practitioner.

Three-stage models

Similar to the three-stage model of presented earlier, Hill (2020) developed the Helping Skills Model comprising exploration, insight, and action. In this model, the helper supports the client to understand themselves before taking their learning to the real world. In exploration, the sport psychology practitioner engages various skills to establish and develop rapport with the client. These skills might include open questions, attending, and reflection of feelings. Next, the helper works to construct new insight and understand issues in relationships through challenge, interpretation, and offering insight. Finally, the helper encourages clients to explore new behaviours and choose actions and development of skills for action with feedback by offering feedback, homework, and role play.

The Skilled Helper Model (Egan, 1984; Egan & Reese, 2021) has been applied to organisational change interventions and counselling. In stage 1, the helper helps the client to tell their story using skills to tune in and listen to the client's verbal and non-verbal communication, reflecting what you have understood, probing and summarising to clarify the story and challenge the client. In stage 2, the helper helps the client to understand what they need and want using skills such as decision-making, goal setting, determining possibilities, and making choices in their commitment to change. In stage 3, the client puts the strategies into place to help the client get what they need and want.

In summary, these models, micro-skills, and three-stage models seem straightforward and practical. The stages offer direction and processes or skills to follow. Although sport settings appear controlling, filled with advice and guidance to fix things, these models orient us to describe and understand a problem before acting. The movement here begins with patience, understanding, and clarity to allow the client to take action and follow through with their plans. In practice, however, this neat process does not fit the client who wants to take action now or the client who seeks understanding but not change. The client's choice remains to determine where and how quickly or slowly to proceed. Being accepted, understood, and trusted remains paramount in the sport psychology practitioner, using their skills to create a relationship in which the client and the sport psychology practitioner pool their knowledge, experience, and resources to meet the client's needs.

A model for counselling skills in sport and exercise

A sport psychology practitioner will encounter many barriers to regular support for a client in the milieu of sport. Some of these barriers emerge with the hectic schedules of training, competitions, medical treatment, travel, holidays, and so on that befall all athletes and teams, and the wider needs of coaches and backroom staff like physiotherapists, strength and conditioning coaches, dietitians, and more. While contact might be regular, it might also be highly irregular. What we think about here is less about the regularity of meetings and more about the process, which can be one of two parts. The first process we usually refer to is the movement between the client and the sport psychology practitioner; this movement or change happens outside the psychologist–client relationship and after the psychologist–client relationship. Through this process, there is usually a second process, like a series of stages to the counselling relationship – beginnings, middles, and endings. We shall explore each of these processes in this book.

The process between the client and the sport psychology practitioner and the series of stages means we need a model to account for this flexibility and the manifold issues presented by the client. One model is the counselling and helping process model of relating-understanding-changing (RUC) comprising the three stages of the principal tasks for the client and psychologist (Nelson-Jones, 2012). Though the model seems to follow a neat order, its purpose is to illustrate the primary task of each stage of the model. First, relating means establishing a collaborative working relationship. Second, understanding denotes assessing and agreeing on a definition of the client's problem(s). Finally, changing refers to working with the client to change the issues and situations more effectively than before. Though the stages seem to be distinct, they overlap and practitioners move between stages flexibly, as we shall see in the next section. We shall aim to present the position of the sport psychology practitioner and client at each stage of the RUC model.

Stage 1: relating

Most helping relationships happen before a client sits in a practitioner's office. What we mean here is the first contact might be an e-mail, telephone call, or meeting at the training arena. Handling those opening exchanges might mean a client books an appointment – or not. The introductions normally comprise meeting, greeting, and seating. In sport settings, the meeting phase depends on whether you hold sessions with clients in a private office offsite or whether you use a space within the organisation where you are employed or contracted. You might have a waiting area where you greet your client before retiring to a private room. Depending on the context (e.g., private practice) and organisation, you might begin with gathering basic information and contracting. Our preference for getting started is to allow the client to share what they are thinking and feeling. It might be that a pole vault athlete presents with anxiety about an upcoming national competition or a rugby player returning from a long-term injury. Regardless of the presenting issue(s), the task for the sport psychology practitioner is to create an emotionally comfortable and safe space to begin with active listening to help the client share their reason(s) for coming to see you.

On the other side of this relationship lies the client. Beginning work with a sport psychology practitioner presents several threats because the client is intending to trust someone they do not know with their secrets. The client does not know if the sport psychology practitioner will share what the client shares with them. In a team setting, the client will not know if the sport psychology practitioner will share their story with the coach or performance director, for example. The client also does not know how the sport psychology practitioner will treat them. They might wonder: "Will she treat me with understanding and respect?" or "Will he dismiss me?" or "Will they rush me to explain my issue?" Clients feel alarmed by the prospect of discussing personal issues; they need to go at their own pace in a calm and reassuring atmosphere. This ambiance of safety, warmth, and understanding means the client might feel reassured enough that there is no power struggle and no one rushing them or diving in with solutions before they share their story.

Stage 2: understanding

Understanding the presenting issue(s) takes time because the presenting issue often requires a supportive, trusting environment in which the client feels safe to explore their issue(s) sensitively and sensibly in all directions. Depending on one's therapeutic approach (e.g., CBT), suitable Socratic methods help the client tell their story and the problem(s) they experience fully. These descriptions normally encompass thoughts, feelings, behaviours, physical reactions, and the environmental circumstances. Their relations with others, patterns of relating, ways of coping, social support, strengths, and resources all play their part in the story. Expanding on the presenting issue in this way means that there is clarity for the client and sport psychology practitioner about what they present and how the client contributes to their presenting issue (where appropriate). The client might uncover their thoughts, feelings, and behaviours more thoroughly. Such junctures offer challenges to the clients, opportunities to clarify points, and summaries to reflect on what has happened so far. These summaries help the client clarify what the sport psychology practitioner understands about the problems and provide an opportunity to change anything that does not seem to fit. This planning prepares the client and the sport psychology practitioner for the next stage.

The understanding stage of the process helps the client feel like their work with the sport psychology practitioner is moving productively. The sense of being stuck lifts somewhat, though the client might be reluctant to tell the whole story; however, discussing thoughts, feelings, actions, physical reactions, and the environment helps to offer a structure to reflect upon. When the sport psychology practitioner reflects and summarises along the way, the client can also reflect and note how their story fits. The summaries from the sport psychology practitioner help keep a hold of facets the client might forget or dismiss along the way. Formulating in this way helps the client to see how there might be a way out of their situation.

Stage 3: changing

This stage involves solving the problem. In practical terms, alongside the sport psychology practitioner, clients clarify their goals and generate options to tackle the problem situations and plans to implement their action plans. To solve the problem, however, a client might need help learning communication skills to interact more assertively with her teammates. Though the sport psychology practitioner helps or coaches the clients to develop these communication skills, the client works on the client's problem. A skill like self-talk can be coached, rehearsed, and practised in the sport psychology practitioner's office before experimenting in real life. The client might continue practising self-talk between sessions and then assume responsibility for their behaviour change in real life now and in the future.

The change process for the client often runs forwards and backwards. What I mean here is that clients might aim to avoid old, unhelpful behaviours and engage in more helpful behaviours. They might well be new to this systematic process of change and so need to proceed slowly and carefully to gain confidence in a new skill, for example, and feel confident working it into real life. The more the client stays at the centre of this work, the more the client will feel in control and empowered in the change process. They can see their resourcefulness and strength to handle setbacks along the way. This responsibility and accountability are crucial to maintain their gains when the therapeutic relationship ends.

Case study: Dom

Dom struggled in his relationships with people in powerful positions, especially coaches and managers. When Dom came to see me (Paul), he explained that he got on well with these people at the professional football club, but resented being swapped in and out of the team without explanation. The consequences of this swapping meant he lost confidence in himself as a player. The manager rarely gave reasons for his team selections and Dom felt he could not raise the topic with him in case the manager put him out on loan or ended his contract. Our work together meant working on two separate but related issues. First, Dom needed to address his need for constant approval by the manager; second, Dom needed to develop some communication skills to bring up the issue with his manager so that he could more ably deal with the process of selection and deselection across the football season.

Attending, observing, and listening

The communication skills you develop as your foundation for working with clients means you are laying a solid base for every structure that lies above them. We will use these foundation skills throughout the helping process. With practice, refinement, reflection, and support, you can develop these and other skills. The skills we begin with here are attending, observing, and listening, followed by reflective and probing skills (Culley & Bond, 2011).

Attending skills

Attending, observing, and listening skills work together because listening requires observing and attending, and attending means you can observe and listen. The four main ways to create communication in a client session are verbal, vocal (e.g., vaper), bodily, and touch. With attending, we normally focus on bodily and touch. Bodily refers to communication by your body through eye contact, facial expression, gaze, gestures, posture, physical proximity, clothes, and grooming. Eye contact helps us to send messages of interest, anger, or attraction. Facial expression helps us to send body messages to others. For example, we might show different emotions: anger, fear, happiness, interest, surprise, sadness, disgust, or contempt. These facial expressions tell others what is being felt by you. Gaze reflects looking at others in an area of their face. We can collect information and show interest in the speaker. Gestures are physical movements to show words like clenching one's fist to reflect an angry feeling. In Western culture, we recognise a nodding head to show agreement. Posture also reflects feelings like crossed arms that we may interpret as emotionally uptight but something else might also be true (e.g., feeling cold). Physical closeness reflects the comfort we feel about how close we are to others physically. We in Britain typically work in the personal zone (from 18–48 inches) for helping work in a therapist's room (3–5 feet). Finally, clothes and grooming present information about status, roles, identity, neatness, and tidiness (Nelson-Jones, 2012).

Attending is the first step in the process to observe and listen to clients because you show you are there non-verbally with them, with a curiosity about their story. This orientation brings weight to your words, alongside your genuineness, acceptance, and understanding. Noting these non-verbal messages previously described, we aim for an open posture, facing the client and leaning forward, yet relaxed. Your eye contact shows interest in the client and their story without staring. Your client reads your facial expressions as you read your clients. You may wish to share the pain you feel through your facial expression to reflect understanding of the client.

In summary, your non-verbal communication communicates care, understanding, interest, genuineness, and warmth. It shows that the client and what the client shares matters to the sport psychology practitioner. As we attend, we also observe. We see how they are dressed, see their gestures and postures, hear their tone of voice, and so on. Their individual ways of communicating become visible to you. I might attach a smile to a happy story or a sad story. These incongruities might be worth exploring because a client might not know what they are feeling or the weight of what they are feeling; however, we observe and enquire gently, simply indicating what we noticed.

Non-verbal communication

Each culture develops its own rules for non-verbal communication, like a pattern of greeting or turn-taking when conversing with one another (Harper et al., 1978; Hill, 2020). We internalise and assimilate these rules for non-verbal behaviours particular to our culture; however, we might find ourselves in another culture unsure of how to relate. As helpers, we adapt our non-verbal communication style (e.g., eye contact) to fit the client's non-verbal style, focusing on individual differences particular to the client. We can easily judge clients using our cultural standards rather than their own, so we need to tread carefully to help the client relax and feel safe in our company.

Much of our communication of attending and listening occurs through our non-verbal behaviours, so we need to recognise what one says verbally and non-verbally, and the resonance or discrepancy between them. Our non-verbal behaviours include *kinesics* (i.e., bodily movements which we can subdivide into different functions [Ekman & Friesen, 1969]) like *emblems* (i.e., a substitute for words) such as waving to say goodbye; *illustrators* complement speech much like a coach shouting to her team and spreading her hands apart to illustrate to players to spread out on the pitch; *regulators* (e.g., head nods) monitor the flow of a conversation. Finally, we have *adaptors* (i.e. acts outside our control with no communicative purpose) such as scratching one's head or playing with one's hair. Emblems, illustrators, and regulators complement verbal messages, whereas adaptors might distract the client (Hill, 2020).

Sport psychology practitioners work inside and outside clinical settings, so it is likely much more of our non-verbal behaviour communicates to those around us. Compared to sitting on a comfortable chair in a clinic, there is comparatively more movement and expression out on a golf course or at a running track such as body posture, body movements, use of space, gestures, head nods, facial expressions, and eye contact. Maintaining an open body posture and leaning towards the client with arms and legs uncrossed makes it possible, whether sitting or standing, to convey our attention to the client. Continuing a particular posture over a period seems unlikely, and so movement becomes part of our relating. For example, we may use hand gestures to present our messages (e.g., presenting a reflection to the client), and in our attempt to do so, our non-verbal leakage from our legs, feet, or face tell another story. For instance, while we are speaking, we are often unaware of our gestures (e.g., a clenched fist, locked arms, steepling one's fingers) which convey different meanings to different people. To steeple one's fingers, for instance, might suggest a confidence, superciliousness, or pride. This sense of superiority might be unintended, yet we reveal it in our non-verbal leakage.

Proxemics means how people use space in interactions. In intimate relations, we are closest to others, while personal, social, and public distance zones usually mean progressively more space afforded to both parties. In work with clients, we use personal to social distances (from 1.5–12 feet) which vary according to cultural background. From personal to social distances, we are aware of others' facial expressions, eye gaze, and head nods. A head nod usually confers that one is listening and following with the client. While too many head nods can distract, too few might signal that the listener is not listening. A client might look further for clues that the helper is listening to them, such as facial expression or eye contact. Eye contact or gaze shares information with another, ranging from intimacy and interest to submission or dominance. We understand through our eyes when it is our turn to speak, as well as pauses in conversation. Gaze avoidance signals different feelings or intentions, such as anxiety or a desire not to communicate. Different clients will feel comfortable with less or more eye contact – but too little eye contact (e.g., he is not listening to me) or too much eye contact (e.g., I feel controlled, intimidated) signals discomfort. We need to attend to cultural differences also to make sense of what seems reasonable, suitable, and appropriate.

Our facial expressions also give meaning to our verbal message. Our facial expression communicates our feelings and other information to the listener (Ekman, 1993). We might smile, frown, squint, roll our eyes, shake our head, and so forth, conveying meaning to others. Smiling when happy or crying when distressed appears universally. We can 'see' fear or anger in one's eyes. Working pitch-side, we might perceive anger in the eyes of a team member about to return to the field of play following a hostile tackle by a member of the opposition team. Our facial expressions towards the player might convey calm rather than disgust or anger, helping the player to return to the field of play without needing to exact revenge and get 'sin-binned' or sent off.

Paraverbal messages

Paraverbal (or paralinguistic) messages refer to the manner in which we speak. We can hear someone's tone of voice, pitch, delivery, and rate of speech in their verbal communication. We might notice a soft and encouraging tone of voice and how it contrasts with a harsh and haughty voice. How might a client respond to each tone of voice? We, as practitioners, might match the rate of speech of the client, but with a client speaking quickly, for instance, feeling anxious, we might slow our rate of speech to encourage the client to slow their pace. As you develop as a practitioner, you will notice how you move from thinking (e.g., observing, judging, summarising) to feeling (e.g., gut or emotional response, smiling) to understand the speaker from the speaker's frame of reference. You will hear the utterances, pitch, volume, and tone of speech to understand your client rather than needing to direct, influence, and control to meet your needs for direction and control. We can easily stray into non-acceptance of our client by analysing, advising, lecturing, praising, preaching, probing, and solving, but we can also bring ourselves back to the client and listen for the content and feeling to hear and respond appropriately.

Part of this process is to facilitate client exploration using minimal verbal behaviours: minimal encouragers, approval reassurance, disclosures of similarities, avoiding interruptions, and silences (Hill, 2020). A minimal encourager (e.g., "um-hmm" or "yeah") acknowledges what the client shared and shows we are listening and attentive, and encourages the client to keep talking. A minimal encourager at the end of a sentence allows the client to choose to continue exploring because you acknowledge you have heard the client and are happy for the client to continue rather than taking your turn to speak, which is typical of a conversation.

Similar to head nods, too few minimal encouragers might feel distancing, while too many can interrupt and distract. Interruptions distract most clients' self-exploration – we do not give them a chance to keep exploring what they are thinking and feeling. Waiting a few seconds at the end of a client's statements allows the client to think about whether they wish to continue thinking and talking. Of course, there are times, occasionally, when we need to interrupt. Here are a few examples. For instance, a client might talk nonstop but only at a surface level with little exploration, or perhaps the client is stuck and does not know what to say. To bring the client back on track, we can use exploration skills (e.g., restate or reflect feelings or use open questions for thoughts and feelings). We might say "I'm sorry to interrupt you; however, I wish to make sure I understand what you're saying" or "I want to make sure we process how you are feeling about the situation".

Approving or reassuring a client is a helpful skill to use occasionally. Approval and reassurance reverberate around sports grounds – "Good try" or "Well done" or "Unlucky" – so it is likely to be part of your vernacular. Providing emotional support and reassurance shows how much we empathise with the client-athlete, and those feeling are normal and expected. Working with a client, however, although we aim to approve and reassure them that their issues are normal and they are not alone in their feelings, they have their limitations because we do not want to stop the client from exploring and accepting their feelings. It is understandable how we might wish to reassure someone about how they are feeling: "Everyone feels that way before a game" or "Don't worry about missing a penalty". Minimising or denying how clients feel does not allow clients the right to their feelings. As practitioners, we help clients to identify, express, and accept feelings; however, not all practitioners feel comfortable excavating this emotional landscape and would prefer to move the client on from their feelings. Reassurance and approval often mean more to the practitioner than the client, and it is worth exploring these personal needs and their meaning in our lives. When we disclose our similarities with a client, we highlight the universality of problems in living or problems in performance we all face; we present honestly and openly to the client, but for whose benefit? Our goal ought to be to return to the client's frame of reference after our disclosure (e.g., "I had trouble adjusting to national level competitions at the beginning, too. Please tell me more about your experience") (Hill, 2020).

Many trainees feel concerned about silences between them and their clients. These silences might feel uncomfortable initially because they remind us about silences in everyday conversation. But in therapeutic work, silences communicate. A silence by the client might mean they are reflecting, worried, bored, or uneasy. You might decide to let the client break the silence in the client's own time. A silence offers space to weigh and reflect but also encourage the client to face their uneasiness which might require the sport psychology practitioner's intervention by sharing what the sport psychology practitioner notices or asking questions: "What's happening for you now?" or "What are you feeling now?". These are examples of 'process' questions. 'Process' questions differ from 'content' questions. The 'process' reflects the dynamics of the relationship – how a client and sport psychology practitioner work together and what is happening between them. 'Content' is what the client brings to the interaction such as thoughts, feelings, behaviours and experiences. 'Process' questions keep you following the trail of the client's experiences.

Listening skills

The goal in listening will be to understand and agree about what concerns the client and how the client experiences concerns. This listening process means sifting information, deciding what and how to respond. While you decide to attend to some information, you will dismiss or omit other information and follow to a point of clarity to be clear about what the client shared and left out. This active listening means two things: listening with purpose and communicating what you have heard. Culley and Bond (2011) presented a helpful framework to classify what a client shares comprising behaviour, experiences, feelings, and thoughts. With behaviours, we listen to what clients say and do. Experiences comprise what happens to clients and the roles others play or do not play in their lives. Feelings are the client's responses about their experiences and behaviour. Finally, thoughts reflect what clients understand about their actions and inactions, the sense they make of their own and others' behaviour, and the beliefs about themselves, others, and the events in their lives. With these components, we hear about behaviours, experiences, feelings, and thoughts. What seems more challenging is what the client omits. For example, we might hear about what an athlete does, how others behave in competitions, what she thinks about herself and others, but rarely – if ever – does she mention feelings. Noticing this omission, you might encourage the client to express feelings that offer self-awareness, self-knowledge, and self-understanding. Reik (1948) discussed listening with a 'third ear' or trying to hear (or understand) what the client really means, not just what someone communicates overtly. Joining verbal and non-verbal messages helps the listener to hear what the client is thinking or feeling at a deep level (Hill, 2020).

Reactions and filters to listening

Listening to a client means following what they share, verbally and non-verbally. You are making sense of how you think and feel, as well. A client might cultivate annoyance or excitement within you and the feelings usher you to notice what happens in the 'process' between you when you feel annoyed or excited. Sharing your thoughts congruently with a client and inviting their exploration might help the client understand others' reactions to the client's behaviour and their meaning for their relationships. The filters of values, culture, and one's personal life also influence the listening process. Values, for example, that we as sport psychology practitioners hold or those within sport might influence us and how we listen to our clients. Though particular values hold merit in sport, it remains the client's choice how to lead their life. Our cultural norms and values ought to be explored so we do not impose them on clients. Finally, our lives as practitioners involve difficulties like all people experience; however, we need to manage our issues to create space for the client's issues.

Our defences as people and sport psychology practitioners also hinder our listening. For instance, we might be anxious about what the client is sharing and unwilling to hear it. We might behave defensively after making a mistake that the client spotted, or jump in to solve the client's problem because you 'get things done'.

Reflecting skills

Attending and listening skills are two-thirds of the support process; the clients need to know you hear them and understand them. To achieve this goal, the last third is reflective skills (we shall include probing at the end). Hearing and understanding the client's internal frame of reference – how clients view themselves and their concerns – can be approached using three reflective skills: restating, paraphrasing, and summarising. Probing, however, reflects the practitioner's perspective or an external frame of reference. You might probe, seeking more information or changing the course of a session. Culley and Bond (2011) believed that reflecting skills encourages trust and rapport through communicating empathy, understanding, and acceptance. The skills of restating, paraphrasing, and summarising mean you show the client you understand what they are sharing and wish them to continue without influencing the direction of their story. The client, through these skills, hears that you are listening attentively, reflecting on what you heard in their words or in yours.

Restating: Restating means repeating to the client single words or short phrases they used to prompt elaboration. Here are some ways to introduce a restatement: "It sounds as though . . ." or "You say that . . ." or "From what I hear you saying . . ." or "So . . ." or "If I'm hearing you correctly . . .".

Following is an example of using a single word in a questioning or inviting tone.

Client:	I felt humiliated.
Practitioner:	Humiliated. [restating]
Client:	Yes, I felt I had worked so hard for the team – worked my socks off – and for him to say what he said made me feel useless, worthless even. I just don't know where to go from here.

Restating 'humiliated' meant staying with the client's frame of reference and encouraged the client to take the lead in the client's story again. This 'one-word question' with an enquiring tone does not encroach on the client and the client's story telling. The value in these reflective skills lies in their judicious use, so paraphrasing might be necessary for another stage.

Paraphrasing

The skill of paraphrasing is restating what you understand to be the central message of the client's communication. The goal of paraphrasing is to show the client you hear and understand their point of view. Again, we stay with the client's frame of reference. In doing so, we communicate empathy, understanding, and acceptance. Through paraphrasing, we gather information from clients about how they see themselves and their issues without judging or evaluating what they share to build a trusting relationship. To paraphrase well means attending and listening accurately to the client's story. It is the client who hears what they have said through you so they can understand and change what we have communicated.

Following is an example:

Tom:	I'm not the achieving athlete I used to be. Somehow, I'm working harder and things are turning out worse than before. How can that be? I thought success was all about effort and hard work and never quitting.
Practitioner:	You're comparing your achievements now with past achievements and seem confused about why your efforts do not guarantee more achievements.

Tom:	Yes. I feel like I'm doing all the right things. Don't get me wrong, I'm happy with what I've achieved. I thought I'd be further ahead . . . [looking upset]
Practitioner:	You sound sad. It sounds like you're saying "What I have achieved is not good enough".
Tom:	That's it. It's not enough. But then again, how could it be? I've always had to fight for everything.
Practitioner:	You're annoyed because others have had it easier than you.
Tom:	Oh, absolutely. Where I come from, you get nothing. You fight for everything. You fight for support, encouragement, funding, training – everything!
Practitioner:	You resent the help others got.

[The practitioner follows the client to show her understanding. She encourages her to express her feelings. There is no challenge, argument, or collusion. Paraphrasing helps when you are challenged about knowledge, understanding, and experience of the client's situation.]

Client:	What would you know about it? You're not the one shaking like a leaf on the final tee, knowing this final hole will make or break your playing rights on the tour. You just swan around the putting green taking it all in. I'm the one who has to get the job done!
Practitioner:	You're annoyed that I'm not there to share the load . . . to know what you're going through?
Client:	Entirely! And it's not just you. It's my coach, my agent, the whole damn team.
Practitioner:	And I, and the team, don't know what things are like for you.
Client:	No . . . no one truly gets it. I feel alone . . .

Paraphrasing, like all skills, requires practice to improve. We attend to offer tentatively what we felt the client said. We respectfully offer our perception, but we are not telling or defining for the client. We use our words, keeping our tone level and aim to reflect the feeling the client shared. We are not adding or interpreting, rather; we aim to understand. When we do not understand, we can say: "Let me check with you about what you've said . . .".

Summarising

A summary is a summing up of the main points. These are longer paraphrases bringing key points together, in an orderly manner. Not only are summaries useful within treatment sessions, they are helpful in beginning a session by recapping the past session and present a focus for the upcoming session. Summaries also help close a session by summarising what was covered. Culley and Bond (2011) referred to summaries in the initial stages as 'attending summaries' that capture what the client said but do not include your hypotheses.

These attending summaries present order and unity to what the client shared and an overview of what we have covered so far.

Let's now summarise what we presented earlier.

Practitioner: From what you shared so far, you seem to resent how you were treated by others. You compare your achievements now unfavourably with achievements from your past and you expected more at this stage of your career.

In this summary, there is content and feelings. The client can hear what sense you made so far and can correct misunderstandings, add clarity, or reassess what they said. There are several other benefits to summarising, such as clarifying content and feelings, reviewing the work, finishing a session, beginning a new session, prioritising and focusing, and moving the helping process forward.

Summaries allow the client to hear what another person – the practitioner – heard of their story. Often, a client feels confused or overwhelmed by their problems, so hearing a summary helps them to evaluate what they are thinking and add any missing pieces, and it provides a moment to reflect on whether they believe what they have shared is true to them. In a summary statement, the helper shows the client what they have understood of the client's story. The client struggles to tell their story sometimes, so it can be a struggle for the helper to get a handle on it. This struggle is progress, though it might not feel that way. It is also likely that clients prefer a cognitive appraisal (i.e., thinking about their thoughts) rather than an emotional appraisal (thinking about or feeling their feelings), especially at the beginning of a therapeutic relationship.

Probing skills

We, as family and friends, overload athletes in training and competition with well-meaning suggestions, guidance, and advice. But probing – the practitioner's perception of what is imperative to address – takes control of the content from the client and places it with the practitioner. Although such a move might go unnoticed by most athletes, this approach moves beyond reflecting, paraphrasing, or summarising to a more directive stance. It is not about whether probes are right or wrong; rather, it is how practitioners use probes. A probe ought to be used sensitively because it may render the client wholly passive in the helping process or make them feel interrogated by the practitioner. When we use probes, we use them to gather some further information which we feel is important to explore, and we can do so with statements and questions.

STATEMENTS

Before we address questions, we can use a statement as a gentler alternative. For example, instead of asking "What does your coach think of your plan?", you might say "I wonder what your coach thinks of your plan". Statements gather information specifically, allowing the client to share their thoughts, feelings, and behaviours. Statements also offer the chance to move the focus from others to the self. For example, a client might discuss the professional environment, the backroom staff, and their treatment of the players.

Practitioner:　You have spoken a lot about the people at the club and how they treat players and you. This is a clear summary of what they say and do. I wonder how you respond to them.

Another example might be a client not getting promoted to the first team. He shows little feeling about not being promoted.

Practitioner:　You have mentioned several times how important it is to make the first-team squad. I imagine you have some feelings we have not explored yet about not being in the first team squad.

These examples show a gentler way to explore issues that a client might be defensive about.

THE VALUE AND LIMITS OF QUESTIONS

Practitioners use several types of questions (e.g., open, hypothetical, closed). Some types of questions are helpful; others are less so. Open questions, for example, demand a more detailed response than 'yes' or 'no' answers – questions that begin with 'who', 'what', 'where', or 'how'. A practitioner might ask the following questions to an athlete who argues with a teammate.

"When do you usually argue?"
"How do your arguments begin?"
"What usually happens when you argue?"
"Who tries to end the argument?"

Hypothetical questions often arise in the helping process with athletes because they help athletes explore thoughts and feelings in a relatively safe, helping relationship. An athlete might have a fear about an upcoming national trials. A practitioner might ask: "What do you imagine would happen if you were to find yourself in the chasing pack rather than leading the race?" In this way, the athlete identifies and explores her fear of being in the chasing pack rather than leading the race as she likes to do. She might explore the challenges in coping with worries as the race unfolds. Hypothetical questions also offer the client to consider positive outcomes: "If you were running confidently, what would you be doing?" or "If you were managing your worries, what would you be doing?"

One open question we did not include in the opening paragraph of this subsection is 'why' questions. One reason is that 'why' questions can put clients under pressure to justify or find a cause. These questions rarely bring clients to a new understanding and a possibility to think or act differently. What we explore are the thoughts, feelings, actions, values, and beliefs for clients to make sense of themselves, their relationships, and the world. Leading on from 'why' questions are closed questions.

Closed questions ask clients to answer "Yes" or "No" but do not explore. Closed questions often present the practitioner's agenda rather than the clients, and the space for restating, paraphrasing, and summarising is squeezed out. Sometimes, perhaps in an intake assessment, practitioners might ask the client, "Are you receiving treatment for your injury?" to establish facts or clarify a point that seems unclear. Leading questions propel a client towards an expected outcome. In sport, many feelings, values, and beliefs appear as the only ones to experience or hold. The implicit message might be that an athlete would want to train to the best of his ability to prepare for the Olympics, and everything or anything less is unacceptable. Without being aware of our wishes as practitioners, we might – through leading questions and non-verbal communication – lead the client to answer questions in a way that fits with the values or beliefs of a sport.

Clients also ask questions. Sometimes the questions are in search of information. At other times, the questions are a defence against exploration. Questions do not need to be answered immediately or directly. Athletes often wonder what they should do when there are a few or several options, such as "What do you think I should do now?" We can respond to this question with an open question: "What would you like to do?" or "What do you imagine yourself doing?"

Immediacy

Immediacy in practitioner–client relationships refers to commenting on what is happening in the interaction between the practitioner and the client. At the beginning of a therapeutic relationship, immediacy helps to establish, monitor, and maintain the relationship (e.g., "How do you feel about working with me?"). As the relationship develops, it helps to understand how the client comes across in the relationship, such as "As you were sharing your story, I was aware of my sadness" to resolve problems in the relationship. Here, the practitioner refers to the 'here-and-now' response to the client. How one relates within the therapeutic relationship helps to understand how one might relate in the outside world. A compliant client may well be compliant in the outside world, and an arrogant client may be arrogant in the outside world. In short, a snapshot of a client's interpersonal style emerges in their relationship with the practitioner while acknowledging that their interpersonal style might differ depending on the relationship (e.g., to someone in authority). Reading the non-verbal signals of the client might involve noting gestures, pace and tone of speech, breathing, and facial expression. Perhaps a client relates a story about preparing for competition without referring to any emotion, yet speaks hastily about the process. The practitioner might say, "I notice how hurriedly you ran through your preparation for competition. I'm wondering if you're feeling uncomfortable about it" (Hill, 2020).

The skill of immediacy takes much practice because we need to notice what is happening within us as practitioners and in the therapeutic relationship and be confident to relate what we notice. In our personal relationships, we might be reluctant to share our immediate feelings and so we need to be courageous and compassionate in our work with clients. We say courageous and compassionate because we need to proceed gently yet keenly so that how the client relates to others reveals itself in the therapeutic encounter.

Immediacy feels threatening to beginning practitioners because they feel unsure about how their client will receive their immediacy, or they do not trust their own feelings (e.g., "I'm not sure if I should share how contemptuous she sounds when she speaks about her teammates"). A direct and honest sharing in a relationship feels so open and defenceless that it may bring conflict and the practitioner struggles with conflict. While one's empathy helps the client acknowledge their sadness, for example, working through interpersonal problems forms a critical professional skill to help the client (Hill et al., 2014).

Summary

Our learning journey grants us opportunities with no predetermined destination. Though that statement excites some trainees, it frightens others. In postgraduate study, we normally undertake our training pathway to become a sport psychology practitioner; however, this journey requires your active participation because much of your learning depends on your organisation, motivation, commitment, and curiosity. You freely chose most of your learning hours to suit your circumstances. In short, universities and training pathways offer you a chance to learn for yourself. For this reason, being at university or on a training pathway brings out the best in some trainees and the worst in others (Moran, 2018). To explain, if you enjoy independence, take responsibility, and feel accountable for your actions by learning new knowledge and skills, you will flourish. But if you cannot take responsibility for your learning, training to be a sport psychology practitioner can be agonising. If you find yourself in the latter category, take heart. You can learn to help yourself and prosper by revving up your curiosity. Learning refers to a relatively permanent change in our knowledge and/or behaviour from our experiences, which might emerge through active learning (planned) or incidental learning (unplanned). Active learning is deliberate, which means it is purposeful, while incidental learning happens by chance. If you hold a goal to become a good listener for your counselling skills classes, you will feel motivated to read books, watch videos, and practise basic listening skills at home. Incidental learning might occur on your learning journey because you noticed how appreciative your friend became because you listened to her crisis without judgement. Following the story so far, you see that our deliberate intention to answer a question, for example, helps us to find the answer and along the way, we might learn other helpful things. Our curiosity – our drive to explore and understand – grows with a questioning outlook when you create space and time to learn skills to motivate yourself, organise your time, focus effectively, and think critically (Moran, 2018).

6 Beginnings

Introduction

The models we presented earlier (see Chapter 5) captured processes and stages of a counselling journey with a client-athlete. We shall use those stages but within broad labels of beginnings, middles, and endings to reinforce the movements that might happen in a sport psychology service delivery relationship without forcing the journey from beginning to end. At a simple level, we aim to help the client-athlete feel safe, which we can do through focusing and connection. The emphasis here remains on the skills in this type of introductory textbook to counselling skills in applied sport psychology.

Before the first session

The first session usually follows an orientation when the client books a time to meet the sport psychology practitioner, perhaps after reading about the sport psychology practitioner, how the sport psychology practitioner works, and what to expect in the first and following sessions. Many sport psychology practitioners have websites which offer an online booking system so a client can book a session to meet face-to-face or remotely (i.e., online). Websites also offer space to inform clients about the clinic, sport psychology practitioners, services, the process of support, and location and contact details. Some intake procedures mean completing online assessments or a telephone call before attending a session (i.e., pre-therapy), so the sport psychology practitioner can offer the best service to the client. Many of the online digital systems request a name, contact number, next of kin, and so forth. These intake procedures help the sport psychology practitioner and the client to work better together when each party follows the practical procedures for booking, for example. The sense of welcome, respect, and hope grows from the experience a client has before the first meeting and sets the scene for what they hope will follow.

DOI: 10.4324/9781003453857-6

The first session

The thought of a first session with a sport psychology practitioner draws the client into a world of possibilities. How will they treat me? Will they judge me? Who is the sport psychology practitioner? Is the sport psychology practitioner like a coach? Will they accept me? With all these possibilities, the client seeks to feel at ease, safe in the setting, and accepted. If this is the first session for the client, and knowing what we know about how the client might feel, our first meeting offers a chance to create a warm, safe, and understanding environment to navigate the worries they might have about this uncharted territory. This uncharted territory is also relevant for the sport psychology practitioner meeting a new client, so sound preparation pays off.

People are natural storytellers. The stories people tell shape how they think about themselves, who they are as people, and how they go about their lives. These stories, however, need to be told so the client can create a clear picture about what they are thinking and feeling. Sometimes stories are coherent; sometimes stories are a muddle. In the latter case, clients need to tell their story to make sense of it so they understand their problems and how their stories got them to where they are now. As helpers, we want to hear the clients consider their issues, slow down the process, and make sense together in a supportive and non-judgemental way. In telling their story, the client considers, evaluates, and reflects rather than telling the story without comprehending it.

Meeting, greeting, and seating

Nurturing trust and safety raises several challenges at the beginning of a therapeutic relationship, especially when the client feels uncomfortable and perhaps reluctant to be there. These meetings usually begin at the sport psychology practitioner's premises. When a sport psychology practitioner works for an organisation (e.g., in football, tennis), initial sessions might begin at the training arena, where the clients feel familiar with the territory; however, the privacy afforded by a private clinic gives way to the challenges of an office on a busy thoroughfare. In practical terms, whether at a private clinic or a training arena, we strive for a comfortable and well-lit room, free of belongings, so that this room feels as much the client's as the sport psychology practitioner's. Having water and tissues available is a sensible preparation. We can focus on meeting, greeting, and seating to breed neutrality, safety, and trust from the outset. The final part for preparing the room is seating. Chairs of the same height, positioned slightly at an angle, offer the client a sense that there is no power difference between the client and the sport psychology practitioner, and it offers the client comfort to speak without needing to make direct eye contact. Maintaining a clear space – where we minimise the intrusions of mobile phones, computers, or telephones – offers the client the attention they need and deserve. Having a clock in your line of sight means you can note the time so you do not run over without showing disinterest to the client by looking at your watch, for example. In sport, we often conduct successful sessions in crowded spaces, walking around the training ground, or in a café. Clients often choose these spaces because they feel comfortable there; our role is to adapt and engage the client.

The space we provide, literally and figuratively, clears a vantage point, a haven, to reflect upon where the client is right now and what the client might wish to change. Sport psychology practitioners play a critical role in the first session because they orient the client about confidentiality, risk management procedures, an overview of the first session, and time for clients to ask questions. This opening procedure follows saying hello, introducing yourself, and settling the client in the client's seat. After this opening procedure, whether face-to-face or online, reassures the client about the next steps. Depending on therapeutic mode, after these housekeeping notices, we offer time for the client to explore the client's concerns in an atmosphere of warmth, understanding, and acceptance with hope for the future.

This first session feels like there is much to fit in, so some sport psychology practitioners take 90 minutes, for example, to address intake, assessment, and the process of support. With a longer opening session, the client gains a sense of direction about goals, possibilities for the future and how to achieve goals, and realises strengths and resources and the shared sense of purpose between client and sport psychology practitioner in an atmosphere of humility and hope (McLeod & McLeod, 2022). Many trainees enquire about the opening question for a client to begin the session. The intention here is to ask an open question so the client can interpret and begin where the client feels comfortable. Open questions such as "What brings you here today?" or "How can I be of help?" or "Where would you like to begin?" help, especially with an empathic and engaging tone. Child and adolescent athletes might be anxious about the process, so we might begin with what we notice: "Emma, I sense you are a little nervous and perhaps unsure where to begin. Would it help to begin by telling me a little about yourself?" Sometimes a little more structure helps the client along. For instance, "What might be helpful to us is if you could tell me what has brought you here today and what you hope to get out of our work together. How does that sound to you?"

Discussing a concern, problem, or issue means the sport psychology practitioner understands what the client wishes to gain from therapy. The process of questions to clarify and understand the client's problem and goals means the sport psychology practitioner can understand what they present and the outcome the client seeks. For instance:

Practitioner: Can I check I am hearing you correctly? Are you saying your lack of confidence is troubling you greatly at the moment and preventing you from playing your best?
Client: Yes, that's it.
Practitioner: I wonder how you see our work together helping you – perhaps you have a sense of what you want from our time today or what you hope to achieve by the end of our work together.

A summary later in the session to capture what the client shared about their goals might be:

Practitioner: From what I have heard so far, it sounds like regaining your confidence is the most pressing issue for you now. I'm a little unclear about whether you wish to say how you feel and gather a better understanding of the whole situation at the club and make sense of how this situation developed or whether you wish to focus on developing skills to cope better for now? Whichever direction you wish to travel works for me.

Part of the first session ought to establish the client's strengths emerging from the client's personal exploration of the issue, the ways the client handled the issue so far, and their understanding of the issue. The first session means an opportunity to build trust and establish boundaries. We shall explore each element before starting the listening project.

Building trust and rapport

Engendering the trust and rapport with the client often means a challenge from the first session, especially when trust in support services left the client in a state of suspicion or disbelief about what sport psychology might offer them. As sport psychology practitioners, we aim to develop rapport with the client and the client's trust with active listening and considerate responding, reflecting feelings, empathy, unconditional positive regard, and modelling trust with an open, honest, reliable, and consistent stance (Sutton & Stewart, 2017). The feeling of harmony, compatibility, and affinity lays the foundation for a therapeutic relationship.

Healthy boundaries help clients feel safe with a sense of direction about the process of service delivery. When we discuss boundaries in this section, the boundaries apply to the sport psychology practitioner and the client because our boundaries might be rigid, enmeshed, or healthy. With rigid boundaries, people aim for self-sufficiency whereby they do not need others' help and keep others at a distance. When they keep others shut out, they keep what is personal to themselves personal, but also emotional connection and intimacy. Looking beyond these boundaries, we might see hurt and rejection in one's past, so the wall one builds helps to protect against further pain; this plan makes sense to the person because "If nobody gets close, then no one can hurt me" – and this is the message sent out to others if they try to get close. With enmeshed boundaries, a person is open to hurt and pain because the person does not see their separation in a relationship. We might see a coach develop overly close relationships with athletes to compensate for inner desolation. When boundaries are inappropriate, fragile, or ignored in one's past, perhaps in childhood, the developing athlete might not know that their boundaries are being dishonoured. With healthy boundaries, a person chooses who enters their space and honours the space of others. In these healthy spaces lie safety, security, autonomy, agency, and self-respect. These resources cultivate emotional connection and intimacy for healthy relationships and, concurrently, let the person know where others crossed their boundaries (Sutton & Stewart, 2017).

Boundaries in sport psychology service delivery

The healthy boundaries we need in our lives we also need in a therapeutic relationship. These boundaries help the client and the sport psychology practitioner to work safely and beneficially together. Boundaries might include what we agree about the duration of support, time, length, and places of sessions, limits of confidentiality, when phone calls are received and returned, sending and responding to messages (e.g., text, e-mail). We usually agree with these conditions before service delivery begins, verbally or in written contract signed by client and sport psychology practitioner. Contracting respects both parties' participation and autonomy. You will see an example contract in the Appendix.

The value of boundaries helps each party. Within sport psychology service delivery, we will see clients with different needs. How these clients meet these needs vary; however, it is possible that some clients with strong needs for liking and acceptance or attention might test the agreed boundaries. For example, a client might turn up at the sport psychology practitioner's office without an appointment, message the sport psychology practitioner between sessions without agreement, or bring gifts to the sport psychology practitioner. On the other side, a sport psychology practitioner might well alter the boundaries with the client. A sport psychology practitioner might create unhealthy dependence or increase the problems the client brings through emotional or psychological harm by, for example, letting sessions continually run over, meeting outside the appointment times, accepting gifts, inappropriate self-disclosure, withholding, or delaying in referring a client. One issue for sport psychology practitioners working with organisations and teams means they are often in the company of the athletes they support in hotels, at mealtimes, and while travelling and relaxing. These logistical challenges mean that the onus rests upon the sport psychology practitioner to establish with clients how best to establish and navigate healthy boundaries. It is best to clarify what a client can do about out-of-session boundaries and agree these with clients. Clarity about when a client can contact, how (e.g., telephone, text, e-mail, face to face) and for how long they can contact you (e.g., 15 minutes on the telephone) saves much misunderstanding and ill feeling. If you cannot meet a client, can you arrange other support (e.g., a necessary referral) or offer alternative times or settings? In informal settings (e.g., around a clubhouse, a sports centre), you can clarify how you will greet them by discussing what works best for each party.

Time of sessions

The time of session' usually revolves around the '50-minute hour' or the therapeutic hour, which is practical because it guarantees time for the sport psychology practitioner to make notes, rest, and prepare for the next client. There are several considerations for the time to see clients (e.g., purposes of session, fees). Some sessions are shorter than 50 minutes if delivering a specific intervention or longer than 50 minutes if you are supporting a client in a performance or training environment (e.g., over nine holes at a golf course). The 50-minute hour works well in private practice in your clinic to keep work scheduled for you and your clients, a break between clients, and to avoid keeping other clients waiting.

Though the image many people might hold of a sport psychology practitioner in practice – whether on a training pitch, track, or poolside – several other images are possible, from the consulting room with an athlete, meeting each week over several months, to consulting over telephone or video call. What we try to remember here is that learning and change happen in different ways, settings, and modes of delivery. Perhaps more than other settings, sport embraces the breadth of modes of delivery to the benefits of what is on offer finds its way to those in most need, most often. Issues about time, place, clients, technology, and materials help us do what we do better, more often.

Some therapy approaches advocate using an extended initial meeting (e.g., three hours) to establish a solid contact with a new client (Barkham et al., 2017; McLeod, 2019). Dr Bob Rotella, for example, shared his working practice for initial sessions, especially with golfers. He explained he invited clients to work with him from his home office over one to two days. They spent part of this time playing a round of golf on the golf course, where Dr Rotella attends, observes, listens, and interacts with the golfer. Such day-long sessions allow the client to show the practitioner their responses in troubling or feared situations with the attendant support of a skilled helper. Though the rhythms of a client's life on the golf course might differ, immediate concerns become the focus of assessment and formulation.

Frequency and number of sessions

The frequency of sessions ranges from daily to weekly, fortnightly, monthly, or ad hoc. These arrangements might be formal in a private clinic, but informal sessions with unstructured contact with clients are common in sport because we see athletes at training grounds, travelling to competitions, staying in hotels, eating meals, and so on. In my (Paul) practice, I usually see clients on a weekly basis because I am keeping the client's problem in mind, especially with pressing concerns in their athletic lives; occasionally, I will see clients more frequently than once weekly.

Though many of the clients we see benefit from 6–10 sessions, sometimes working with broader problems can last from several sessions to 25 or more sessions. Working with athletes who play sport professionally (e.g., golf, tennis, cricket) might require sessions online because they are travelling across the world for long periods (e.g., up to three months). Working with these clients means reviewing and supporting what the client is doing to change. Because of the infrequency of sessions or the long-term support provided to clients, perhaps preparing through an Olympic cycle, appointments explore current events in the athlete's life and anticipations over the coming months. Mostly, brief, time-limited interventions resonate with the pressing needs of clients for efficiency and effectiveness.

The nature of sporting careers such as season-long commitments to a club, playing on tour, Olympic cycles, and so forth, means that long-term support makes sense for meaningful change. Developing a trusting relationship with a practitioner takes time, and the volatile nature of sport means issues arise unexpectedly and require addressing. Many athletes with support teams (e.g., coaches, physiotherapists) will have multiple related problems (e.g., technique changes or recovering from injury) that need attending to sequentially, and sometimes in parallel. One issue arising in long-term support is the limits of how far a practitioner can take a client. Sometimes, changing practitioners lies in the best interest of the client; however, some clients in sport present a valuable source of financial income, so letting the client develop independence poses problems. These ethical and moral issues ought to be addressed with a supervisor and the client to recognise what happened and why.

Ending sessions on time

Another healthy boundary for a client and practitioner means ending a session on time. If the agreed time means 50 minutes, then the practitioner and client are clear about what will happen after 50 minutes of the session beginning. Boundaries like ending a session on time ought to be clear, appropriate for the context, respectful, and firm without being controlling or manipulative (Ballantyne Dykes et al., 2017). A practitioner might have scheduled sessions which begin on the hour, each hour, for a few hours in succession. A client will also have other commitments, and these time boundaries mean we set the scene and everyone knows where they stand and what to expect in a session. Closing a session forms a critical element of the therapeutic hour, so what we open together (e.g., exploring a complex relationship with a teammate) we can close together, sensitively. The intention with all sessions is for the client to return to their world safely after a helping session ends. We need to allow some time to close a session, which means offering the client a sign of the time remaining. The skills of summarising capture what they have shared today, illustrating your understanding of the client and the client's story. Inviting the client to share what they experienced and valued about the session, and what changes they would like in the next session, not only allow the practitioner to improve their work with their client but also allow the client to weave together the threads of the session.

Clients sometimes share 'doorknob comments' or 'doorknob confessions' for several reasons. For example, a client might disclose comments at the end of a session, as they are about to leave, leaving little time to discuss them. Sometimes clients feel anxious about discussing or receiving feedback about a topic, so they leave it to the end of the session. It takes much courage to disclose, and sometimes it takes the whole session to feel comfortable to disclose. Occasionally, clients share these confessions at the end of an early session so they can leave unsatisfied with their treatment, which did not address what they wished to address. We need to acknowledge the 'doorknob confession' and suggest adding it to the next session's agenda so it receives the time it deserves. In this way, the session ends on time and the 'confession' will be addressed.

Assessment

An assessment forms part of the helping process. Although there are different schools of thought on the value and place of assessment (and diagnosis) in the helping professions, it forms an integral part of the beginning stages of support because it helps the practitioner to understand the client as a person and an athlete. It helps the client to understand themselves, the process of applied sport psychology support, and how the sport psychology practitioner seeks to help them (Taylor, 2018). In this triptych, we consider the athlete (e.g., age, competitive level, needs, goals), context (e.g., coach, family, organisation, sport type), and practitioner (e.g., competencies, training, psychotherapeutic approach), and how these components fit (Vealey & Garner-Holman, 1998; Vealey et al., 2019). Assessment falls into each stage of the helping process because clients and their issues change as the work unfolds. With a preliminary assessment, you hold that this assessment changes as the information gathers from various sources. In applied sport psychology, for example, we normally assess presenting issues with semi-structured interviews, questionnaires or psychometrics, and observation.

For athletes, there might be physical, psychological, technical, tactical, lifestyle, and social support dimensions to their understanding of psychological well-being and performance. As practitioners, our focus emphasises the psychological domain; however, other aspects remain present throughout, so we often relate to an athlete's coach, conditioning coach, physician, equipment providers, biomechanists, dieticians, and so on to include or exclude these areas of the athlete's presenting issues. Sport psychology practitioners use assessment to gauge: (1) athletes' needs, (2) clinical assessment, (3) change over time, (4) evaluate an intervention, (5) cross-validate observations, (6) selection, and (7) offer structure to the service delivery (Vealey et al., 2019).

Gathering data through assessment emerges through your approach to supporting clients and your education, training, and experience. We shall explore three forms of assessment here, beginning with questionnaires, then following with observation before exploring the details of an intake interview.

Questionnaires/psychometrics

We value the information we gather in questionnaires and psychometric instruments, owing to their validity, reliability, and appropriateness. A valid measuring instrument measures what it purports to measure. One issue we encounter in sport settings means that although researchers may test an assessment's validity in a general population, they might not evaluate it with your current working population (e.g., athletes). In testing for validity, researchers explore construct, content, criteria, and internal validity of the measure. Our judgement as practitioners means choosing what serves the client before us. A reliable instrument means it calculates similar scores each time we administer it. This stability or consistency of scores means the assessment measures the same thing each time you use it.

To progress scientifically, we need to identify, define, and measure constructs (e.g., motivation, confidence) accurately. If we develop and validate a scale for use with athletes, for example, a sport-specific self-report measure of identity foreclosure (Brewer et al., 2021), we need to submit acceptable psychometric properties. Surveying an athlete's thoughts, emotions, perceptions, intentions, and behaviour helps us to understand, explain, and predict athletic performance and well-being. Not only do we need valid and reliable measurement instruments to achieve these goals; we need to use them appropriately. Carlstedt (2013) argued that practitioners do not use psychological inventories discriminately, especially portraying predictive validity. Predictive validity reflects the degree to which test scores accurately predict scores on a criterion measure. A practitioner working with a strength and conditioning coach might wish to know whether components of physical fitness (e.g., aerobic capacity) influence performance (e.g., points scored in basketball). If a strong correlation emerges between scores on physical fitness tests and average points per game per player, the strength and conditioning coach can argue for the validity of physical fitness tests to predict the points per game of the players. When we plan interventions with athletes, we need to know the function and purpose of the inventory rather than collect data that is false or inaccurate. As for the athletes, they need to perceive them as helpful to their needs and complete the instruments honestly (Beckman & Kellmann, 2003).

When considering an assessment tool, we sensitively consider age, culture, education, ethnicity, gender, religion, and sexual orientation. An assessment tool suitable for an adult population often falters among those in late childhood and early adolescence. Having assessment tools at our disposal is not a justification for using them. We ought to consider how the assessment tool helps the clients to understand themselves and you to understand your client. Sometimes a questionnaire, though it may have strengths, it may also be harmful because it might produce an expected and harmful response relating to memories of painful experiences or troubling relationships.

Psychological inventories pass by names such as profiles, questionnaires, scales, surveys, and tests (Vealey & Garner-Holman, 1998). Psychological inventories might focus on personality traits, psychological characteristics, dispositions, orientations, styles, or behavioural tendencies. Is it any wonder practitioners get confused without clear definitions, purposes, and applications of these instruments?

Vealey et al. (2019) examined the specific inventories used by sport psychology practitioners, comparing data from 2003–2017. They showed a remarkable similarity, as the Profile of Mood States (POMS) (McNair et al., 1992), self-designed questionnaires, Test of Attentional and Interpersonal Style (TAIS) (Nideffer, 1976, 1993), Test of Performance Strategies (TOPS) (Thomas et al., 1999), Athletic Coping Skills Inventory (ACSI-28) (Smith et al., 1995), Competitive State Anxiety Inventory-2 (CSAI-2) (Martens et al., 1990), and performance profiles (Butler & Hardy, 1992) were within the top ten questionnaires used by sport psychology practitioners in both 2003 and 2017. In the top four were self-designed questionnaires, performance profiles, and POMS. Even with this consistent use by sport psychology practitioners over the past few decades, using psychometrics in applied settings comes with limitations. Martin et al. (2000) used the POMS to monitor high-intensity training in cyclists, but the relationship between POMS scores and individual performance was unpredictable. The authors recommended coaches use an idiographic approach to record and examine individual histories of training and responses to taper to recommend the most favourable schedule for athletes.

Common errors in assessment

Assessment forms one stage of service delivery. Often, assessments form part of the evaluation stage of service delivery to determine the effectiveness of the intervention. How one selects to assess depends on professional (e.g., one's training, background, skills), interpersonal (e.g., type of relationship with the client), and situational (e.g., athlete's needs) factors (Anshel & Brinthaupt, 2014). For one practitioner, a structured interview or direct observation of the client's behaviour serves the assessment needs adequately. One challenge here, however, means we have no psychometric evidence that the intervention caused the changes in the inventory scores following the intervention (Smith & Sparkes, 2009).

Vealey et al. (2019) analysed the practices and attitudes of sport psychology practitioners' use of questionnaires in sport psychology consulting. They reported that practitioners in 2003 rated questionnaires as more useful than practitioners in 2017, though the specific questionnaires used did not change extensively over that period. On a practical day-to-day level, a practitioner may choose – depending on workload and time demands – to take a shortcut in assessing or interpreting the scores of an inventory or perhaps use an inventory generated for – and applied in – non-sport settings (Anastasi, 1992; LeUnes, 2008). Practitioners also misuse psychological inventories, such as using a trait measure to gauge an athlete's state (e.g., situational) or asking child athletes to complete an inventory developed and validated for adults. To use inventories properly, we need valid and reliable instruments for the sport setting and a judicious consideration of the client's needs (e.g., age, skill level, sport type). This latter scrutiny depends on one's educational background, training, experience, and competence in administering, scoring, and interpreting the scores on an inventory.

Are we choosing the right test for the right function? We have tests for selection and tests for development. In a selection context, a test might help organisations choose among candidates. These tests detect maximum performance (test of one's ability or aptitude). In a development context, tests might help highlight candidates' strengths and areas for development. Some organisations use personality tests in selection and development. Inventories also serve diagnostically, whereas others describe, explain, and predict a characteristic of an athlete. A practitioner might design a checklist to observe behavioural patterns on a basketball court but realises that this checklist of observable behaviours does not contain psychometric properties.

The relative certainty proffered by inventories might skew one's work practices to rely on inventories only and dismiss interviews and observations. When we consider the circumstances of sport, we need to include skill level, experience, and personal and situational resources to gather a holistic view of the client. This rounded view also depends on securing the athlete's trust and openness to share and involve oneself in the therapeutic process. Developing such trust for self-disclosure challenges most practitioners, and without it, the likelihood of resistance and reluctance to disclose grows (Singer & Anshel, 2006). Openness and honesty from the practitioner about the aim and value of an inventory and the link to the athlete's performance and well-being ought to be made clear from the outset. In this collaborative alliance, the athlete completes the inventory and the practitioner scores it and returns the scores to the athlete. On returning the scores to the athlete, the practitioner reviews, interprets, and validates the scores with the athlete so that together, they can make sense of what these scores mean. An athlete may score low, moderate, or high on an inventory but the practitioner will need to discuss what these scores mean for the athlete.

Inventories help us determine sources of performance impairment, performance dysfunction, and potential clinical treatment in an accurate, valid, and ethical manner (Gardner & Moore, 2006). Anshel and Brinthaupt (2014, p. 412) listed 16 guidelines for proper use of psychological inventories in sport psychology practice.

The eight guidelines before administration are:

1. Determine the inventory's purpose.
2. Confirm the inventory's psychometric properties.
3. Determine objectives and the conceptual framework.
4. Determine whether the inventory is intended to assess the athlete statistically or to compare the athlete against norms.
5. Determine the inventory's external validity.
6. Assess the role of inventory scores in consultation effectiveness.

7. Detect multiple applications of the data.
8. Obtain prior written consent and Institutional Review Board (IRB) approval (if applicable).

During and after administration, the practitioner ought to:

9. Establish trust between the consultant and athlete.
10. Be sensitive to group and cultural differences.
11. Determine the client's reading level.
12. Obtain client confirmation or refutation of inventory scores.
13. Ensure data accuracy.
14. Interpret scores with norms.
15. Have a data disclosure plan.
16. Document the experience of using the inventory.

In summary, several steps before, during, and after administering an inventory help practitioners to do good work with their athletes. And because psychological inventories in applied sport psychology serve several purposes (e.g., selection, development, diagnosis) in applied research and practice settings, we need to tread carefully in a critical and ethical manner. Athletes and sport psychology practitioners might also consider questionnaires irrelevant or impractical, undermining the practitioner–athlete relationship, and lacking the validity of the specific population or context. We need to alter our approaches to assessment, perhaps by shortening questionnaires in the applied sport psychology setting, to improve athletes' return on investment (Horvath & Rothlin, 2018).

Performance profiling

The performance profile empowers clients to govern how they appraise their performance and any developments emerging thereafter. Butler and Hardy (1992) presented the performance profile as a theory-driven, client-centred tool to analyse performance. Since then, practitioners have shown how clients applied the performance profile to boost various psychological outcomes such as self-awareness (e.g., Castillo & Chow, 2020), motivation (Castillo et al., 2020), and cohesion (Weston et al., 2010). The performance profile is an autonomy-supportive assessment encouraging athletes to identify meaningful skills and qualities they believe meet their needs. This athlete-led assessment counterbalances the challenges of boredom, lack of buy-in, response bias, and social desirability of psychometric tools (Chow & Gilson, 2018; Taylor, 2018). Though most practitioners and clients manoeuvre the profile towards deficits, Castillo and Bird (2021) proposed a strengths-based performance profile to help athletes, coaches, and practitioners better understand, assess, and profit from standing strengths for coming performances. In a strengths-based performance profile, the clients appreciate what works for them now (e.g., strengths and virtues). Researchers have revealed that those applying their strengths are more confident, energetic, happy, resilient, and task-engaged than those who refrain (e.g., Govindji & Linley, 2007; Linley & Burns, 2010).

The personality profile appears as an assessment (e.g., to analyse performance) and a standard intervention (e.g., to enhance a range of psychological outcomes) in applied sport psychology. Over the past 30 years, sport psychology practitioners continued to use the performance profile as an assessment tool (Castillo, 2022; Vealey et al., 2019). Its theoretical footings lay in personal construct theory (Kelly, 1955/1991). Personal construct theory is a theory of personality and cognition to understand the psychological reasoning for people's actions. People develop personal constructs about the world and use these constructs to make sense of what they observe and experience. This meaning-making guides behaviour. A performance profile nudges the athlete to explore the idiosyncrasies of their construing (i.e., how they interpret and make sense of events they experience) and meaning-making processes about their athletic performance.

The performance profiling technique works for individuals and teams, and can include four corollaries (i.e., individuality, commonality, sociality, and experience) from the personal construct theory stance. To illustrate, we can use the performance profiling technique to gather an athlete's perspective (individuality corollary), a team's perspective (commonality corollary), and further social interaction among the team and backroom staff (sociality corollary), and gather changes in construal over time (experience corollary) with repeated profiling.

Although the performance profiling technique sets its foot in personal construct theory, it plants its other foot in cognitive evaluation theory (Deci & Ryan, 1985). Cognitive evaluation theory binds social (e.g., feedback, coach behaviour) environmental (e.g., competition rewards and punishments) factors to support or spoil an athlete's intrinsic motivation. Also, satisfying basic psychological needs (competence, autonomy, and relatedness) and an internal locus of control cultivates self-determined motivation, flowing toward complementary cognitive (e.g., focus), affective (e.g., fun), and behavioural (e.g. flow) outcomes.

Practically, when athletes undertake a performance profile, they choose (i.e., autonomy and an internal locus of control) what they wish to include in the profile about aspects of training and competition. They can cultivate competence through monitoring progress working on their chosen goals (i.e., competence) from one profiling session to the next. Athletes might conduct performance profiling alone or with the guidance of a sport psychology practitioner and coach or in a group setting in which all members share their construal of performance issues. This three-pronged approach harnesses intrinsic motivation.

Performance profiling serves several purposes, such as performance assessment, self-awareness, intrinsic motivation, a basis for setting goals, building confidence, monitoring progress, and enhancing team functioning. Here is a brief description of the performance profiling procedure with an athlete. We can present performance profiling in circular targets, tables, flowcharts, or worksheets. There are several ways to generate profile qualities, scoring, and implementing the technique (Weston et al., 2013). One case study of performance profiling comes from Jones (1993). The athlete-rated constructs (e.g., tactical, technical, physical, and psychological) on importance from 1 (not important at all) to 10 (of crucial importance), on ideal where 1 (could not be any worse) to 10 (could not be any better) and subjective self-assessment where 1 (could not be any worse) to 10 (could not be any better). Subtracting the subjective self-assessment from the ideal self-assessment, then multiplying that value by the importance score, produces a discrepancy score:

$$D = ([\text{ideal self-assessment}] - [\text{subjective self-assessment}] \times I [\text{importance}]) \quad (6.1)$$

Those scores with the largest discrepancy highlighted the qualities needing the most pressing attention. Planning an intervention follows this formulation.

Observation

Watching athletes, coaches, and teams in their natural habitat of training and competition offers practitioners a pastiche of information about behaviour, emotion, performance, social interaction, and so forth. Behavioural observation involves gathering information, formally (e.g., checklist) or informally, about athletes from their behaviour in their natural settings (e.g., training). The behavioural evidence we gather by watching and listening to an athlete in practice and competition tells us about who this athlete might be and how the athlete responds to other athletes and the world in which they belong. Observation is a dominant assessment modality for practitioners who work with their clients in training and competition arenas rather than exclusively in an office setting. Although a client might recall an athletic experience, a practitioner might also be present to observe. This direct observation gathers specific information about the person, the physical and social environment, and especially how these influence their thoughts, feelings, physical responses, and actions.

We wrote earlier about how assessment runs through beginnings, middles, and endings when working with clients. For example, our behavioural observation guides us about the effectiveness of an intervention. We can measure and evaluate changes or lack thereof, following an intervention. We might observe a client over several occasions in practice and competition to capture specific behaviours under investigation. Our behavioural observation, blended with feedback from the athlete and coach, tells us about what we, as practitioners, observe and how we interpret those observations by the athlete and coach.

Martin et al. (2020) offered four practical guidelines for effective observation practice. The guidelines steer us towards observation, its challenges, and how we might engage best with observation practices. The first guideline establishes when to observe, while the second, third, and fourth guidelines describe how to observe.

When to observe

Most clients operate in training, competition, and social environments where a practitioner might be present outside of typical office time. At the outset of work with a client, a practitioner might observe the client in training and competition to gather information directly about the presence or absence of a skill (e.g., diaphragmatic breathing) before closed skills (e.g., serving in tennis). This macro-level information contributes to the formulation with a client before intervention. There is much to observe here in each setting, such as psychological constructs (e.g., motivation, commitment) with time-keeping, attitudes towards teammates and coaches, interpersonal interactions, skills practice, coping with success and failure, and so on. At a micro-level in one-to-one work in the office setting, a client might display non-verbal responses about their experience of anxiety at this phase of play (e.g., serving in tennis).

The opportunities for learning about a client depend upon context, availability, and accessibility. For example, it may not be possible to observe a client in competition because you cannot be where the client is working (e.g., competing internationally) or because of your availability to travel, or there is no access granted to support staff at events or the client wishes service delivery to remain private.

Embedding observation

The practitioner's time outside office hours costs, yet practitioners hesitate to charge for this time (Martin et al., 2017). Without observing the client where possible, part of the assessment phase remains hidden from the practitioner. One might consider observation a period of inactivity on the practitioner's part because the practitioner does not appear to be working, like a coach, for example. To illustrate its necessity, let us consider the case of a journalist attending a game with a deadline for her report a few hours later. Without observing the game and taking notes, how might the journalist write her report? Similarly, practitioners gather information for their job – service delivery. This time in observation serves the client. The challenge for practitioners means working with the client (e.g., athlete, parent, coach, organisation) to create a contract for working that includes this time and effort in observation.

Elevating contextual understanding

The third guideline amounts to gathering contextual material about the client and the demands of the sport. Through observation, the practitioner amasses information about social, cultural, and historic contextual factors operating in the performance arena (Eubank et al., 2014). The practitioner creeps towards appreciating the client's reality and the data for a formulation. Sometimes, a practitioner will work on site with a squad, meaning the practitioner immerses in the milieu as part of the organisation's set-up. A practitioner employed within an organisation usually works with and alongside the backroom staff at training sessions, travelling with the squad and supporting the coaching staff.

Structuring observation

Trainees seek guidance about observation as a matter of course because they attend training and competition without knowing why they are attending, but attending seems like the right thing to do. One reason for this uncertainty falls under the goals of attendance. Without goals and structure, trainees wonder what to focus on and present concerns about their ability and competence as practitioners. Practitioners always move along a continuum between structured and unstructured observation. For example, a structured observation usually means recording specific behaviours using frequency counts, while an unstructured observation might encompass witnessing the 'felt sense' of the squad training together.

For best practice, beginning with an intention for observation seems functional. First, determine which aspect of observable behaviour presents most readily for a frequency count. This aim emerges from the intake assessment and the client's presenting issue(s). Later in service delivery, the practitioner might observe a difference between baseline and intervention. The frequency count might be for training and/or competition, with opportunities to observe discrepancies in each context and the transferability of a client's behaviours from one setting to another. Issues of days of the week, times of the day, and segments of the season all play their part in the contextual patchwork of the client's performances.

The material gathered might form part of a formal feedback report to a client (e.g., an organisation) or informal feedback added to the client's reflections and observations relating to the context. Our observations as practitioners offer a lens through which performers see themselves in a setting so we can work sensitively and sensibly with them for their goals in service delivery.

Contracting

An effective therapeutic relationship requires a contract. A contract defines the commitments of the practitioner and client to a course of action meaningful to each party. The client engages in this working relationship voluntarily to explore an issue in depth with a systematic structure. A working therapy contract displays the formal aspects, such as purpose and agenda for the work with boundaries and roles of the practitioner and the client. There are legal, ethical, therapeutic, and psychological benefits for the client because it corrals their expectations and standards to judge progress and determination of when to finish the work and contract. A contract ensures a professional and mutually beneficial relationship, accounting for the ground rules so healthy boundaries offer a vital sense of one's own identity. You will see detail about confidentiality, venue, address, fees, frequency of sessions, number of sessions, missed or cancelled appointments, process of referral, responsibilities of each party (e.g., homework, data storage), practitioner's supervision, ethical guidance, ending service delivery, accreditation, and signatures of each party. We present an example of a sport psychology service delivery contract in the Appendix.

Is Single-Session Therapy (SST) sufficient?

Talmon (1990, p. xv) defined single-session therapy (SST) as "as one face-to-face meeting between a therapist and a patient with no previous or subsequent sessions within one year". Dryden (2017) felt this definition did not discount other forms of contact (e.g., telephone) that might happen across the year and suggested SST comprises:

> One main face-to-face meeting between a therapist and a client with no previous or subsequent main sessions within one year; up to two non-face-to-face brief meetings prior to the main session to arrange and get the most out of the main session; and one follow-up session.

Dryden (2017) conceptualised single-session–integrated CBT having four points of contact between the practitioner and client. The first contact entails a person seeking help and contacting a practitioner. Next, an extended pre-session contact (e.g., by phone) formalises this initial decision to gain the most from the third contact – the single face-to-face session with the practitioner. The final contact, about three months later, covers the follow-up session. One might argue that one face-to-face session seems insufficient for a client's benefit; however, following SST with a practitioner, a person might find that they can now put things in perspective, settle on a new way of thinking about an issue and associated factors, and realise they could deal with issues better than expected (Dryden, 2017).

SST flourished since publication of this pivotal book in 1990 (Talmon, 1990). Much of the SST work began in family therapy to maximise the time when family members attended because of the challenges of assembling family members in ongoing therapy. Similarly, practitioners in sport settings wrestle with coordinating calendars among groups of athletes, or the pressing concerns of an athlete about an upcoming performance suggest that SST might fit suitability. Also, practising sport psychology practitioners need to deliver effective, efficient, and meaningful interventions in return for investment from national governing bodies, performance directors, coaches, and performers (e.g., Portenga et al., 2012; Fletcher & Wagstaff, 2009).

Formulation

Service delivery in applied sport psychology comprises assessment, formulation, intervention, evaluation, and communication. In an assessment, we gather information about the client, but how do we make sense of it? We need to combine all the information from the client with the theory we learn in teaching components of training. The challenge does not finish there because we also need to identify a suitable intervention strategy. Trainees often find it challenging to explain a client's presenting issues – and so the formulation process, though critical to the process, remains superficial. It is, however, a skill one learns and hones through training and supervision.

One reason trainees find formulation challenging is because it is a complex skill and requires a step-by-step approach to build a sound formulation. Also, depending on your therapeutic modality (e.g., PCT), formulation is understood and presented differently. Useful formulations also encourage the active participation of the client. If we place ourselves in a sport setting, having learned about theory and practice in applied sport psychology, we still have much work to do because we need to engage the client so the client feels safe to share and explore their dilemma. Next, you need to make sense of their problem(s) with them, which they could not do alone; although they might have a working hypothesis of what is going on for them. Then you need to communicate your combined understanding of their problem in a way that makes sense to the client. Finally, these words need to become an intervention to address the presented issue for the better. These steps in the process seem daunting, especially when the issue presented is time-limited, either by the number of sessions available or the event (e.g., Olympic trials).

With so much information and decision dilemmas along the way, we need a process to follow. A formulation is a working hypothesis of the problems presented by the client. This working hypothesis is a psychological understanding of what the client is experiencing. With this idea in mind, we need to keep our theoretical knowledge aligned with the presenting problem as we explore the basis, development, and maintenance of the problem(s). In the end, we link all the information gathered (e.g., intake interview, observation, psychometrics) with our therapeutic orientation, theoretical knowledge, and research to identify those parts amenable to change and begin our intervention. Much information lies within a client's personal history, current functioning, and circumstances that tell a story which links with your therapeutic choices, theoretical knowledge, current research, and practice experience (Corrie & Lane, 2017).

Several components comprise a formulation. A formulation sorts the information gathered during assessment into a coherent narrative. Some practitioners use the 'five Ps' formulation to conceptualise an individual's presenting problem in the wider system in which they operate. The 'five Ps' comprise factors such as predisposing (i.e., historical factors), precipitating (i.e., triggers of the presenting issue), perpetuating (i.e., elements that maintain the presenting issue), and protective factors (i.e., resilience and strengths), alongside the presenting issues (i.e., a description of the client's thoughts, feelings, and behaviours). With this formulation, the problem holds structure, which helps to set goals to address it with an intervention and a timeframe to achieve the goals. In this picture of a presenting problem, the unwieldy trove of information coheres. If you consider all the information gathered from a client's story; your observations in session, training, and competition; the results of psychometric tests; and reports from a coach or backroom staff, it is daunting to fit the pieces of the puzzle into a coherent whole. The simple questions we might ask will have complexities attached to them. For example, we might ask the following questions:

1. Which factors influenced this client to develop this problem?

    a. Is there a family history of a similar problem?
    b. Is there early trauma?
    c. Are there any significant developmental experiences?
    d. Are there any social or economic challenges?

2. Why did the problem begin in this way?

    a. Are there any specific 'trigger incidents' at this time?
    b. Are there any specific life stressors?
    c. Are there any specific developmental transitions?

3. How did the problem develop?

    a. What improves the presenting problem?
    b. What exacerbates the presenting problem?

4. What is maintaining the problem?

    a. Personal circumstances.
    b. Social circumstances.
    c. Performance circumstances.
    d. Psychological processes.

5. How is the client coping with the problem?

    a. What is helping the client to cope?
    b. What is not helping the client to cope (e.g., drugs and alcohol)?

6. What resources does the client hold?

    a. What are the client's strengths?

7. Knowing this information, which intervention might work best?

These questions and answers mean hearing the client's story blended with your best understanding of your therapeutic approach, theoretical understanding, research knowledge, and practice experience. Remember, this is a blend – not a blender. We are not forcing everything into a specific way of understanding; rather, we blend our sense and sensibility to arrive at a workable understanding of the whole.

Together with the client, you can construct a formulation that keeps you headed in a chosen direction with clarity about the goals and tasks of therapy. Trainees and qualified practitioners find formulations helpful to manage their own worries when several issues are presented together or when uncertainties crop up in the process of service delivery. Some practitioners, however, working with humanistic, phenomenological, and existential frameworks, see therapy as a process unfolding rather than a prepared action plan. For instance, a process of 'being' rather than a process of 'doing' and imposing one's world view on the client, perhaps with a disease model of mental distress in mind. If we frame our work as 'problem-setting' rather than 'problem-solving', it emphasises a different journey with a client (Strawbridge & Woolfe, 2004) and perhaps a crossover where 'being' and 'doing' coalesce for the betterment of all (Corrie & Lane, 2017). Your training programme will mandate a view of formulation according to the therapeutic modality (e.g., cognitive-behavioural or psychodynamic approach) in use. These requirements from our practicum placements and training course assessments mean tensions ensue about what works best, and we are often shaped by lecturers, supervisors, and our readings. These tensions lead to confusion and sometimes withdrawing from thinking, reading, and arguing for what fits, acknowledging the prevailing views and course requirements.

Constructing a formulation

Notwithstanding all the tensions written about formulations in the preceding paragraph, we can create a formulation that fits for your theoretical approach and the context within which you work. For example, a psychodynamic formulation will differ from a cognitive-behavioural formulation, emphasising different aspects of the client's narrative and collected data (e.g., observations, psychometrics) to arrive at a working hypothesis. In a person-centred approach, a practitioner might focus on an athlete with low mood being burdened by conditions of worth that stifle the authentic self-expressing in practice and competition. The conditions for growth – acceptance and unconditional positive regard – only emerged when high standards were achieved. The athlete might have internalised specific conditions of worth which interfered with clear and consistent self-expression when playing and performing. The athlete learns to play and compete, but without their own authentic experience and tendency towards growth. In the same case, a cognitive-behavioural practitioner would develop a formulation emphasising how the client's thoughts mediate emotional experience and behavioural outcomes, examining links between unpleasant thoughts and feelings. It may transpire that the practitioner formulates links between low mood, poor performance, and a negative bias towards one's self, others, and the world.

In sport settings, we might work with client-athletes from ages 8–80. We might work with amateur and professional athletes who lead us towards issues relating to the individual or towards the systems in which they live and work (e.g., family, professional organisation). We might formulate a specific incident (e.g., triggers that led a client to perform poorly after sustaining steady progress) or perhaps how an athlete sustained difficulties with managers' and coaches' links with attachment difficulties in childhood. Yet, it is this richness that might mean we feel utterly confused, so we need to focus on what is most useful for the client now. We need to justify our choices and actions for (and with) our client, our employers, and ourselves. We do so considering theory, models, research, experience, and the presenting issue(s). Written assessments in our training programmes require these coherent formulations and these are typically encouraged in all logbooks where we store case notes and reflections on our practice.

Corrie and Lane (2017) offered a generic approach that focuses on three elements: purpose, perspective, and process. The purpose comprises what you and your client intend to achieve. The perspective reflects your values, beliefs, knowledge, and therapeutic approach, including personal, interpersonal, and systemic models that inform your work. Finally, the process (any method or tool) then follows from this psychologically informed approach to decide and answer questions along the way. The case and formulation we present next reflects Corrie and Lane's (2017) example following a CBT therapeutic modality.

Case study: Sonny

Sonny had not been feeling his best and could not seem to put a string of good performances together. His coaches kept telling him he needs to "up the effort" and "help the team". Sonny, a 24-year-old, second-row forward, had been playing professional rugby since he turned 18 years of age. Sonny lived with his wife and their two young boys. The young boys struggled to sleep well at night, so Sonny did the night shift, putting the boys to sleep when they woke because his wife felt permanently exhausted and struggled with the boys at home each day. Despite Sonny looking after the boys at night, his wife rarely slept well. She also felt quite tearful and felt like she was "failing all the time". She was quite critical of Sonny and would yell and tell him "how hopeless he was", which reminded him of his mother who criticised Sonny heavily as a child (e.g., "How could you be so stupid?" and "You get nothing right"), especially when she was drinking.

Sonny spent five days at the training ground and travelled for away games and international duty as the season unfolded. Sonny described himself as "a willing worker" and "a team player", but the concerns about his wife weighed heavily, especially when travelling for games abroad. His current performances in training and games worried him, and he saw these as personal failings ("I should man up and just get it together" or "I am failing as a husband, a dad, and rugby player") and problematic cognitions about his employment and future ("What if I lose my contract? Where will we be?"). He spoke disparagingly about himself, labelled himself (e.g., weak, hopeless), and discounted his strengths and resources (e.g., resourceful, disciplined, kind, patient). With each passing training session, the tiniest mistake played on his mind (e.g., "I missed that last tackle and that's not the performance of a Lions player"). Sonny felt appreciated and resourceful, kind and patient, working with the

Early childhood and adolescent experience

Sonny's longstanding criticism at the hands of his mother. Constantly trying to be good by doing all the right things so he could stay in control in an uncontrollable situation.

Critical incidents

Sonny's reflection on a string of poor performances at training and games. A stream of worries about his boys, his wife and how she is not coping, especially when he travels away from home with the team or international squad. His wife's negative reactions towards him at home especially if he did things to relax (e.g., train the academy boys, play golf).

The cognitive triad

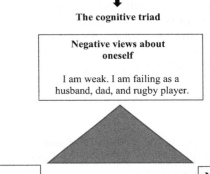

> **Negative views about oneself**
>
> I am weak. I am failing as a husband, dad, and rugby player.

> **Negative views about others and the world**
>
> My life is all over the place. Nothing is going right for me at work or at home.

> **Negative views about the future**
>
> Things will never change. I'll lose my contract and then where will we be?

Content: Themes of loss, isolation, devaluing self in personal narratives and thinking style (see the cognitive triad above).
Process: A selective view of perceived difficulties and failures at work (e.g., ruminating over one mistake) and at home. An interpretative bias (e.g., labelling, all-or-nothing thinking). A ruminative style of reflection upon incidents at work and at home.
Vulnerability: Activation of negative core beliefs about himself formed in childhood in two environments: home and work.
Behavioural coping: Playing with his boys at home; taking training with the academy squad, getting out of the house.
Personoal resources: Beliefs about himself as resourceful, disciplined, and patient.

Figure 6.1 A formulation of Sonny's presenting difficulties.

academy players because they recognised and appreciated him without reservation. His depressive thinking style kicked in at home when his wife criticised him or blamed him for the most insignificant things he had not addressed. His wife also felt anytime spent playing golf or training the academy boys is time he could spend at home, which made him feel guilty rather than as a time to access a few positive experiences in his life. When his wife went to rest in the later afternoons, his mood improved because his time with his little boys was so relaxed and he "didn't get anything wrong".

When Sonny sought support, he did not know where to begin because, although he wanted to do whatever was required, he could not identify what was required. Sonny also wanted to understand why all these problems seemed to spiral at work and at home. It seemed sensible to address his mood first before addressing other parts of his life. He could change unhelpful patterns of thinking and behaving which were affecting his mood before deciding how best to help his wife and little boys. The formulation helped Sonny to see how the pieces of his life fitted and which did not and how his ways of thinking and behaving were his ways of coping and not a sign that he was a 'weak' man. He could take any incident at home or at work and deconstruct it into thoughts, feelings, and behaviours that maintained his low mood. The formulation also helped him to recognise how change is possible because he could see a way to recover his situation. The route to recovery depended on developing cognitive problem-solving skills to manage challenges at home and at work, leaning into those activities that afforded mastery and pleasure, and focusing on reappraising those unhelpful thinking styles and biases including some core beliefs laid down in childhood. Sonny could use his personal resources of discipline, kindness, and patience to think more helpfully and act compassionately towards himself along the way. The formulation instilled great hope in Sonny as he began his journey to help himself first.

Summary

In this chapter, we introduced components of the first session, from meeting, greeting, and seating to building trust and rapport. A critical element of this stage is to outline boundaries in service delivery, such as time of sessions, frequency and number of sessions, and ending sessions on time. Assessment forms the core of beginnings, often involving intake interviews, psychometrics, and observation, especially in sport and exercise contexts. An assessment may take one or a few sessions, but once it is complete, we begin with formulation. Formulation presents a critical step between assessment and intervention. It requires much learning and support from tutors and supervisors. In Chapter 7, we turn to the middles phase of service delivery.

7 Middles

Introduction

The middle phase of service delivery involves exploring and understanding the problem as we present it in this book. Just as therapeutic support over 12 weeks, for example, contains beginnings, middles, and endings, individual therapy hours encompass a similar structure. Outside the therapy hour, practitioners have a preparation phase, and after the therapy hour, a review phase. These five phases vary in length, purpose, and outcome, and we shall explore each one.

Preparation phase

While this preparation phase differs for practitioners at different stages of their career, the principles in play remain the same. For example, arriving early, preparing the room for the client, reading over client notes, and relaxing before the session. With online sessions, similar principles apply, especially preparing oneself for the session. For instance, if you intended to introduce behaviour recording sheets or thought record sheets, you are ensuring you have the materials you need. With a large caseload, especially if you are working with a squad of 25 players, you will need to familiarise yourself with the client's notes from the previous session so you can begin efficiently when the client arrives – and though you may be prepared, we still ask the client how the client wishes to proceed.

Beginnings

After a few sessions, clients familiarise themselves with the structure of sessions (e.g., meeting, seating, and greeting). Many practitioners begin by re-establishing the working alliance, reviewing homework, and assembling the agenda with the client. Starting the session might happen with the client or the practitioner, but it is helpful to slow things down and check in with the client. Practitioners can establish this safe space for the client to share where they are at just now. Many events might have occurred in the client's life that they wish to share with you. Also, we aim to review how the client progressed

DOI: 10.4324/9781003453857-7

or otherwise since the last session, and to explore the homework and experiences. Part of this whole process is to establish an agenda for the session which the client and the practitioner develop together. These agendas offer structure and flexibility, which means the client or the practitioner can alter the items on the agenda to focus on specific developments within the agenda. The client lives in the client's world, not ours; so, we attend to the client's wishes, mostly, when setting an agenda.

Middles

The middle section of support during this phase works on the agenda. We refer to an agenda here, which is typical of traditional CBT, which other practitioners following different therapeutic modalities might not follow. Following a formulation, the client and the practitioner work through the chosen intervention. For some practitioners, there might be a tendency to lead the session and do most of the talking. One way to address this concern is to record some sessions (e.g., audio recording) and reflect upon the split of time between the practitioner's talking and the client's talking. You can share this audio recording with your supervisor and put it on the agenda for your supervision session.

Developing skills within sessions might require many rehearsals. For sport psychology practitioners, these sessions might mean working with an athlete in their athletic setting. Within sessions in a therapy room, communication (e.g., assertiveness) or mind skills (e.g., imagery) ought to feel comfortable to the client in the sense that they can take this skill with them to practise at home and in real-life settings. In a 50-minute session, for instance, it is likely that we will address some items; acknowledging, however, that items on the agenda take time means finding a pace that fits. What seems most likely is that we move too quickly or too slowly. As practitioners, especially at the beginning of one's training or career, we are eager to get things done quickly to show competence and efficiency, and so rush through delivering an intervention without catering to the client's learning needs. Part of this rush to get things done might mean we press the client rather than allowing the client to travel at a pace to suit them. At the other end of this spectrum lie the aimless sessions that meander with little being achieved and neither the working relationship nor the tasks receiving the support they need. Though it may feel as if you are controlling the sessions, summaries and a focus on the agenda help to establish productive sessions. What the practitioner does here means offering a choice to the client about pace, timing, and choice about the next item on the agenda rather than a statement to say "Let's move on".

Endings

Closing a session offers the client and practitioner a chance to review the session and clarify the homework or activities between sessions before arranging the next session. If you begin with the homework, followed by an assessment of the session and then complete arrangements for the next meeting, you will need sufficient time to do so. Taking approximately ten minutes to close seems sensible, and you can adjust as you go. Maybe you have discussed the details of homework in the middle phase and the client knows what to do; however, clarity for both parties seems sensible and emphasises the value of homework or activities in between sessions. Also, this collaboration on planning manageable assignments with clear instructions that expect and address difficulties along the way means that the client gains autonomy to pursue meaningful learning in between sessions. A review of the session allows the client to share what works or what does not work, as well as raising issues the client wishes to put on the agenda for the next session. Finally, you negotiate the date and time of the next session before ending the session (Nelson-Jones, 2012).

Length, frequency, and number of sessions

A '50-minute hour' seems most common for many helping professionals, such as sport psychology practitioners, with the final ten minutes to write notes, rest, and prepare for the next client. Outside these typical office hours, several other factors are worth considering, such as workload, purpose, and place of the session and a fair return of time for money. A practitioner might arrange time differently for working with a golfer on the golf course or a rugby player developing a pre-performance routine for her kicking. For these sessions, the practitioner factors in travel to and from the location and the length of session with the client. Maybe on these days, it is possible to work only with one or two clients. When practitioners work in informal settings (e.g., a sports club), sessions depend on what is possible or appropriate for both parties with other ongoing commitments.

Depending on settings (i.e., formal, informal), the frequency of sessions range from daily to weekly to fortnightly to monthly or on an ad hoc basis when the need arises. In informal settings (e.g., football club), there is usually much unstructured contact with clients around meal times, training venues, travel to and from games, and so on. In formal settings, sessions are typically weekly unless a critical upcoming event (e.g., competition) deserves more frequent sessions (e.g., two sessions per week) in the two weeks leading to the event.

Though the practitioner estimates the number of sessions in the initial session, the practitioner adjusts this estimate according to the progress of the client. While the number of sessions may range from a few to 40 sessions or more, many fall between six and 10 sessions. The nature of an athlete's career, training, competition, travel, and other commitments means that we, as practitioners, need to make reasonable adjustments to length, frequency, and number of sessions.

Making sense of emotions

It does not take long before we touch on emotions in a session with a client. Though we might not speak explicitly about these emotions, the emotional dimension of the work begins. It is often these troubling and painful emotions that bring clients to your practice. What to do with them, however, is also perplexing because we need to work with our emotions for their benefit. After all, our emotions travelled with us through evolution.

Defining emotion remains a puzzle, but we know about the characteristics of emotion, such as their immediacy and short-lived physical responses in our body with directions for action. When we are fearful, we might flee, fight, freeze, or fawn. In today's world, much of the challenge we face is choosing a sensible response rather than taking the emotional information from our fear, for example, as directions for action. In this way, it appears as if our fear is getting in the way rather than playing a key role in our survival.

Watching a golfer on television with a chance to win a major championship, we can subjectively interpret her feelings, but we are not sure how we would feel in similar circumstances. At any moment, we can walk out of the room and the intensity of the emotion fades. For the golfer, however, permission to feel and express emotion goes with the territory of being in contention to win the major championship. In a therapy room, we cannot recreate the experience from the major championship; however, we can interpret feelings as an indicator of meaning for the golfer.

While the golfer might wish her cognitive system to process information and help to execute the correct course of action on the golf course, it is her emotion system that influences physical responses such as muscular tension, heart rate, and breathing rate. We can witness the fear, worry, anger, joy, and pleasure on the face of the golfer. This ever-present signalling on our faces suggests that there is meaning happening in a person's life all the time. For a golfer in this situation, they might wish to know why they feel as they do and how to feel more calm and assured at these critical moments. It is the unknowing, the sense of confusion about one's feelings, that usually brings them to the sport psychology practitioner's clinic. Sometimes, it is those feelings that seem out of control, intolerable, and overwhelming that press most on the mind of the athlete.

When our feelings seem less well known to us, it is often because socially and culturally, people encouraged us to neglect our feelings. In sport, it might be that mantras like "show no fear", "keep your cool", and "show no mercy" abound, so feeling or expressing feelings does not fit. A man who feels as if he cannot be sad after a losing a competition might get angry. A woman might become fearful because she cannot show her anger after a similar loss. Though this broad brush misses many nuances, the issue remains that many people express the acceptable emotions and hide the unacceptable ones. In the privacy of our own home, for instance, we might cry at the moving experience about how an athlete overcame seemingly insurmountable hurdles to win a gold medal at the Olympic Games.

We might use the words feeling and emotion interchangeably in our everyday lives, yet they have different meanings for us as sport psychology practitioners. Feeling and emotion are sources of information with an internal sense responding to the world, but while a feeling might be ongoing always with many parts, an emotion is more specific, consuming the body, like anger (McLeod & McLeod, 2022). This distinction between everyday feelings and emotion might enter the therapy room when a client recalls a strong emotion (e.g., shame, anger) in relation to an event in their lives. But often, feelings are unclear or concealed. Sometimes, emotions are unexpressed or emotions are overwhelming and require some management in their expression. In all three cases, the sport psychology practitioner requires a thoughtfulness about feeling and emotion, because without this alignment, the emotional life of a person and the opportunity to explore feelings ends and the emotional significance of events in a client's life goes unnoticed.

Though a client might not share feelings directly, when we listen for feelings, we hear them in the client's story, in the client's words. Of course, the client might not include any feeling words; however, the sense of direction in their story, the orientation of their body, and their tone of voice might hint at feelings that go unexpressed. Skilfully, the sport psychology practitioner can tentatively suggest a feeling word or words that might fit the client's experience. Maybe one's anger hides behind one's sadness, yet acknowledging this anger requires the greatest sensitivity. This sensitivity to another's feelings means attending to our feelings as a sport psychology practitioner. We can become more aware of our feelings by noticing and labelling them. We can 'check in' before a session to sense whether we are bringing our feelings to the session and reducing the space for the client's feelings. The sport psychology practitioner, after bracketing (setting aside their emotional processing), concentrates on the client's feelings which the sport psychology practitioner might feel and can clarify through sensitive enquiry. Sometimes, the feelings we receive from a client show a broader experience among others in the client's life. If we, as sport psychology practitioners, feel overwhelmed or annoyed in the presence of a client, we can explore these feelings and the implications these feelings might have on the lives of those in the client's life. For instance, perhaps your feelings as a sport psychology practitioner resonate with the client's partner, who complains to the client about their behaviour. Tuning into our feelings helps us to understand and remain sensitive to the feelings of the client. Through personal development, we can gain an awareness of our emotional lives – and so the emotional lives of others (McLeod & McLeod, 2022).

Greenberg and Pascual-Leone (2006) presented four empirically based principles to guide therapeutic intervention when working with emotion: awareness and arousal of emotion, enhancing emotional regulation, reflecting on emotion, and transforming emotion. Before beginning this work, we must distinguish between adaptive and maladaptive emotional experiences and also among primary and secondary emotions. In sum, we bypass secondary emotions to reach primary emotions and clients access these primary emotions in awareness for their adaptive information and capability to organise action. Maladaptive emotions, once accessed, transform through new experience and, therefore, generate new meaning.

Awareness and arousal of emotion

Primary emotions, like sadness following a loss, represent a person's initial and direct response to a situation. To gain awareness, we need to approach and accept our emotions rather than avoid them and to use the emotion for its rewards. When we see our emotions as offering information for our regard, we can see the goal or need it prompts us to attain. Greater emotional awareness means greater impulse control. Once we arouse emotions, we can learn to process them; however, we also hold a strong tendency to avoid emotions. One example might be that a coach feels angry (primary emotion) with an athlete who continually turns up late to training. The coach learned to be afraid of his anger during childhood when he was chastised for losing his temper within his family. Worry represented a more acceptable emotion, so the coach gets anxious when the athlete turns up late to training ("I don't know what to do here. I'm worried"). Sustaining our attention through painful feelings in the short term brings sound long-term benefits. This experience resonates with a line from Robert Frost's poem, "the only way round is through" (Frost, 2015). While the first steps of approach, arousal, acceptance, and tolerance of emotional experience are necessary, so too are the cognitive processes to explore and reflect upon the experience and draw in other emotional resources to transform the maladaptive state.

Emotion regulation

Regulating our emotions seems a most sensible and valued process for any athlete. From a practical perspective, it is the secondary emotions and maladaptive emotion that we need to regulate. For example, an athlete might feel hopeless (secondary emotion) when there is an underlying or unspoken feeling of anger (primary emotion). The feelings of being stuck, hopeless, and helpless, for example, are learned responses (maladaptive emotions) that no longer serve an adaptive advantage. The competitive, transparent, and public displays of sport usually mean regulating high distress, which entails emotion regulation skills. These skills involve identifying and labelling emotions, allowing and tolerating emotions, forming a working distance, growing positive emotions, decreasing vulnerability to negative emotions, self-soothing, breathing, and distraction (Greenberg, 2002). The sense of despair and hopelessness an athlete might feel can be overwhelming and the athlete needs some distance initially before developing self-soothing methods to calm core anxieties and humiliation in the longer term. Self-soothing might involve diaphragmatic breathing, relaxation, developing self-empathy, compassion, and self-talk.

Reflection on emotion

Developing new narratives to explain one's experience requires reflection. A player, upon reflection, realises he becomes angry at his coach because he feels abandoned being left out of the team and his anger relates to a history of abandonments. This reflection and understanding brings therapeutic relief because the new coherent story solves older experiences in emotion memory to better understand the self and the world. This reflection might happen through expressive writing (Pennebaker, 1995). Language offers the chance to organise, structure, and integrate emotional experience and the events that triggered the emotional experience. In this space, people can reflect on what they feel, generate new meanings, and evaluate their emotional experiences to share with others.

Emotion transformation

The last part of emotional processing is transforming one emotion into another. Here, one changes one maladaptive emotional state with a more adaptive emotion – we transform one emotion into another. In a sport setting, for example, an athlete might cope best by recruiting positive emotions to regulate negative emotional experiences. An athlete feeling angry, sad, or hopeless, one who activates alternative emotions and needs, changes their view of self or other. In this process, they evoke another feeling to transform the maladaptive feeling. Adaptive sadness could transform a maladaptive anger before arriving at acceptance, or an athlete could transform maladaptive shame into self-acceptance by accessing anger at harm, self-soothing, compassion, and pride.

Opening up to emotion

The prospect of working on one's emotions frightens many people, and athletes are no different. At some level, the athlete might feel embarrassed or ashamed about acknowledging or expressing their privately held emotions. The challenge for the sport psychology practitioner is to feel comfortable with the client expressing feelings at a time and pace that suits the client. On the other side, the athlete might be worried who can hear them outside the room or see them leave the therapy room. Understanding these circumstances means the accessing sources of emotional safety (e.g., a soft voice) or self-soothing (e.g., using an object such as a cushion or blanket or imagining a safe space sitting on a beach). A soft, slow-paced voice might give space and time to an emotion or feeling being felt at that moment. Reflecting on what the person said, allowing silence, and speaking gently can have the effect of helping the client to stay with the feeling at the moment (McLeod & McLeod, 2022). This feeling and emotion occur in the body and the mind so we can invite a client to notice where in their body they feel (e.g., sadness, joy, worry). Some people say they "feel a tightness in [their] chest" or a "knot in [their] stomach" or they might not realise their clenched fist or that they are stroking their arm. We might invite them to attend to the meaning of this expression in the body. The client might not realise how they hold their breath to hold an emotion inside or breathe a sigh to show relief. Breathing offers a place to focus one's attention and its effect on the body and mind of the client.

Making sense of one's feelings and expressing one's emotions, as we have seen, challenges many people. In Eugene Gendlin's view, the meaning of a situation, event, or relationship is captured as a 'felt sense' in the body (Gendlin, 1996). But in Gendlin's view, we block our felt sense of a problem by talking, busyness, and not focusing on bodily feelings and sensations.

Two-chair work

This theoretical exercise of two-chair work dialogue offers a client who struggles with the emotional facet of situations and relationships a mechanism to express feelings. Two-chair dialogue helps a person to express underlying emotional processes (Elliott & Greenberg, 2021). Although normal one-to-one sessions with a sport psychology practitioner offer a client space to share feelings, they might consider an emotion rather than entering directly into the emotion. This 'talking about' feelings with a sport psychology practitioner often involves monitoring what one says rather than feeling one's feelings by going into and through those feelings.

To go into and through one's feelings, the client enacts their relationship with the object of their emotions (e.g. another person). The client in one chair talks directly to the imagined person in the second chair. The sport psychology practitioner guides the client: "Tell him what you wish to say as if he were here". To heighten the emotional intensity of the interaction, the sport psychology practitioner might say, for example, "Tell him how he demeans you". The sport psychology practitioner might sit beside the client rather than opposite them to set the scene for the enactment and raise its intensity. The client expresses strong feelings towards the object of their emotions rather than to the sport psychology practitioner. The dialogue softens, bringing in different feelings. The athlete resenting the controlling team captain might notice the sadness of what she has not expressed as a player.

Two-chair work weaves in those empirically based principles when working with emotion in a therapeutic intervention (Greenberg & Pascual-Leone, 2006): awareness and arousal of emotion rather than talking about an emotion, expressing emotions linked to relationships, staying with feelings to reach one's primary emotion, and a chance to make sense of what one learns from the two-chair enactment with the help of a guiding sport psychology practitioner. Two-chair work allows a client to express feelings and emotions they may well have held tightly for years. This process, though healing, also raises other questions about how the client relates to others.

A theoretical orientation towards emotions in sport

There are several ways to explain how emotions arise in a sport setting and how they might influence the performer and performance. For example, the cognitive-motivational-relational theory (CMRT) of Lazarus (1991) proposes that individuals evaluate events in their lives about the significance of these events for their well-being. Generating and regulating emotions involves two processes: cognitive appraisal and coping. The situations we might find in sport matter less than the appraisal we make of the situation, which influences the emotional response. This appraisal categorises events or situations according to harm, threat, challenge, or benefit. One may represent a source of harm if a loss occurred; threat with a potential for loss; challenge if there is an expected, but demanding, gain; and benefit if the gain already occurred. One's emotions arise from a core relational theme comprising six separate appraisals: primary (goal relevance, goal congruence, type of ego involvement) and/or secondary (blame or credit, coping potential, future expectations). Appraisal joins with a relational meaning as the individual considers personal factors, environmental demands, constraints, and opportunities.

The coping process begins with the experience of emotion. Coping mediates the response to the emotion-provoking relationship and the ensuing emotion. One's appraisal and coping response influence the emotion that follows from the emotional encounter. To perform at one's best requires at least focused attention; however, emotions might trigger ruminative thoughts that disrupt one's attention. The core relational theme of each emotion will influence the performer's response. It is the balance action tendencies (impulse to act when we experience an emotion) derived from the core relational theme and task demands that eventually influence performance (Lazarus, 2000; Moran & Toner, 2017).

The process and outcome of athletic performance remains closely related to emotions. One's emotions (e.g., anger, sadness) influence one's actions (e.g., to train or adhere to a rehabilitation programme), so we need to remember the theoretical foundations of emotion when working with clients.

The change stage

A significant part of the middle stage of service delivery and the RUC model is change. Change means addressing problems and problem situations so we can handle them better next time. The change process depends on the relating and understanding phases. Nelson-Jones (2016) suggested two overlapping approaches to the change stage: (1) helping to solve problems, and (2) developing mind and communication or actions skills. When solving problems, the client remains central to the problem-solving process, so as helpers, we lean on the client's frame of reference and suggestions for change. Helping clients to develop mind and communication or action skills involves teaching or coaching.

Learning to solve problems

When clients bring 'problems with living' to us, they often wish to solve the problem quickly, but we run into more problems when we do not know the exact problem to begin with, or the boundaries of the problem or the goals a client may hold regarding the problem. As skilled helpers, we listen to the client – but depending on our therapeutic orientation (e.g., CBT, PCT) and the client's preferences, we might have different roles to play. For instance, a golfer might wish to have a skilled listener to create the emotional climate so she can judge what feels right for her and then solve the problem doing her own work. But on other occasions, you might be more involved, leading the process until the client feels ready to lead. Maybe in the first few sessions when the problem itself seems so overwhelming, the client needs some steerage to think reasonably and rationally about their goals.

One issue we encounter often in sport is goals. Most students know about outcome goals, performance goals, and process goals, but fitting these goals together takes understanding and practice. These goals also fit into solving problems when working with clients. A badminton player might wish to feel less anxious before and during competitions. The client can achieve this outcome goal (i.e., to feel less anxious) by pursuing some performance and process goals along the way. An outcome goal focuses on the result (e.g., to win a race, to feel less anxious). A performance goal means improving your ability (e.g., reducing your heart rate by 10% in a stressful condition). Finally, a process goal means a undertaking a basic activity to execute a higher goal; to illustrate, practising diaphragmatic breathing to lower one's heart rate and calm oneself before or during a performance. One structure for the goal-setting process is using the SMART goal-setting strategy. SMART is an acronym for the parts of the goal-setting process: specific, measurable, achievable, realistic, and time-tabled. Specific means your goal states precisely what you wish to change or improve. Measurable means you can assess your progress. Achievable means your goal is possible. Realistic means your goal challenges you but it lies within your capacity to achieve it. Time-tabled means you put targets in place for when you wish to achieve your goal. The key to this goal-setting process is to remain flexible and adjust as you go.

When clients set goals for change, we as practitioners help them consider pitfalls along the way. A few questions help to clarify what the client wishes to achieve and avoid, and to address pitfalls as they arise. Setting goals within one's values and strengths erects a scaffolding to keep the client's goal on track if there are setbacks along the way. Clients usually have options about which goals to pursue or how they pursue these goals; however, many clients feel stuck and cannot see a way to proceed.

Whatever options amass, we also help clients to tease out the consequences of their options. But the first step is to generate the options. This creative outflow might be on a notepad, flip chart, or whiteboard so each person can see the collection of options. Next, we plan to implement one or two of them. Following the SMART goal-setting structure, clients assume responsibility and accountability for what happens and how they will manage any hiccups along the way. Written plans offer the chance for the client to be accountable and responsible for their actions, while also helping them to follow the steps designed. Sometimes, an immediately pressing issue (e.g., trial game) requires attention. Offering a calm and supportive structure to work through one's plan(s) means reducing the chances of engaging in self-defeating thoughts and actions.

Part of the change process might include teaching or coaching skills. This 'how to' approach requires preparation so that the client can work systematically through the skill learning process in a calm, supportive environment. Respecting the client's ability to lead their own recovery lies at the heart of good coaching or teaching because we do not overstep our role; rather, we encourage and trust the client. Athlete-centred coaching respects the autonomy and capacities of the client, engages the strengths of the client, works with the client, and builds upon existing knowledge and skills. Two elements of learning remain critical here: pace and direction. Each client learns at their pace and often wishes to follow a direction of their choosing. We wish for the clients to gain confidence in the skill (e.g., breathing technique), so we need to check that the client's skill is developing and encourage the client to judge their performance and then we can add our feedback. Offering feedback forms a discussion rather than a diktat.

Teaching skills (e.g., imagery, relaxation, assertiveness) means that we ought to prepare content and develop our delivery through our body language and voice, demonstrating effectively and rehearsing with the client (Nelson-Jones, 2012).

Preparing the content

Some practitioners feel that if they prepare content, most of the task is complete, but this mistake often leads to costly effects for the client later. For good outcomes for the client, we need to prepare and deliver. We shall delve into processes of delivery after this section. Some practitioners find it helpful to prepare audio-visual content on a Microsoft PowerPoint presentation that a client watches and listens to at home after they have presented the content in a session. At other times, a flip chart or whiteboard suffices, whereby illustrations plus explanations help the client grasp the concept presented.

Using your voice

Any demonstration usually involves sending effective voice messages. Using the VAPER assessment, we can examine how volume, articulation, pitch, emphasis, and rate of speech coalesce. With volume, we may speak a little louder and project our voice when showing or presenting skills. Next, we clearly articulate to help the client understand the content during delivery; the pitch of your delivery often rises above the typical responding in helper–client encounters. After that, our emphasis usually leans on words or phrases of the principal points conveying interest and commitment. Finally, the rate of speech ought to be slow and smooth so you have time to think as the client has time to comprehend. Pauses clarify and emphasise points, while the client might feel these as spaces to ask questions for clarification.

Using your body

As much as we convey verbally to a client, we also share messages non-verbally through our body posture, our physical openness and proximity to the client, clothing, grooming, and facial expressions. Try to notice how you gesture when you speak and how the client gestures in return. For example, a symbolic gesture for understanding in most cultures is nodding your head for 'yes' and shaking your head for 'no'. Coaches and managers often use descriptive gestures to illustrate points like movement or positioning on a football pitch. Another non-verbal message comes through eye contact. When we instruct, we gain some awareness about how the client receives the messages we are sending through reading the client's reactions. We can relate directly to the client with gaze and eye contact when emphasising key points, for example.

Though most trainees learn about the criticality of active listening skills, it can sometimes slip by how important our way of communicating is to the listener. The more you practise describing skills to a client, the easier the process becomes because you can record your work on your own, listen to the recording, make adjustments, and improve. Rather than talking only while educating, we combine talking and listening when working with clients so they feel valued in the training process.

Using demonstrations

Demonstrations form a central feature of sports coaching. The sports performer observes as the model (e.g., coach or player) demonstrates a skill. For example, a practitioner might display assertive body posture and combine it with motivational or instructional self-talk. We typically use live or recorded demonstrations with clients. A live demonstration of an assertive body posture combined with motivational self-talk offers the client hooks to see and hear one's voice (e.g., VAPER) and body messages (e.g., shoulder and head position). A recording offers the client a chance to see and hear the demonstration repeatedly. There are several models in sport, for example, if one wishes to follow their example of assertive behaviour on the basketball court. We can see these live and recorded demonstrations on television and through social media outlets.

Visualisation aids most clients' learning. Visualisation represents one of several skills common to the sports milieu, and some clients visualise more easily than others. Some clients can more easily visualise another person performing the communication or action, but with practice, their imagery ability and vividness improves.

The demonstrator has two challenges when demonstrating for the client. First, there will be a sequence of 'telling', 'showing', and 'doing' with the client. In this sequence, telling the client what you are doing and why you are doing what you are doing before showing and doing helps the client to attend to specifics (i.e., key points). A central feature of this demonstration is checking for understanding; we might ask the client what she understands about your demonstration. A little at a time maximises the client's learning. Second, the client rehearses to gain knowledge, understanding, and confidence in the skill. In rehearsals, creativity and autonomy means the client can rehearse and make mistakes in different scenarios. For example, a client might wish to manage his anger after receiving feedback from the team captain that displeases him. In a role play, the practitioner plays the role of the captain while the client rehearses voice and body messages to prepare for the actual event. Sometimes, when the setting allows, this rehearsal might happen on the playing pitch to match playing conditions. Here, the client shows what they currently do (voice and body messages) before planning how to respond next time.

Case study: Tom

Tom, an international rugby player, struggled to manage his responses (voice, body, and behaviour) to perceived criticism from within his own team. For instance, following perceived criticism, he typically withdrew from his role, somewhat 'hiding' on the pitch. He dropped his head and shoulders, losing his assertive posture. Together, we developed a formulation and intervention. Tom practised listening to the content of the perceived criticism for its instructions: what is he trying to tell me to do? Then he would respond positively and supportively with his words ("I'm on it!") and a sense of his duty to follow the orders of the captain, who has the best intentions for the whole team. He would take a deep breath and fix his body posture to signal his intention to play his role for the team. We practised this role play on the pitch where Tom ran, tackled, kicked and passed the ball in various scenarios while I played the role of a team member, critiquing his performance. Over several short sessions on the training pitch, Tom transferred his learning to the training ground for squad sessions and then onto the international stage. One part of our work together involved a role reversal, with me playing Tom's role while Tom played the role of the captain to see himself as others (i.e., coaches, teammates) experience him. In these role plays, while Tom played the role of the captain, Tom admitted, "That looks dreadful, that victim posture you talked about, and that's me". This role reversal helped Tom and me to explore the thoughts and feelings generated in each role.

Monitoring progress

A principal feature of change programmes involves systematically monitoring behaviour. When clients self-monitor, they gain an awareness of what they think, feel, and do. While systematic monitoring might occur in the assessment and formulation stages, it also occurs in the intervention stage to establish a baseline and general awareness of the entity under consideration. Self-monitoring helps us to check our progress – or lack of it – and reminds us about what we are aiming to do. We have several methods to monitor our thoughts, feelings, and actions. For instance, we might use diaries or journals, frequency charts, or various logs (e.g., stimulus, response, consequences). Diaries and journals help us record instances when we used a skill well or where the skill broke down over a day or week, for example. Frequency charts help track behaviours, for example, over a day or week. Beyond these forms of self-monitoring, some clients prefer to capture the story of what happened (i.e., stimulus), how they responded (i.e., response), and what happened next (i.e., consequences). A player working on anger management skills might complete this log after training and games to understand the triggers, thoughts, feelings, and consequent actions.

Self-monitoring or self-observation are effortful tasks. Clients might wish to avoid recognising how they think, feel and act, so we need to explain why self-monitoring matters and how beneficial it will be for change. We, as practitioners, also need to design simple, accessible, and meaningful recording logs and teach the client how to use the log. When we offer a client sound reasons for self-monitoring and relate the self-monitoring to effective changes in their lives, clients then have reasons to adhere. For example, we might say, "When we know how many times you chastise yourself on the tennis court during a game, we can judge its severity, lay it as a baseline and then measure your progress against it". Clients also need to know what, how, and when to record the behaviour under review. To help us here, when we design clear, accessible, and simple logs that clearly define what we are intending to measure, clients feel comfortable recording accurately. We ought to recognise and reward completed frequency logs, so the client understands their value in the intervention process. These logs help the client understand their behaviour and begin the change process (Nelson-Jones, 2012).

Scheduling

Client-athletes vary in the ability and desire to schedule activities in their lives. For some athletes, a third party (e.g., coach or manager) schedules all their sport-related activities for them, but for others, their time is their own to marshal as they please. Skills and activities emerging from working with a sport psychology practitioner ought to be scheduled into a weekly timetable with reminders. Minimum goals help the client begin a change process without overwhelming the client. If, for example, a client wishes to meditate, then three 20-minute sessions across the week would suffice. The client commits to a time (e.g., 8 am), a task (e.g., meditation), and a place (e.g., at home) as a minimum and can do more if they wish; however, minimum goals help the client achieve and gain confidence from doing and completing the task.

Scheduling pleasurable activities for oneself daily or weekly encourages self-care. These pleasurable activities (e.g., a walk, coffee with a friend, reading a book) reinforce the value of doing things for oneself. These commitments to oneself sit alongside the commitments to others (e.g., coach, children, partner), but some clients falter because they believe that commitments to others always trump commitments to oneself. In a healthy, balanced lifestyle, we can create a time and place for both. When we schedule activities, we learn to work with our schedule but not feel enslaved by it. Scheduled activities help clients commit to activities. Many clients have mobile phones with calendar systems and reminders. Clients can input chosen activities to suit their lives and other commitments. Though some clients feel reluctant to schedule activities, learning and practising this new skill pays many dividends. A patient, understanding approach, acknowledging the client's anxieties and concerns, helps to address pitfalls along the way. For example, some clients feel trapped by a timetable, meticulously planning each task each day rather than devoting time to the tasks on the timetable. Other clients feel anxious that they will not complete their commitments and so need to alter the predicted times for completing the tasks. A gradual and graded exposure to scheduling helps most clients develop a skill for life. In subsequent sessions, the client and practitioner can review progress and setbacks. Sometimes a setback reveals another presenting issue (e.g., perfectionism), such that the client fears failing at the scheduled task and instead avoids them. Through practice, feedback, and encouragement, clients develop their ways of developing schedules that work for them and their lives.

Graduated progress

Sport environments teem with athletes, coaches, and backroom staff demanding too much too soon for themselves or others. Any early progress seems to spark a desire to do more, which is encouraging, only to find they fail at the task or withdraw from it altogether. Practitioners can tackle this mix of motivational ambivalence by gradually building confidence and skills together. The maxims of 'one step at a time' or 'little by little' hold much wisdom here. We can begin by working on tasks from least threatening to most threatening, least challenging to most challenging. The goal remains to break large tasks into little tasks and progress from there, as we explained earlier about goal-setting. Using the steps of stairs as an analogy, taking one step at a time helps the client reach the top of the stairs. Achieving small goals or small wins motivates and encourages clients as they progress towards more difficult tasks. In all of this work, some failures are inevitable. Whatever these failures might be, they present an opportunity to learn about oneself. Encouraging clients to share their experiences with success or failure helps them to know themselves better (e.g., how they think, feel, and act) and progress towards their chosen goals.

   One feature often missing from change programmes is a reward system of internal and external rewards. Internal rewards from oneself (e.g., praise and encouragement) or external rewards (e.g., a relaxing bath or new item of clothing) each play a role and one can administer these rewards for progress. These rewards are contingent upon change in the targeted behaviour and are meaningful to the client. Most clients know what feels rewarding to them, and between the client and practitioner, they can find a blend that fits.

Rewards, especially rewarding activities – listening to music, reading a book, eating a good meal, seeing a beautiful view, visiting a friend, helping someone, or wearing fresh clothes – are often close at hand but might go unnoticed. We encourage clients to reward themselves immediately after performing the targeted skill or behaviour. Some clients give themselves a token for each performance of a targeted behaviour and after five tokens, they trade them for a meaningful reward.

Changing rules and expectations

Many people live with demanding and overbearing rules for living. In sport, these rules for living and expectations often lead to despairing outcomes in people's lives. Demanding rules, rather than preferential rules, one can hear by words and phrases such as 'must', 'should', 'have to' and 'ought to' – such as "I must score in this game" or "I have to make a good impression". Along with these demanding rules come unhelpful feelings for the situation (e.g., fear, anger) or physical reactions (e.g., muscular tension). Some athletes, owing to the weight of the demanding rule, feel angry and out of control in the performance arena, and their physical arousal impairs their judgement and decision-making in critical situations. An athlete's behaviour might be self-defeating. Some rules like "do your best" are preferential; so clients need to know what their best looks and feels like so they can stick with the realistic part and discard the unrealistic part. Doing one's best and performing competently seems preferential, although never making a mistake is an unrealistic goal.

We need to unearth our demanding rules and expectations to query and challenge them so that favoured rules fit in their place. We, as practitioners, can help the client check evidence, logic, and practical value of such rules. With reason, logic, and facts, clients can choose whether to change or discard their rules. You can help the client to move towards rules the client prefers, but loosening old demanding rules usually forms part of the process.

Rather than demanding that I play well, we can state our preference to play well as: "I'd prefer to play well but there's no reason I absolutely have to play well". Whatever the outcomes might be, athletes can learn to tolerate anxiety and discomfort as they make plans to keep improving. Once clients develop an awareness of the demanding rules and expectations governing their lives, they have a choice about changing them. Considering facts, reason, and logic, the client can understand their subjective reality and can test the reality of their insights instead of jumping to unjustified conclusions. Many sports generate data about distances covered in a game, shots on target, lap times, and so forth. These facts and the extrapolations clients make from them ought to be explored to see which inferences fit best. In summary, we might: (1) search for the evidence, (2) seek other ways to explain the situation, and (3) understand how one's perception best fits the facts.

A role for self-talk

Self-talk plays a motivational and instructional role for many athletes. Gaining awareness of one's self-talk often startles athletes because they did not know how they were talking to themselves. Unbeknownst to ourselves, we might use soothing (e.g., "You're doing fine"), calming (e.g., "Deep breath; I can manage"), or motivating (e.g., "Come on – you can do it!") self-talk. We might use self-talk to denigrate ourselves (e.g., "You're a waste of time") or our chances of succeeding (e.g., "No point in carrying on; you're a loser"). We might use self-talk to instruct ourselves helpfully before executing a sports skill (e.g., low and slow take-away) or unhelpfully (e.g., "Don't hit it left").

For our work with athletes, self-talk presents a way of coping because we can remember our preferential rules rather than our demanding rules. We can revise our perceptions and we can soothe and instruct ourselves. Most athletes use a diary to record their training, nutrition, and valuable psychological strategies (e.g., recording one's achievements). This diary also serves to record their preferential rules, ways of coping, and records of progress towards chosen goals. Any setbacks, once recorded, offer athletes an opportunity to write about how they coped with the setback. The diary represents a daily reminder about how an athlete fills each page with psychological support and opportunities for change.

Homework

The example of using a diary represents a homework activity common to some therapeutic approaches (e.g., CBT). Homework – like many other activities in the therapeutic process – is a negotiated activity encouraging autonomy, responsibility, and accountability in a client's life. Some examples from earlier include completing a self-monitoring sheet or composing a schedule of activities for the week. Other common homework activities include reading self-help books, watching modelling or instructional videos, and practising meditation. Homework assignments often mean practising skills learned in a session with a practitioner so they can speed up the learning process through deliberate practice. Doing, reflecting, and merging one's learning means the client can transfer skills learned in a formal session with a practitioner to real-life settings. What the client notices in these experiences forms part of the agenda in the next formal session with the practitioner.

Because homework represents a negotiated activity, it needs sufficient time in a session for the client to understand what is being asked of them. Also, many homework activities require practice within a session so the client feels comfortable and confident about completing the task(s) on their own. In addition, Greenberger and Padesky (1995) suggested that homework assignments ought to be relevant, collaborative, manageable with graduated difficulty, and practised in sessions. Together, these elements show first, that time negotiating and practising at home is critical; and second, managing progress, difficulties, and setbacks means the client can progress rather than stagnate in their quest to change.

A homework assignment ought to be relevant because, without the client's input, cooperation, and intent, it is unlikely that the client will pursue the activity. Keeping the client involved in all processes honours their strengths and capacities to help themselves. Clients offer a tailoring of homework to their unique life circumstances. Homework assignments need to be manageable and graduated in difficulty. Reasonable and manageable homework assignments mean the clients feel confident they can execute what they believe is right for them. As clients progress, the difficulty of the homework increases in line. Early success generates confidence and persistence. When clients practise homework assignments in session, they gain an understanding of what is required of them and any gaps in their understanding the practitioner can address in the session. They will also need a summary of instructions to complete the assignment. I encourage clients to bring a diary with them for their sessions so they have clear instructions for their homework.

Homework brings several challenges to working with clients. For some clients, strained school experiences put them on alert hearing about homework, or having to do the homework well generated much anxiety. A collaborative formulation expects some difficulties in completing homework assignments. When asked, clients can think realistically about the hurdles preventing them from doing their homework assignments. When clients schedule their tasks and set up reminders, they tend to complete them because they have considered the impediments along the way and chosen what suits them best. Brief, engaging homework assignments ensure that clients have meaningful yet achievable tasks to complete. Not all tasks will be completed or perhaps not completed successfully – so together, the client and the practitioner can learn from the experience and adjust the task or the expected outcomes to suit. Developing skills takes time, so we need to appreciate progress along these lines for the client. For many athletes, seeing tasks as learning experiences emphasises persistence and encourages reflecting on experiences rather than dismissing or withdrawing from them.

Like many instances in sport settings, efforts go unrewarded when an athlete or team does not realise an expected outcome (e.g., winning). In therapeutic settings, we continue to emphasise learning, process goals, reflections, and when necessary, altering the task, effort, strategy, or help from others. Two points are critical here: first, we discuss homework assignments in follow-up sessions so that the client realises the centrality of homework; and second, we explore the thoughts and feelings related to the homework assignments. Clients need to see how the cycle of setting homework assignments includes a process of understanding and reflection with the practitioner in sessions. Some clients have social support to help them with their change goals, while others do not or work counter to their best interests.

A helping hand

Most change programmes depend on others to succeed. Others may play minor or major roles in this change process. Knowing that others play a role, we need to consider who helps and who hinders. We need – where possible – to strengthen our connection with supportive people and weaken our ties with unsupportive people. Athletes who feel tired and exhausted gain a lift from those who are relatively upbeat rather than those complaining and despairing about their circumstances. One might need to loosen ties with those working counter to the client's goals (e.g., those who are unsympathetic or withering about the client), or at least limit their influence.

At other times, the helping hand we are searching for lies at the end of our own arm. We might need to seek resources (e.g., books, manuals, videos) and support groups (e.g., coaches, specialist teachers) or online learning. These supports – whether informational, human, or educational – work best when they are of the client's choosing and using.

The changes we desire

There are at least four categories within which most people seek change (Norcross, 2012). These include bad habits (e.g., overeating), new goals (e.g., running long distance), interpersonal relationships (e.g., maintain good relations with colleagues), and life satisfaction (e.g., to be a better person). Though these categories appear quite different from each other, the process of change remains quite similar across diverse goals and problems (Norcross, 2012). Norcross (2012, p. 21) simplified the path to change into five steps:

- Psych (get ready/contemplation).
- Prep (plan before leaping/preparation).
- Perspire (take action/action).
- Persevere (manage slips/maintenance).
- Persist (maintain change/maintenance).

The further along one is in the steps, the more likely one is to succeed and the progress one makes is a function of the step in which the person is in. Taking one step at a time allows the client to consolidate changes and keep moving. The challenge for most clients remains to match where they are at the correct stage; thus, personalising treatment for the client and their specific step works best for change. Though taking one change at a time seems sensible, sometimes two changes at once work best when the two changes relate (e.g., eating and exercising). Similarly, improving one's relationship might fit best for developing communication skills.

Summary

The middle phase of service delivery is typically the longest phase, with its own beginning, middle, and end. One element of the middle phase that is challenging to explore is emotions. Gathering an awareness, reflection, and regulation of one's emotions often feels overwhelming, so we take things slowly with the client and move at their pace, opening up to emotion in safe and graduated steps. The middle phase of service delivery reflects the change stage as clients learn to solve problems, but do so with our help in sessions and outside sessions. Scheduling change and noting progress with the use of homework, for example, allows the client to see that the helping hand they sought was also at the end of their own arm. In Chapter 8, we turn to the final stage of service delivery: endings.

8 Endings

Introduction

Ending a relationship means sifting through several questions alone and with the client. The first question is: when does the process terminate? Sometimes the client terminates the relationship before the sport psychology practitioner feels that they are ready. There are several reasons for their choice to terminate, which might include feeling they can continue on their own, change of job, travel, or change in a professional playing contract, among others. At other times, the idea of change with an impending ending to a helping relationship becomes so overwhelming that the client's feels it would be a major setback to end service delivery.

Sport presents several time frames, which means clients seek help to prepare for a competition, for example, and end at that point. In sport organisations, like a football club, where there is formal and informal support, contact might end when the player transfers from one club to another. Sometimes, the client feels they have changed sufficiently and so they continue on their own. Apart from these circumstances, when the sport psychology practitioner reviews when to terminate a contact, they usually do so by reviewing four main sources of information (Nelson-Jones, 2016): (1) the client's report of feelings and progress, (2) the sport psychology practitioner's observations of the client's progress, (3) feedback from those in the social and working lives of the client (e.g., coach, spouse, fellow athletes), and (4) the evidence relating to the goals established in the therapeutic plan and the progress towards these goals.

Early termination and prolonging service delivery

Clients do not always attend their next appointment. My (Paul's) experience in private practice suggests that athletes tend towards conscientious and committed progress from the beginning to the end of the therapeutic process. On those occasions when clients miss an appointment, we can explore the evidence. There might be good reasons for missing an appointment, and after some time, we can enquire about the missed appointment and whether the

DOI: 10.4324/9781003453857-8

client wishes to reschedule. Early or premature termination occurs for several reasons – sometimes the reasons relate to a mismatch between the client and the sport psychology practitioner; for example, the fit between the client and sport psychology practitioner did not feel right, or the client felt that their fears about the helping process increased rather than decreased. Issues about lack of money, defensiveness, fear of abandonment, and fear of rejection might also play a part.

A challenge for most sport psychology practitioners, however, is to explore those occasions when, consciously or unconsciously, they wish to prolong a contract. Maybe a client sees you appreciatively, and this admiration feeds your narcissism. Or you feel erotically attracted to your client and wish to keep on seeing the client. Perhaps the organisation you work for holds much veneration from an adoring public (e.g., professional football club, Olympic squad) and being attached and involved meets your 'shadow' motives. Shadow motives are those motives you wish to keep private and hidden lest someone know why you do what you do. Sometimes the sport psychology practitioner breeds a passive, dependent relationship with the client, leaving them worse off than when they first began (Nelson-Jones, 2012).

Shadow motivations

All sport psychology practitioners hold an array of motives for practising as sport psychology practitioners. Choosing our current role for work ought to be explored because pure motives (e.g., wanting to make a difference in society, to understand people better, or to help people in the way it has helped you) are not our only motives. Our mixed motives help us understand what urges a sport psychology practitioner to work with athletes in emotional difficulty, angry and demanding managers or performance directors, tired and withdrawn players and teams? These mixed motives mean facing the shadow side of our helping impulse and how we meet our needs by helping others. Our shadow motives are not negative; however, not being aware of them means they can unconsciously affect how we relate to others.

Hawkins and McMahon (2020) presented four common 'shadow' motives: the drive for power, meeting our own needs through others, the need to be liked, and the wish to heal.

The drive for power: this encompasses a need for power and control in our lives. When this need remains hidden, we might not notice how we surround ourselves with people worse off than us or a need to direct the lives of those who ask or appear to need help. As sport psychology practitioners, we might process our fear of powerlessness through the client by presenting a premature solution. Jumping in with a solution means creating a dependence on oneself rather than exploring the issue fully with the client.

Meeting one's own needs: the helping role of a sport psychology practitioner might feel like it is the client's needs that are the only focus; however, our needs as sport psychology practitioners have not disappeared. If we get something back from our work, then a need is being met (e.g., self-esteem from our ability to give help). When we cannot see ourselves in the helping process, we might also deny our needs.

The need to be liked: to be liked, valued, to do one's best shows the good sport psychology practitioner to others; however, the client might not see it that way. A client might say we are 'greedy', 'cold', or 'power hungry'. Hearing such feedback might tempt several avenues of action. For instance, we might aim to 'please' more, counterattack, or find a way out of the helping relationship or 'conceivable' reasons. We have a choice here to make sense of the client's feelings. If the client feels vulnerable, the client might wish for you to feel as the client feels so criticises you to meet that end. Sometimes, there might be public criticism of the work of a sport psychology practitioner (Moran & Toner, 2017). Consider what the golfer Gary Player said about sport psychology:

> When you need to put a two iron on the back of the green to win the Open, how is a psychologist going to help you? If he hasn't got the experience, what can he tell you? I'm not totally against psychologists but you have to do a certain amount yourself.
>
> (cited in Buckley, 2005, p. 12)

The wish to heal: the realities of working in sport might raise questions about why we do the work we do. The central position remains to understand why we do what we do and the pure or shadow motives for this work. If we hold a wish to heal but deny it, we cannot see how our denied motives influence our working relationships. The better we know ourselves, the better a source of real help we are to our clients. Rather than using our clients to meet our needs, we can see how we become stuck. Rather than projecting parts of ourselves, which we cannot abide onto our clients, we reflect upon them, work on them in supervision or personal therapy.

These 'shadow' motives often exist because we do not explore them sufficiently in personal development or professional development. Our helping work means different things to different people, so we need to understand what applies to us. Our personal frame of reference means we can see ourselves, our biases, and our basic assumptions more clearly. Doing this work alone is challenging, and we benefit from the process of supervision here.

After all, our role as a sport psychology practitioner means we learn to cope with the demands of our work and be a role model of the skills to handle stress, conflict, demands, and emotional and psychological discomfort. To be of value to a client, we need to meet their needs – not ours. Yet it is easy, especially in sporting milieus, to seek to fulfil one's own needs (e.g., to be seen as important, superior, wise, powerful, a saviour) or to use clients to gather social friendships and win financially from significant associations. One might need to question whether the client is progressing in their work with you – and if not, what steps ought to be taken in the client's best interests.

Types of endings

There are several types of endings to a working alliance. Nelson-Jones (2016) presented the following endings: fixed, open, faded, and booster sessions. In sport and exercise settings, sport psychology practitioners encounter a range of endings that ought to be explored to understand more about the service delivery and the needs and preferences of the client. Trainees often raise concerns about endings in supervision because they feel responsible for the ending, especially when the helping relationship ends without notice. In supervision, the supervisor and supervisee can explore why the helping relationship ended. For instance, the client may feel happy with their progress and wish to proceed alone. Or perhaps a change in personal circumstances (e.g., a professional club transfer) meant a move happened without sufficient notice for the client or the sport psychology practitioner.

When the client and sport psychology practitioner hold the choice about ending helping, then the ending to fit the needs of the client and the practitioner unfolds. In a fixed ending, the sport psychology practitioner and client may have agreed to a contract of eight sessions to address a presenting problem. Knowing the limits of the helping relationship means both parties see the finish line and progress towards it with clarity and independence; however, other issues that arise might not be dealt with sufficiently. For example, if a client were learning a set of skills to communicate assertively with colleagues, the client may not feel thoroughly competent in those skills by the final session. One way to address this fixed nature of ending is to hold an open ending that finishes once we meet the goals set. In this way, the client and practitioner can judge the right time to end the working alliance. In sport settings, depending on training and competitions, a faded ending helps because it allows time for the client and practitioner to move from weekly to fortnightly or monthly intervals and assess progress at those time points. Maybe you choose to schedule a booster session after two or three months to consolidate skills learned during your work together and work through any current difficulties, perhaps using the skills learned in your sessions. In sport settings, clients often schedule booster sessions – or follow-up sessions – as a check-in on their progress. These check-ins might be face to face or over a telephone call, e-mail correspondence, or an online meet-up.

Regardless of the type of ending presented, sport psychology practitioners begin with the end in mind. This end means we begin with the client understanding that their independence and self-sufficiency will show they are ready to continue on their journey without the support of the sport psychology practitioner. Depending on your therapeutic modality (e.g., CBT), you might work with homework to ensure the client learns skills as you go. The client learns, develops, practises, and tests these skills in real-world settings to the satisfaction of the client and you. Homework forms the basis of support when the helping relationship ends. With each passing session, the sport psychology practitioner gathers information from the client about how the client feels they have progressed and how they would use their skills to cope with problems in the future. One difficulty in sport performance settings relates to process success and outcome success. For example, a tennis player might have coped with the strain of competition using sound process skills, yet did not achieve the outcome of winning. To the outside world, the match ended in failure, yet the tennis player achieved the process goals and these processes will be available again for the next competition.

Evaluating outcomes and skills

When trainees meet for supervision after the helping process with a client ends, it is likely that the supervisor and trainee will explore how the work unfolded and whether the goals and tasks set at the beginning materialised. The supervisor and trainee will also like to know about the process of therapy – the details of the unfolding relationship between the trainee and client. Trainees and supervisors use several types of feedback to make these assessments. For instance, the trainee usually records attendance, notes of progress, feedback from the client, perceptions of progress through the service, audio or video recordings of helping sessions, homework compliance or lack thereof, quantitative measures, and feedback from third parties (e.g., coaches and backroom staff) and their supervisor. Some trainees prefer to separate the outcomes of the service (e.g., intervention) from the relationship and counselling skills within the service with the client. A sensible, balanced appraisal is necessary, and supervisors offer a sounding board to make sense of the various sources of feedback. Making sense of outcomes feels complicated because it is complex. As an example, a client may attend just one session and feel that the session with the sport psychology practitioner met their needs and goals.

Case study: John

John, a professional football player, missed out on a transfer to a successful foreign football club team. John told the story of his entry into football and the multitude of challenges to get a professional contract. To miss out on this "once-in-a-lifetime opportunity" seemed incredibly unfair to John because his current club would not agree to terms with the new club. At the end of the session, John said he felt sanguine about his future. In his own words, he said, "There is nothing I can do about what happened, but in the past, I would bottle all of this up and drive myself crazy. I'm feeling excited about the future now. Talking helps, doesn't it?". At the end of the season, John ended up transferring to the club he followed as a child. He sent a thank-you card with tickets to the first home game. Inside the card were the words "Talking helps, doesn't it?".

The end of a therapeutic relationship brings feelings about the future and about the therapeutic relationship for the client and the practitioner. The stepping off point might bring feelings of apprehension and uncertainty for the client about coping on their own with the skills they have learned. Other clients might feel confident about what they have learned and how they will put their skills into action on their own in their own lives. The practitioner could raise this issue as an item for the agenda as they move towards ending the therapeutic relationship. Dealing with doubt about the future might mean reinforcing the plans and schedules developed and maintained during the intervention. On the other side of the therapeutic relationship, the practitioner also will have feelings about the relationship, the work completed, the skills demonstrated and learned, and the level of dependence or independence of the client.

Ultimately, the client carries the responsibility for success or failure of their choices and actions. Each person – client and practitioner – plays a role in the outcome and the practitioner can reflect on their part played. Accounting for what happened seems sensible rather than dwelling on what did not happen. It seems as if success and failure depend heavily on the client because the practitioner can only travel as far as the client will travel, so their pace is paramount (Sutton & Stewart, 2017). Keeping with the client's frame of reference keeps you – as a practitioner – on a helpful path. Pressuring the client to work through difficulties too early or too quickly when the client does not feel ready to do so can rupture the therapeutic relationship or cause emotional harm with the client breaking off the therapeutic relationship. When we keep within the client's frame of reference, they remain safe and move at the pace that best meets their needs.

Keeping records

Practising sport psychology practitioners record their work with clients to fulfil a basic competency. We need to keep and manage full and accurate records under relevant legislation, protocols, and guidelines (e.g., HCPC, 2016). Keeping clear, accurate records of our work with clients might seem like an afterthought when the busy work of supporting a client finishes. We might wonder: who has time for paperwork? Although demands on our time from swelling roles and responsibilities increases, we remain accountable to clients and employers. This accountability rubs against clients' needs for privacy and demands upon one's time in precarious work settings.

Training routes for sport psychology practitioners place intense focus on developing these professional duties (i.e., record keeping) in logbooks, for example. Logbooks typically include session notes and reflections following each session with each client. These systematic clinical records offer several benefits to the practitioner. To begin, our regulatory bodies (e.g., APA, APS [Australian Psychological Society], BPS, HCPC) and ethical codes of conduct require these records in line with legislation, protocols, and guidelines. These records protect us as practitioners and our supervisors, clients, and employers. Our employers, or those who pay for our services (e.g., clients, third-party payers), assign contractual obligations for our work with them. From a habitual practising perspective, our records support our work with clients, allowing us to assess, formulate, and outline interventions. At any stage of our training or professional practice, our supervisor can see how we work safely and we can note issues within sessions we wish to take to supervision. Part of our training or professional development might involve writing reports for employers (e.g., legal documents) or formal assessments like client case studies or process reports for our assessors, which require accurate records (Luepker, 2010).

Consider this circumstance for a moment: a complainant has raised a grievance against you as a practitioner. Your legal representation requests your records of the support provided to the complainant. You search frantically for something, anything, to support your view of yourself as a competent practitioner. You realise either you have no notes, or whatever notes you have are incoherent. This lack of care for you as a person and as a practitioner puts you in a tailspin as you put your reputation and career in jeopardy. On mature reflection, most practising professionals do not wish to find themselves in this predicament, so let us start as we mean to go on.

As a conscientious, compassionate, and client-centred practitioner, you will need to take care of yourself, your clients, employer, and supervisor by keeping competent records. These records protect all our professional relationships. The better the records you keep, the better you satisfy every professional relationship you serve (Bond & Mitchels, 2008).

What do good records look like?

Though we now have many service providers offering digital systems to record our work with clients, how we keep these records online usually depends upon how we construct our notes on the system. A good set of case notes or records will address the process of work with clients, including assessment, formulation, intervention, evaluation, and communication. A logical process from an initial meeting to finishing a treatment leaves a clear and indicative trail of your work with a client. The client can also explore where they began their work with you and what unfolded over the treatment – what worked and what did not work.

Digital or handwritten notes need to be chronological, legible, efficient, accurate, and reliable (i.e., CLEAR).

- **Chronological:** organise notes by date following from assessment, formulation, intervention, evaluation, and communication.
- **Legible:** write progress notes for any reader to understand.
- **Effective:** write notes with sufficient detail to note progress or otherwise.
- **Accurate:** write relevant and sensitive information.

- **Reliable:** describe actions taken to serve and protect the client (and practitioner), such as emergencies or absences.

In this format, we can see when the work began, with whom, and the processes followed throughout the contract. For instance, if a supervisor were to read our notes, it would be clear with whom we were working, the referral process, and our initial assessment and contract. Next, the supervisor would see our case notes and reflections listed by date. Then, the supervisor could interrogate the detail of our formulations, reformulations, interventions, and outcomes. In short, the rationale we offer for our choices and client choices at any point. If at any point an emergency arose, the supervisor could see where and when it occurred and our actions (e.g., protection of a vulnerable client). A complete set of client notes ought to contain at least:

1. A referral letter or notes (if a service provider referred the client).
2. Initial assessment (e.g., self-report questionnaires, intake interview notes).
3. Contract and informed consent forms.
4. Case notes (i.e., for each session) with reflections and issues for supervision. Case notes (or progress notes) normally include formulations, reformulations, interventions, and evaluations.
5. Referral letters (if you refer the client to another service provider).
6. Continuity of care among service providers (e.g., physiotherapist, clinical psychologist) when working in a multidisciplinary team.
7. Correspondence from related service providers or coaches or backroom staff.
8. Correspondence with coaches, parents, and performance directors.
9. Summary of treatment and termination.
10. Billing record (e.g., dates, services).

In this section, we outline how this information might present itself in your secure online notes or password-protected files. Practitioners vary in their work practices, depending on how they work in private practice or with whom they work (e.g., an organisation). Good habits formed in your training programme last a lifetime, so it is sensible to start as we mean to go on (Luepker, 2022).

Intake assessment notes

Intake assessments vary among practitioners and organisations. We typically set aside 90 minutes for an initial assessment and then 60 minutes to write up our notes from notes taken during the assessment. When you write notes after each session, you save time and strain that comes with procrastination. We can use an intake questionnaire to gather substantial information that helps with formulation and intervention later. We can understand the presenting problem using the 'five Ps' (Johnstone & Dallos, 2013), for example, which you will see in the next subsection for the formulation. Gathering information depends upon your chosen modality (e.g., CBT, PCT, REBT); however, the history of problems normally explores when the problem began, how it began, and what one has done to solve the problem, which tells us what has worked or has not worked. These descriptions usually capture the complex biopsychosocial world we live in, such as family, friends, school, work, sport, and so on, along with any relevant medical history. We combine this information with the information we gather in the session with the client who presents to us. We will notice their appearance, thoughts, feelings, behaviours, and non-verbal communication. Some practitioners set out a battery of assessments related to well-being (e.g., CORE-10) and specific presenting concerns (e.g., performance anxiety, self-confidence) to amalgamate in the treatment plan.

Formulation and intervention notes

The plan for the journey ahead means discussing and deciding together between the client and practitioner what seems best. Some practitioners use the 'five Ps' formulation to conceptualise an individual's presenting problem in the wider system in which they operate. The 'five Ps' comprise factors such as predisposing (i.e., historical factors), precipitating (i.e., triggers of the presenting issue), perpetuating (i.e., elements that maintain the presenting issue), and protective factors (i.e., resilience and strengths), alongside the presenting issues (i.e., a description of the client's thoughts, feelings, and behaviours). With this formulation, the problem holds structure, which helps to set goals to address it with an intervention and a timeframe to achieve the goals.

Session or progress notes

Every time a client attends a session, they will present information relating to the presenting problem and treatment. This collage tells the story of treatment and how the client is progressing – or otherwise – with their agreed plans. Some practitioners keep extensive notes (e.g., a few pages), while others keep narrow, focused notes (e.g., a few paragraphs). Our guidance remains to complete your notes as soon after each session as possible. Your notes on the client's progress captures what has been happening for the client between sessions. The client may respond well to treatment or may struggle; whatever the status, your notes help you and the client will know where you are and what you plan next. Most session notes will address homework or activities, notes for supervision, and reflections on the session.

Correspondence with others

The sporting milieu usually means working with others (e.g., coaches, performance directors, health professionals), and the care of an athlete might involve several of these professionals who correspond in scheduled meetings (e.g., player care) or other ways such as electronic correspondence (e.g., e-mail, player welfare systems). These meetings and relevant notes can be added to the file of that client; however, we need to ensure privacy and confidentiality of these individuals (e.g., supervisor, health professional) and their contributions to the client's case.

Summary of treatment and termination

When work with a client ends, maybe the client returns at a later date because she is a member of the squad to whom you offer ongoing services. Rather than reading through everything in the client's file, you can read the summary to review the presenting issue, treatment, and outcome (including how the relationship ended). Another benefit of a summary relates to the ongoing care of the client who seeks treatment elsewhere or a relevant third party (e.g., employer). The summary of treatment captures what is necessary without disclosing everything, such as personal reflections and issues for supervision. Most practitioners separate these elements (e.g., personal reflections, supervision notes) because though they apply to the practitioner, they unnecessarily burden the client (Luepker, 2010, 2022).

Summary

Ending the relationship involves a particular set of skills because sometimes the relationship ends without warning. There are several types of endings we can prepare for at the outset of our work with a client, but we must also know how our shadow motives in the helping process influence the helping relationship. It is at the end when we evaluate the outcome of our work and make sense of the next steps for the client and ourselves. An ongoing focus of our work with the client is keeping records. These records include intake assessment notes, formulation and intervention notes, session or progress notes, correspondence with others, and a summary of treatment and termination. In Chapter 9, we explore working in practice and some problems we encounter.

9 Working in practice
Ethics, challenges, and referral

Introduction

Working in private practice or for an organisation offers a multitude of opportunities, yet there will be problems along the way which challenge our competencies and require referral, for example. As sport psychology practitioners, we work within legal and ethics frameworks for the safety of our clients and ourselves. For instance, we create contracts to work with clients, we conduct assessments, and we refer clients to other health care practitioners. Working within an organisation, for example, means addressing ethics, the law, policy, governance, and work practices particular to that organisation, working within our limits, and managing ethical dilemmas. In our work, we can ask ourselves:

1. Am I working within the law?
2. Did I negotiate informed consent?
3. Am I maintaining confidentiality?
4. Do I have a dual relationship with this client?
5. Am I safeguarding the child-athlete?
6. Am I aware of and working within my competencies?
7. Am I aware of my use of touch?
8. Am I aware of risk to the client?

The answers to these questions might trigger ethical dilemmas, so we need to be aware, be sensitive, and act in the best interests of all involved. Training programmes encourage trainees to develop their ethical sensitivity, ethical reasoning, ethical motivation, and ethical implementation, so let us begin with a definition of ethics. "Ethics is defined as the rules or standards governing the conduct of members of a profession" (Committee on Professional Practice and Standards, 2003, p. 595). In applied sport psychology, ethics encompasses practice and process, and we can reflect on ethical codes as prescriptive (i.e., imposing a rule or method) and proscriptive (i.e., forbidding or restricting something). Ethics encourages us to explore and evaluate our beliefs, values, knowledge, and practices to the benefit of those who seek our assistance (Hays, 2006).

DOI: 10.4324/9781003453857-9

Ethical practice in applied sport psychology

To practice within an applied sport psychology setting, we begin by developing our formal and informal knowledge. Formal learning usually begins with academic degrees, specialist masters, and doctoral training programmes or independent training routes (e.g., BPS Stage 2 Training in the UK). With this formal training comes different degrees of informal training, including performance experience, informal training opportunities, and formative life experiences (Hays & Brown, 2004). In one's formal academic training in the practice of applied sport psychology, it is usual to develop skills in assessment, counselling, and therapy skills to work with individuals, families, groups, and teams. Performance consulting emphasises cognitive, behavioural, and short-term approaches; however, longer-term approaches also matter.

Informal preparation combines performance experience, informal training, and formative life experiences (Hays, 2006). With performance experience comes an orientation and appreciation of a performer's life in sport. A former professional football player understands her life as a football player, though it may differ appreciably from the lives of the clients she now consults. Holding this playing experience enhances credibility and develops rapport more easily with one's performer clients. Many practitioners, however, do not have this direct experience, but through their sport experiences appreciate lives of others in sport – and with passing time, a practitioner's professional learning transfers from one domain to another while generalising and differentiating among these domains (Hays et al., 2002). Informal training combines reading, observing, and experiencing a domain, but one might also receive mentoring, coaching, and supervision. Though supervision remains critical, one might supplement supervision with a network of colleagues to support one's development and offer guidance throughout one's career. Finally, formative life experiences bring with them a unique yet shared experience of life that helps to understand, appreciate, and accept the lives of others. Each practitioner – with a set of values, beliefs, and perspectives bound to a personal history and personality – shapes the work they do with the clients they help. Life experiences bring with them universal life experiences such as love, loss, fear, sadness, happiness, and joy, among so many others tied to life events (e.g., birth, friendships, education, marriage, parenthood work, retirement, and bereavement).

Moral and ethical dilemmas

We do not venture far into our work with clients without bumping into moral and ethical dilemmas. What clients bring to therapy often involves some element of what they believe to be right or wrong, or how others and society around them see as right or wrong. The sport psychology practitioner in the room helps the client to decide what is right for them – but does not decide for them. In sport, the practitioner might be equally thrown by others' expectations to do the 'right' thing with their client without the certainty of what is the 'right' thing to do for the client. To arrive at a stable base for the work we do as sport psychology practitioners, we need to lay foundations for the moral and ethical dimensions of our work. Our professional code of ethics guides us to serve the best interests of clients who might be vulnerable, searching for support, and without sufficient guidance to help themselves. But even with these guidelines, institutional demands, directives, and disagreements with colleagues add to the complexity of the cases we encounter – so where do we begin?

Gathering our ethical knowledge

If we ask ourselves where our moral and ethical knowledge comes from, we probably begin by thinking about our sense of what feels right in a situation. But if we ask ourselves, "Where did this sense emerge from?, we will probably think about our values and what we have learned as people growing up in the world. One's personal intuition – a sense of what feels right – seems like a strange place to consider what feels right for the client, especially if our personal intuition is incomplete or we find ourselves in unusual circumstances (McLeod, 2019). Many cultural mantras in sport espouse "Never give up" or "Winners are workers" or "No guts, no glory", but when one's personal moral beliefs do not chime with the client's moral beliefs, we might see unethical behaviour ensue. For example, a practitioner who believes that elite athletes ought to dedicate their whole lives to pursuing excellence might struggle to tolerate their clients' differing views. Though complications arise, our personal moral reasoning helps to engender trust, a dependable moral position, acknowledging one's boundaries and an openness to the lives and experiences of others. In the privacy of our work, are we willing to do what is right for the client? To answer this question more thoroughly, we need to address our values.

Our values represent our belief about preferred modes of conduct. We might value ambition or trust or equality. We might value all three, but value ambition over equality or trust. Our values as practitioners, therefore, find their way into our therapeutic alliances, leading to value conflicts between the practitioner and their clients. An example might be around resolving conflicts in professional relations for an athlete. One practitioner might inadvertently advocate for a behavioural perspective focusing on removing dissatisfying relationships and pursuing more satisfying ones. In this way, one's happiness might increase momentarily, but the client's benefits arising from conflict or disagreements in professional relationships fall. For example, the client's clashes with her professional support staff might be upsetting, but also generate new ideas, new perspectives, and honest processes for change.

Although we hold a personal moral and ethical stance, influenced by our values, we as practitioners follow professional ethical codes which address autonomy, beneficence, fidelity, justice, and non-maleficence (Kitchener,

1984). Autonomy refers to the right people have to choose and act freely as long as these freedoms do not interfere with freedoms of others. For example, we begin therapeutic support when a client freely takes part through their informed consent. Proceeding without a client's understanding of what is involved and their permission to do so is unethical; however, many challenges arise in therapeutic support, such as age of consent, suicide risk, and danger to others. Beneficence means to pursue human welfare. And non-maleficence means "above all, do no harm". Together, the practitioner who trains to meet competencies fulfils supervision and ongoing training, and works within these limits. The process of therapy involves risks and costs, yet the practitioner – along with the client – judges whether the benefits outweigh the costs. Fidelity incorporates dependability, loyalty, reliability, and acting in good faith (McLeod, 2019). In sport settings, one need not read too far into the daily sport pages to find instances of lying, deception, and exploitation across all sports, from amateur to professional status. One's contract with a client assumes the practitioner offers their best to the client and they handle any challenges along the way to prevent breaches of fidelity. Justice refers to the fair distribution of services. In applied sport psychology, we might ask: who receives support from a practitioner? Is there a fair distribution of services and resources? The possibility of fairness when distributing services might depend on assessment, those in greatest need, feasibility, and so forth.

Each of these moral principles forms the foundation of our work with clients, yet we might imagine several situations in which one principle bumps into another. In upholding fidelity, we act in good faith for the client; however, we might not uphold justice and fairly distribute services.

Ethical dilemmas in sport

The unfolding demands of athletic populations and settings complicate the traditional adherence to ethical practice guidelines in applied sport psychology (Moore, 2003). The sport psychology practitioner, therefore, faces the typical ethical challenges for counselling and clinical psychologists – but also the unique service demands that come with practice and clients from the sport milieu. Working as a sport psychology practitioner, we face similar issues to psychologists in a rural setting because of the smaller size of such communities such as confidentiality and dual or multiple roles. A psychologist in a rural area will meet clients in stores, restaurants, and at community events similar to a sport psychology practitioner working in a self-contained sports setting with increased contact between athletes, backroom staff, and management. When we add time spent in practice facilities and travelling with the team, the sport psychology practitioner will meet athletes in professional and social settings, such as with group meetings and back-to-back individual meetings alongside brief contact at competition and practice sites.

The role of the sport psychology practitioner is to help the athlete function optimally to reach personal goals and the specific goals of the greater organisation/team. Thus, the sport psychology practitioner is in the service of the larger organisational goals. Tensions arise when the goals of the individual athlete clash with those of the organisation. For instance, challenges in the athlete's life might require time away from the sport, but the organisation needs the athlete to fulfil his or her occupational duty rather than disrupt the organisation's greater goals. Moore (2003) listed issues of confidentiality, competence, ending the practitioner–client relationship, and balancing roles, relationships, and organisational demands. We shall explore these next.

Applying moral and ethical codes in sport

Professional bodies within the UK, such as the British Psychological Society (BPS) and the Health and Care Professions Council (HCPC), function to ensure ethical standards of practice using ethical guidelines for practitioners and procedures to handle complaints and unethical behaviour. Such guidelines and codes present limitations because they cannot cover every scenario, but protecting the client and the practitioner remains paramount. When ethical challenges arise, the practitioner consults the professional body's guidance to manage, for example, confidentiality or disclosure of intention to harm self or others. Professional bodies, through committees and special-interest groups, present current consensus across their membership. The challenge for the sport psychology practitioner is to be ethically mindful and lean on the guidance provided to decide what is best. Unfortunately, the ethical frameworks do not give us all the answers; rather, we use their structure and guidance to decide on a course of action. Remember, we use ethical guidelines, not ethical rules.

Confidentiality

Privacy, confidentiality, and privilege combine as three interrelated ethical constructs we encounter regularly in sport settings. Privacy reflects the rights of people to hold personal data, thoughts, opinions, and beliefs to themselves and control over whether such information could or should be in the hands of others. Privacy, therefore, presents the foundation for the moral necessity and duty of what we value in confidentiality and privilege (Andersen, 2005).

> Confidentiality is the cornerstone of trust on which the therapeutic relationship is built, [and as such], clients must understand the limitations to their confidentiality if they are to make informed decisions about whether to enter into treatment and whether to disclose personal information during sessions.
>
> (Glosoff et al., 1997, p. 573)

Without assurances of confidentiality, how can a client develop a trusting relationship to share experiences otherwise held secret? Occasions arise when confidentiality clashes with practitioner accountability. In professional sport settings, we raise several questions about who the client is and on whose behalf the practitioner is working. Even with a client-centred focus, moral and ethical courses of action mean considering others. For instance, a company employing a sport psychology practitioner might expect particular results from a client such as winning an Olympic medal because their funding depends upon such success, or parents of an adolescent athlete might seek information about their child's progress. We can address such scenarios in the contract at the beginning of the helping process to include stakeholders and the bounds of confidentiality we require and appear acceptable to all.

With practitioners working for private companies or national governing bodies, several contractual obligations emerge. These contractual obligations might be to assess the strengths and weaknesses of athletes and coaches to achieve performance excellence. The ensuing interviews and observations present as general themes to the organisation without disclosing who said what exactly. Following this initial assessment, a formulation, intervention, evaluation, and communication unfolds. Another contractual obligation might be to work towards performance targets or collaborate with a multidisciplinary team on performance targets. The performance director will need to know how valuable and effective psychological services are for their athletes alongside sport injury treatments or strength and conditioning programmes.

In short, when sport psychology practitioners work for larger sport organisations, issues of confidentiality and privileged communication ought to be discussed and agreed before service delivery begins. In this way, all parties can witness the limits of confidentiality and the difficulties this process minimises. The organisation employing the sport psychology practitioner holds broad and detailed goals for all its members so the individual client is considered alongside the obligations to the organisation.

Competence

The word competence derives from the Latin *competens* and refers to 'being fit'. When we address fitness to practise, we imply health and capacity to practise, which falls into sufficient preparation, competent practice, and responsible risk management (Hays, 2006). Keeping the client and practitioner safe ought to be uppermost in one's mind undertaking service delivery. To do so, the practitioner ought to work within their limits of competence, intervening only when they are competent to do so. Working on one's personal and professional development to remain within safe boundaries runs throughout one's working life. Our health, well-being, and energy ought to meet the needs of the client and be present in the helping process. When we discuss boundaries in training and supervision, we outline several of these: place, role, time, information, money, self-disclosure, physical contact, language, clothing. These boundaries encourage thoughtful practice so that when one crosses a boundary or violates a boundary, we can manage the consequences.

We all bump into technical and ethical issues in our work in sport. For instance, working with a client in a sport setting whereby you are on a golf course and the session runs over by 45 minutes may or may not be helpful for the client (technical issue) and may or may not be an ethical issue (breach of consent, doing harm by raising insurmountable expectations). Here, the critical debate is context (see Frankel et al., 2012; Pope & Keith-Spiegel, 2008).

McLeod (2019) presented seven dimensions of practitioner competence: ethical sensitivity, interpersonal skills, personal soundness, conceptual ability, mastery of techniques, work within social systems, and openness to learning and inquiry. What these competencies combine is a sensitivity and responsiveness to relate to others for the client's sake with professional skills to formulate and intervene within social systems while remaining open to learning and feedback. Competencies develop with learning, experience, and feedback. This journey as a developing practitioner offers a process to review, revise, and refine competencies in the various systems within which we work.

Boundaries

Sport psychology practitioners work in several non-traditional environments and roles which are less rigid than those typical of traditional clinical practice, especially as a sport psychology practitioner might travel, eat, and share accommodation with clients (Brown & Cogan, 2006; Stapleton et al., 2010). The nature of these environments means adapting to the needs of the client. For example, McCann (2000) described the challenges of working with athletes at the Olympic Games:

> Practitioners learn to perfect the ski-lift consult, the bus-ride consult, the 10-minute breakfast team-building session, the confidential session in public places such as hotel lobbies, parking lots and trainers' tables. These catch-as-catch-can consulting encounters are realities for a sport psychology practitioner in most competition settings.
>
> (p. 211)

These boundary crossings are not unethical. And multiple relationships are not unethical unless they mean harm or exploitation of the client.

Professional boundaries "derive from the rules of the professional relationship that distinguish it from business or social relationships" (Knapp & Slattery, 2004, p. 553). The contextual elements of boundaries help us understand boundary crossings and boundary violations (Guthiel & Gabbard, 1993). A boundary crossing occurs when professionals stray from the outright professional role. A boundary crossing may be helpful, neutral, or harmful. The boundary crossing becomes a boundary violation when it places the client at risk of harm. Sport occurs within the natural environment in public and private venues, whether indoors or outdoors, which means practitioners contend with changing structures, expectations, and outcomes. What does not change, however, are the rules, but the guidelines need to recognise these contexts (Knapp & Slattery, 2004). One example here concerns touch. Physical intimacy – from pats on the back to high fives and hugs – presents an unusual experience for a practitioner occupying a professional role but a more common one for a coach, for instance. The reflective practitioner understands the role of physical intimacy but also acknowledges the slippery slope towards physical intimacy that is exploitative, harassing, or suggestive (Hays, 2006).

Use of touch

The looseness of the working environment in applied sport psychology means increased likelihood of touch such as celebrating a win, commiserating following a loss, supporting an athlete by carrying equipment, and so forth. Why most fear touch is these relations is where touch might lead, such as sexual gratification by the client, practitioner, or both. When we add in social, cultural, or religious proscriptions, touch adds greater concerns about what a client might accuse a practitioner of and so holds a distant and defensive strategy, avoiding all gestures of comfort or contact. Shaking hands, a hug, or a pat on the arm are typical of human compassion, and avoiding these basic expressions might mean the client experiences the practitioner's cold, reserved, and strange way of being. As with all ethical dilemmas, we ought to seek guidance; for example, Hunter and Struve (1998) offered a guide around the ethical use of touch in psychotherapy when it is clinically appropriate and inappropriate. As with all the issues presented in this chapter, one's quiet work reflecting on the meaning of touch for them personally ought to reach supervision, personal, and professional development classes early in their training.

Informed consent

Informed consent means providing the client with all the information we can offer about the therapy we offer and the alternatives. Once the client has this information, they can choose how they wish to proceed, perhaps asking questions, before accepting or rejecting what is on offer. If the client agrees, they sign the contract before beginning work together. Many practitioners make such information available on their websites or within information leaflets for the client, but some might not.

Informed consent ought to be accessible, understood, and up to date for the client. A comprehensive informed consent allows the client to choose which course of therapy suits them best without pressure or coercion to follow the practitioner's leanings – but with changes to one's circumstances, informed consent represents a process rather than an event at the outset of therapy. Some clients feel overwhelmed by the mass of information in the first session about informed consent and need time to read and ask questions. Not only should this choice be available when signing informed consent, but throughout the course of the helping service. With dynamic or process consent, the practitioner routinely checks in with the client whether they have sufficient information and if the course of therapy satisfies their needs.

Dual or multiple relationships

Dual relationships occur when a practitioner engages in another (or more than one) type of relationship with a client. Obvious dual relationships include being a sport psychology practitioner to someone who is a neighbour, friend, or business partner. But the less obvious ones occur where practitioners work in sporting organisations, sports schools, colleges, or universities where the practitioner is also a teacher or tutor. In some sport organisations, the sport psychology practitioner delivers training in coach education, for example, or sits on a promotions panel. Often, a professional sport organisation keeps one post for a sport psychology practitioner and there is no choice for the athletes to see another sport psychology practitioner.

In some settings, the knots of family life, participating in sport, and one's profession cross over. For example, a sport psychology practitioner brings her son (aged 10 years) to athletics training. At the same club, several national and international athletes train under the same coach. While the sport psychology practitioner sits watching her son in training, the coach occasionally drops by to discuss what amounts to best practice to prepare athletes for competition. The coach knows how much this sport psychology practitioner helped athletes in the local community and would like her to join the backroom team, which would involve travelling to national and international events. Although the sport psychology practitioner might act as consultant to the coach and the athletes, she is also a parent to a club athlete, bringing tangles to responsibilities and boundaries.

It is likely that the sport psychology practitioner will share a hotel room with backroom staff, eat meals with the backroom staff and athletes, and meet these athletes around the hotel. The nature of these encounters means a difference between social and professional interactions, but also being alert not to violate professional boundaries (Haberl & Peterson, 2006; Barnett et al., 2007).

Sexual exploitation of clients

Sexual exploitation occurs across all classes of society. With this pervasiveness in mind, what is happening in sport? The precise incidence of sexual abuse might be difficult to determine, but its systematic reports exist in several countries across Europe and in Australia, Canada, and the United States (Leahy, 2008). Athletes in sport – especially young athletes – might experience various forms of harassment and abuse, such as neglect and verbal, emotional, physical, and sexual abuse at the same time. The constituents of sexual abuse in the position paper by Stirling et al. (2011) described sexual relations with the athlete; inappropriate sexual contact; exchange of reward in sport for sexual favours; sexually oriented comments, jokes, or gestures; sexual propositions; and exposing an athlete to pornographic material. While sexual harassment reflects unwanted attention based on sex, sexual abuse involves grooming or coerced collaboration in sexual and/or genital acts whereby the perpetrator entraps the victim (Brackenridge & Fasting, 2005; Owton & Sparkes, 2017).

Maybe the sport psychology practitioner works with a survivor of chronic sexual abuse who struggles with complex, dissociative post-traumatic conditions in their recovery process while driving for high performance goals in sport (Leahy, 2010). Aspects of the culture of competitive sport mean sexual abuse is likely to occur: perpetrator methodology and the bystander effect (Brackenridge, 2001; Leahy et al., 2004). Two key dimensions of perpetrator methodology include engendering powerlessness in the athlete and omnipotence in the perpetrator. By imposing one's version of reality on the athlete and isolating the athlete within that reality, the perpetrator maintains that reality by controlling the psychological environment, silencing and isolating the athlete from sources of support. The bystander effect captures those who knew (or suspected) the sexual abuse but did nothing about it (Leahy et al., 2003, 2004).

In a therapeutic relationship, sexual attraction does not stop at the clinic door; rather, it is a usual aspect of being human, but the erotic dimensions of the therapeutic relationship present a significant ethical and moral challenge for practitioners. The subject of erotic feelings in sport psychology service delivery has received minimal attention (Andersen, 2005; Stevens & Andersen, 2007) but it is likely that sexual attraction and sexual behaviour between practitioners and client-athletes mirrors that in the general field of psychotherapy. Not only do sport psychology practitioners work in various settings with athletes who have qualities most people find attractive, but also the settings are looser, with service delivery occurring pitch-side, at the track, and in the locker room. Some practitioners will travel with the squad and backroom staff, and stay at hotels, eat meals, and socialise with the athletes. Most athletes within psychological service provision are young, talented, and attractive (Stevens & Andersen, 2007). These amassing contexts mean boundary violations could occur, such as touching the client or inappropriate self-disclosure by the sport psychology practitioner. The trial with all ethical and moral quandaries of feelings of attraction towards clients is to recognise and address them by acknowledging one's feelings, separating one's feelings from your work with your client, separating personal problems from the client, and bringing your experiences to supervision.

Ending the practitioner–client relationship

Working in sport organisations, especially professional teams, often means short-term contracts are terminated because of the misfortunes of the team. This situation might be similar for the team management and the sport psychology practitioner. A similar fate befalls athletes who are bought and sold year to year or mid-season. In these settings, sport psychology practitioners seek to continue care despite these abrupt changes in structure or personal employment (Moore, 2003). In the end is our beginning. Because we know services might finish abruptly for the reasons previously listed, we need to prepare for the end when we begin service delivery. Sometimes the organisation terminates the sport psychology practitioner's employment, and sometimes the organisation terminates the athlete's employment. For these reasons, preparing at the outset puts a plan in place for these eventualities. The practitioner might discuss with the client some options for further intervention and continued support, perhaps through a referral.

The process of referral

Referral is a key link in the chain of support for a client. The sport psychology practitioner will not always fit the needs of all clients, and specific issues best handled by another professional is the most appropriate step. There are several explanations for referral, which might include emotional, legal, medical, psychiatric, psychological, and social, which emerge at different stages of the helping process.

From the sport psychology practitioner's perspective, the referral process can be daunting because it might upset the sport psychology practitioner that they cannot help the client or struggle to separate from the client. Take the case of a sport psychology practitioner working with college student-athletes. These student-athletes present with mental health difficulties, such as alcohol abuse, depression, eating disorders, and social anxiety at similarly high levels as their nonathlete peers (Gill, 2008; Storch et al., 2005; Wolanin et al., 2016). A multitude of factors influence college student-athletes' experience of psychological distress, such as pressure to perform well athletically, balancing athletic demands around academic loads, and usual life commitments (Waho et al., 2016). At other times, the sport psychology practitioner is too quick to refer. Sometimes at the outset of therapy, the sport psychology practitioner does not communicate the possibility of referral with the client and so the client cannot see why the referral is required. From the client's perspective, they might interpret referral as abandonment or rejection rather than a process of support to best meet the client's needs. For many athletes, seeking professional psychological support is daunting because of the public stigma such as being seen as weak and teammates finding out about one's use of counselling, which are major contributors to avoid pursuing psychological services (López & Levy, 2013). There are several specialists available to most clients for issues of eating disorders, sexual abuse, mental health, marital breakdown, and so on, which will be in the client's best interests. Building a network of trusted colleagues helps in the transition from one helper to another and also one's readiness to refer in the best interests of the client. Also, this network of trusted colleagues means they will refer people to you, too.

One issue arising in the first session is the suitability of the client to the sport psychology practitioner and the suitability of the sport psychology practitioner to the client. Good therapeutic outcomes often depend on the goodness of fit between the client and the sport psychology practitioner. The first session is a means to consider the help most appropriate for the client.

When someone refers a client

The central position of coaches and backroom staff (e.g., physiotherapists, physicians) in sport organisations means that they often refer a client to you. This process might involve a coach, for example, in a telephone call or e-mail. What seems critical at this stage is the information the referral agent gave to the client because, while this information might be helpful and instructive, it might also be misleading and unproductive for the support process with a sport psychology practitioner. For instance, a coach might say that another player worked with you and benefitted; however, there is no guarantee that you are the right sport psychology practitioner for this referral.

Many athletes find the referral process distressing because they feel that if their coach is suggesting a referral, there must be something awfully wrong with them. Not following the coach's wishes might have short- or long-term implications for their career. Waho et al. (2016) reported that student-athletes were more willing to seek help when referred by a family member compared with a coach, a teammate, or themselves. Student-athletes, as one stratum of the athletic population, are less likely to seek therapy than their nonathletic colleagues, even though they report similar levels of distress (Gill, 2008). Self-stigma and public stigma strongly shape their attitudes towards seeking professional psychological support. Though student-athletes recognise the support coaches and teammates offer when confronted with sport performance problems (Maniar et al., 2001), they paradoxically also act as barriers to seek professional psychological help (López & Levy, 2013).

Regardless of these circumstances, it is the client who makes the commitment to the support service (Feltham & Dryden, 2006). A well-meaning coach might suggest that "She needs to learn how to relax" or "He needs to address his anger", so the client, being compliant, sees this issue as the presenting issue. The key matter for you as the sport psychology practitioner is to uncover why the client is attending your clinic. By gently enquiring about what the referral agent said, we can better understand how accurate and helpful is the information the client holds entering a first session. We can address any misunderstandings or inaccuracies early. For instance, the coach's concern about the athlete's inability to relax might be accurate; however, the client recognises another primary concern, and her inability to relax is one way in which the underlying problem manifests in her sporting life.

Opening this discussion about her coach's assessment, whether she agrees or disagrees, and how she has been feeling since the coach suggested the referral helps the sport psychology practitioner to understand the client's motives and intentions around sport psychology support. It might emerge that this referral was what she needed but was reluctant initially and now feels comfortable proceeding, or that this referral represents one incident, among others, when the client feels pressured to follow orders or accept the consequences.

The challenges for the sport psychology practitioner

Receiving a referral from another professional or referring a client to another professional follows a process. A referral makes up a process, not an event. This process occurs for the client and the professional, referring or receiving the client and a structure of decisions along the way. For the professionals receiving the referral, they must consider the source of the referral, financing, scheduling, and first impressions of the client to judge whether to accept or decline a referral (Shapiro & Ginzberg, 2003). For the professionals referring the client, they must also consider the professional to whom they are referring their client, the financial implications for the client, and the possible scheduling when the other professional might accept the client into their care.

This referral process draws upon ethics, boundaries, confidentiality, and countertransference to inform a practitioner's decision-making to accept a referral. Shapiro and Ginzberg (2003) raised several challenges for the practitioner receiving a referral from a current or past client, including exploitation, dual relationships, confidentiality, and countertransference. For example, a treatment contract means that the practitioner's role is to address the client's presenting issues in return for monetary compensation; however, in Epstein and Simon's (1990) view, accepting a referral from a client means receiving more that one's treatment fee for treating the client. One might consider this referral a gift to the practitioner and the meaning behind the gift might mean we are indebted to our clients. Some former clients also refer clients. Again, each referral draws us into a decision-making process because practitioners need to make a living and decide whether the former client is likely to return for treatment. If the former client is unlikely to return, then accepting the referral seems reasonable without divulging the privacy of the former client.

The therapeutic boundary, which includes a set fee, a defined treatment setting, time and length of sessions, helps the client feel safe in the therapeutic space. Occasionally, a friend might suggest a practitioner from whom to seek treatment; however, the entanglement begins here because the friend's motives may lie hidden. For example, the friend might offer a 'gift' to the practitioner or set up a competition to be the more beloved of the clients. Also, maintaining confidentiality when two clients are closely connected presents problems for the practitioner to ensure they maintain this boundary, which burdens the best memories.

A third challenge for accepting referrals involves dual relationships. A next-door neighbour seeking treatment poses this dilemma of a dual relationship. In sport settings, we encounter several dual relationships whereby we meet people in a club or organisation in our neighbourhood or at the school gates. This criss-crossing of paths might mean the client feels uncomfortable in our office because we see each other in the neighbourhood. Likewise, the practitioner's need for privacy means some tolerable permeability within one's boundaries. Meeting outside the office within the organisation means a further interruption of one's privacy. At many organisations, there might be only one sport psychology practitioner, so we are likely to face this dilemma regularly.

The source of one's referral can create countertransference difficulties when accepting a referral. A simple example of this countertransference occurs when a practitioner receives a referral from a practitioner with a perceived higher status and feels overstretched to impress the colleague. To impress a colleague, we might accept the client even with an overwhelming and immediate countertransference to the client, a heavy caseload, or seeing the client at unsuitable times of the day (Shapiro & Ginzberg, 2003).

What do I include in a referral letter?

The referral letter establishes a process to coordinate care between services. For example, a sport psychology practitioner might refer a client to a clinical psychologist, a physiotherapist, or a physician. Equally, a clinical psychologist, physiotherapist, or physician might refer a client to a sport psychology practitioner. With this referral process happening through a written format, much depends on the quality of the information within the letter. If we write a referral letter without specific points addressed to the reader, it is likely that we lose critical information in translation. Hartveit et al. (2013) presented recommended content of referral letters from general practitioners (GPs) to specialised mental health care using a qualitative multi-perspective study. The following seven headings cover the major themes arising from the study.

1. Personal information and contact information.
2. Important introductory information (check-off points).
3. Case history and social situation.
4. Present state and results.
5. Past and ongoing treatment efforts, involved professional network.
6. The patient's assessment.
7. Reason for referral.

Though specific to mental health and medical care, we explore each heading for the context of applied sport psychology.

1. **Personal information and contact information:** this section means correctly identifying the person and their contact information, emergency contact numbers, and place of residence. This information section also includes the referring psychologist with contact information, such as a phone number, e-mail, and place of work.

2. **Important introductory information:** this section of check-off points (i.e., yes or no) addresses the risks of the client specific to mental health. For instance, is there an immediate need for compulsory care? Is the patient suicidal? Is the patient a threat to others? Is the patient responsible for the care of children? Does the patient have a drug problem or addiction? These questions assess the immediate needs of the client.

3. **Case history and social situation:** the case history focuses on changes such as worsening of a condition over time and the duration of the condition. Any episodes of violence or former suicidal risk guide the reader, along with the broader context of the client's psychosocial circumstances, such as economics, employment, residence, social network, and activities.

4. **Present state and results:** here we hold four categories of information: (1) function, symptoms, and limitations; (2) somatic health; (3) test results; and (4) medications. With function, symptoms, and limitations, we present the problem and the present mental status of the client. Where a loss of function reveals itself, we present the level and duration of the loss. The present state of symptoms and their duration ought to be outlined, as well. One's somatic health includes any diseases or comorbidities. Some organisations ask clients to complete specific questionnaires relating to anxiety and depression. For example, we could include test scores from these questionnaires and any notice of medications.

5. **Past and ongoing treatment efforts and the wider professional network:** here, the referring psychologist presents what they have tried so far and any current interventions alongside other supportive services that the client uses.

6. **The client's assessment:** here we include the client's experience of the situation, desire and motives for treatment, and attitude towards treatment.

7. **Reason for referral:** the psychologist outlines a goal for treatment along with the reasons for referral.

We have provided a sample referral letter in the Appendix. With the increasing flexibility of treatment (e.g., face to face, telephone, online), more sport psychology practitioners receive referrals from practitioners across the world, so we now turn to working remotely with clients.

Working remotely/working online

The conventional view of a sport psychology practitioner and client working together places the dyad in a private office or perhaps at a sports training centre; however, we can use counselling skills online and via the phone (audio/video) with equal success. This remote support and guidance often meets the needs of athletes, coaches, and teams who are travelling for training and competition across the globe. Not only has modern technology offered a cost-effective means of supporting people, but also we can tailor the service to the individual needs of service users. The immediacy and flexibility with which to work with a client preparing for a competition in Rome or a training camp in Switzerland fit the needs of each party immeasurably. Online platforms (e.g., Zoom) tailor their technology so it is as accessible as possible to practitioners.

Although the client and practitioner might prefer to meet in person, telephone and online support means we can jump several obstacles of distance, isolation, travel, finance, emotional and psychological barriers, and so on. In recent years, we have found it most convenient to find times to work with clients in the privacy of their homes (or hotel rooms). The privacy and confidentiality of meeting online matched the needs of athletes who did not feel ready to meet in person or the nature of their sport (i.e., travelling on tour) mean remote support fitted best.

Athletes and coaches have shared several reasons for seeking remote support. Here are some examples:

- "I am well-recognised in my sport and would prefer the anonymity."
- "I travel a lot for my sport and there are no practitioners I feel comfortable around on tour."
- "I'm rarely at home, so working online works well for me."
- "We have a team psychologist here, but I wish to keep working with you."
- "I would rather that no one knows I am seeing a psychologist."
- "I have quite a few calls on my time, so I'd rather not have to travel to your offices."
- "I like the privacy and time e-mail affords, and it allows me to reflect and communicate with a trained professional."

With sport – and its travel, competition, transfers, and so forth – offering services remotely means that effective support can continue despite changes to one's life circumstances, but some clients have also shared the following limitations to working remotely.

- "I do like to work face-to-face; it's how I work with my coaches and physio."
- "I struggle to form a connection unless I'm sitting there with them."
- "I spend so much time alone in my sport; I feel like I'm becoming more isolated."
- "I struggle to express myself through text messages and e-mails."
- "When I'm sitting with you, at least I know the Wi-Fi will not drop out."
- "The time differences can be a real challenge when I'm competing on the West Coast."
- "It can sometimes be challenging to keep my boundaries when working online at home with young children and family commitments."

The fundamentals of safe, ethical, and effective service delivery remain paramount, whether online or on the telephone. Many sport psychology practitioners work synchronously (e.g., videoconferencing) or asynchronously (e.g., text messages, e-mail), according to the needs of clients and their own commitments. Working synchronously means working in real time, while asynchronous means working (e.g., sharing information) without a specific time frame for reply. Synchronous work depends on the technology (e.g., online platform) working and a series of support plans if it does not work. We might prefer working with an online platform, but hold back-up plans like a mobile phone call or a landline telephone call if the mobile signal drops out.

Although we can offer these alternative means of communicating, the visual cues we take for granted in an in-person meeting or video call are absent in an e-mail or telephone call. While you might feel comfortable, competent, and confident working in this way, we need to understand how the client feels and attend more to the accuracy of our observations and understandings to ensure we understand the client's story accurately. We shall share one critical concern with remote working: confidentiality. Working online or over the telephone means the responsibility of confidentiality for both parties: client and practitioner. Although we can ensure a level of confidentiality in a private practice office, when we are working online and over the telephone, we are not sure who else might be listening or accessing the platform. We can address these issues with the client before our work begins to ensure both parties realise their responsibilities when working remotely.

The changing face of applied sport psychology

Tracing the boundaries of one's work as a sport psychology practitioner in an organisation brings swarming challenges, especially because the roles and responsibilities of the sport psychology practitioner appear to be growing (Sly et al., 2020) and the populations falling under the performance title include business, military, health care, education and the performing arts. Although the central theme of this book is working with athletes on a one-to-one basis, we acknowledge the multiplicity of roles and responsibilities that might fall within the role profile of a sport psychology practitioner such as facilitating performance enhancement, performers' well-being, and cultural excellence (Eubank et al., 2014). The socio-cultural–political axis and the legal, economic, and educational dimensions of modern sport draw in a sport psychology practitioner to contribute to attitudes (e.g., race, culture, ethnicity), fairness (e.g., diversity and difference), motivation, stress, and leadership (Cruickshank & Collins, 2015; Sly et al., 2020). This ever-changing landscape means trainees and educators nimbly adjust to meet the current and future demands of clients. Aoyagi and colleagues (2012) highlighted that the future of the applied sport psychology profession will require the following competencies:

1. Competence in the psychology of performance (e.g., theories of performance excellence) and performance enhancement.
2. Competence in mental health counselling.
3. Competence in consulting psychology.
4. Competence in a performance speciality domain (e.g., sport, business, performing arts).

All these domains (e.g., sport, military) mean working with people, and all these competencies (e.g., performance enhancement, mental health counselling) mean trainees need to work with people for a breadth of applied experience (McEwan & Tod, 2015) – but these demands could mean diluting the quality of applied sport psychology practice because several plates (i.e., competencies) are spinning (Winter & Collins, 2016). And whatever demands fall on the trainee, they also fall on the supervisor to provide adequate supervision across these competencies.

Henschen and Tenenbaum (2005, p. 7) wrote that "a prominent issue in sport psychology is the need to develop practice procedures that are accountable and trustful, anecdotal evidence of the effectiveness of applied sport psychology interventions is no longer sufficient to justify the efficacy of the field". Other authors suggested moving beyond the skill-focused intervention work to include diagnosis, psychological testing, assessment, counselling, and providing clinical services (Aoyagi et al., 2012; Gardner, 2001, 2009; Winter & Collins, 2016). The reality for most sport psychology practitioners is that they face counselling, clinical, and personality-based issues in the performers with whom they work. Everyday sport psychology practitioners judge a client's presenting problems; primary, secondary, and tertiary issues; tasks and goals; strategies and techniques (Gardner & Moore, 2004) – and no doubt will continue to develop competencies to best meet need the needs of their clients.

Summary

In this chapter, we explored ethical practice in applied sport psychology alongside the moral and ethical dilemmas we face in sport settings. Issues of confidentiality, competence, boundaries, informed consent, dual or multiple relationships, sexual exploitation of clients, use of touch, and ending the practitioner–client relationship all test practitioners on how to work professionally, safely, competently, and ethically. To work safely and within our competencies also means recognising when a referral to another health professional is necessary and when we can accept a referral. The changing face and delivery of applied sport psychology also means working remotely (i.e., online) and learning how to do so safely. With all the demands placed upon us, we also need to take care of ourselves, which we shall explore in Chapter 10.

10 Taking care of yourself

Introduction

As helping professionals, we often place ourselves outside the loop of the helping process. Some sport psychology practitioners might feel that they do not deserve the support they offer to others, or perhaps taking care of oneself seems self-indulgent when there is 'nothing wrong' and the nature of sport psychology service delivery means looking after others rather than taking care of ourselves. These jumbled thoughts, feelings, opinions, attitudes, values, and beliefs persuade us to excavate further to find a firm foundation from which to build a secure dwelling. Taking care of oneself fits within the guidance of professional bodies (e.g., HCPC, BPS, APA) as an ethical and professional requirement. Minding our physical health and safety and our psychological health and well-being means keeping a healthy balance between our work and the lives we lead. When we work in sport settings, we need to ensure we feel safe from harm (e.g., physical harm). For instance, leaving a training ground at night time might mean you need adequate lighting so you can walk to your car without fear of being attacked, or if you are working in private practice offices past 6 pm when all other staff have gone home. To work safely with a client means feeling safe on both sides – client and practitioner. Our physical and psychological health seems obvious on one level and yet confusing at another. It seems obvious to cancel appointments when you are ill in bed with a sickness bug, but at other times, we might feel well enough to work physically, but psychologically 'struggling' through a bout of depression. In short, we are asking ourselves: when are we fit to practise?

One stumbling block in making this judgement is the ideals and values of the sporting milieu, such as resilience, commitment, teamwork, and so forth. Fans applaud athletes, coaches, and teams for their resilience, commitment, and teamwork to overcome difficulties, to bounce back from adversity and succeed through setbacks. Although resilience presents sufficient advantages (e.g., manage stressful events, overcome adversity) and we can learn to be resilient, we might encounter a "more is better" culture and feel nudged towards matching the work ethic of others within the organisation. In these settings, having supervision means we take time and space to reflect on our work

DOI: 10.4324/9781003453857-10

(e.g., challenging cases, high case load), our work practices (e.g., how we work), and what is in our best interests as sport psychology practitioners. With personal and professional support, the compelling forces in high performance sport, for example, we learn to separate from healthy working practices.

Case study: Darcy

Darcy works at a professional football club. She worked with an Olympic sport previously alongside several colleagues who mentored her through the early stages of her career, but she sought a change of professional challenges. In this professional football club, however, she is the only sport psychology practitioner and her remit means working across all age groups and teams. She frequently travels to games with different teams and does her best to provide support to the players and guidance to the backroom staff. Darcy has a heavy caseload. She meets with her line manager in a small group every Friday morning, but these sessions focus on interventions and ongoing support and action plans for the first team squad. Every evening, Darcy arrives home exhausted and distressed because she cannot possibly meet the needs of the organisation, and typically fatigued with the emotional labour, managing staff needs in the backroom team. Darcy feels as if she has no time for support like supervision or personal therapy.

In your view, could you answer these questions:

Which support options are open to Darcy?
How might supervision help Darcy?
Is Darcy at risk in this workplace?

We all need support to work safely with clients. Several avenues of support mean we can find what we need. Sometimes this support is practical (e.g., child care, a holiday) and sometimes this support is emotional (e.g., personal therapy) or professional (e.g., supervision, coaching); yet we might never examine what type of support we need. Having a supervisor and regular meetings with an experienced and skilled supervisor means we can explore our needs regularly. Attending a music event with friends or going for a walk with a partner in the countryside might offer a much-needed break and an emotional uplift, but we need to know whether we need this social support and/or professional support (e.g., see our GP or a supervisor). Working with a supervisor offers the chance to add items to the agenda that are pressing for us, such as professional fulfilment, work/life balance, personal development, and so on. Only by exploring how we spend our time do we glimpse how we divide our time among our activities, interests, health, relationships, and occupation.

One challenge Darcy faced was that she knew she needed something, but she was not sure what she needed – and a significant personal and professional challenge for Darcy was requesting help. She described herself as a "super-coper who handles everything, always". Darcy felt too busy to go for supervision and without this professional support; she failed to see the warning lights coming on. Reading over her notes following a session with one coach, she saw a reflection of herself: tired, distracted, low energy, feeling overwhelmed and overburdened, lacking empathy, and feeling alone. Seeing oneself as the caregiver rather than the care recipient puts healthcare workers at risk of missing those warning signs. Darcy had not explored those activities that raised her spirits and those that low-ered her spirits. She did not have a safety plan or a care plan in place for herself. In fact, seeking help seemed shameful to her and fraudulent to be working as a sport psychology practitioner and needing help. Darcy worried that the only image she could show to the world was of someone who is healthy, happy, and in control – that was her view of a good sport psychology practitioner. Darcy sought supervision from an experienced supervisor who recognised the warning signs soon after meeting Darcy. When her supervisor enquired about her self-care plan, Darcy dropped her head and lamented "I cannot remember how many of these I co-created with athletes and I never thought about creating one for myself . . . . I cannot believe I am saying these words". Through their work together, Darcy realised she would benefit from some personal therapy, especially to explore her lack of self-acceptance and self-compassion. The insight gained in supervision meant prioritising her self-care and 'checking in' honestly through supervision.

In supervision, I (Paul) often use the principles of impact therapy. First developed by Ed Jacobs and stemming from the work of Milton Erickson, this form of therapy leans on the senses in the therapeutic process that is crea-tive and interactive (Beaulieu, 2006). For example, I often ask supervisees to listen to a metronome with their eyes closed. I ask them to find the rate most comfortable for them, so I raise or lower the speed according to their instruc-tions. Every time I use the metronome to find the beats per minute at which the supervisee would like to live their life, it is always at a tempo much lower than how they are living just now. For one supervisee, the contrast was stark: her natural rate was 60 beats per minute while her working life was 160 beats per minute. It was as though her working life would only work at this speed and intensity. When she explored which reasons lay behind this behaviour, several reasons surfaced. In particular, she felt self-satisfied that she worked at this intensity and delighted in saying "Yes" to more work when she knew she ought to say "No". She also held a belief that she was the only one who could help, so her needs would need to move down the hierarchy. More than any-thing else, she needed to be needed to feel good about herself and her role as a sport psychology practitioner. This jumble of motives, however, meant that the supervisee learned much about herself and what might need to change, because as a sport psychology practitioner, she was the tool of her trade. Being the tool of our trade means we need to take care of ourselves physically, psy-chologically, emotionally, and socially. Our trade, unfortunately, means we are vulnerable in our occupation – and not recognising this vulnerability raises a red flag in teaching and supervision.

A development scheme

We explore the developmental needs of athletes, coaches, and teams throughout service delivery; however, how often do we consider our developmental needs (e.g., trainees) when undertaking training and supervision? (Fogaca et al., 2020; Tod, 2007). Related fields such as counselling and clinical psychology present practitioner development models which help us benchmark our development such as the Integrated Developmental Model (IDM) (Stoltenberg & McNeil, 2009) and a similar model by Rønnestad and Skovholt (2003) suggesting development unfolds linearly. In the IDM, Stoltenberg and McNeil argued practitioners develop competence in eight domains of clinical practice: (1) intervention skills competence, (2) assessment techniques, (3) interpersonal assessment, (4) client conceptualisation, (5) individual differences, (6) theoretical orientation, (7) treatment plans and goals, and (8) professional ethics. A practitioner passes through three stages or levels of development in each specific domain. Three overriding structures offer markers to assess professional growth: (1) self- and other-awareness: cognitive and affective, (2) motivation, and (3) autonomy. The structure of self- and other-awareness: cognitive and affective combines cognitive and affective components indicating where the practitioner is regarding self-preoccupation, awareness of the client's world, and enlightened self-awareness. This structure reflects the practitioner's cognitive and affective knowledge base and their ability to use this knowledge in a professional setting. The motivation structure captures the trainee's interest, investment, and effort in training and practice. This structure is affected by the trainee's awareness of cognitive and affective components of training and practice settings, which vary considerably from clarity to ambiguity, self-absorption to empathy, and anxiety to confidence. A trainee might find himself confused, self-absorbed, and anxious, perhaps stalling his perceived control and motivation to engage willingly in learning and practising within his profession. The autonomy structure reflects the degree of dependence or independence a trainee feels. Beginners often depend heavily on their supervisors at the outset of training, growing counter-dependent (i.e., professional adolescence) and eventually independent.

Here is an illustration of levels using one domain, intervention skills competence. At level one, a practitioner might feel anxious and self-focused working with a client, which means the practitioner falters in focusing on the client's content and in responding to the client or intervening. At level 2, the practitioner feels more comfortable with intervention skills, and connects through self- and other-awareness. At level 3, the practitioner blends insightful self-awareness with awareness of the client's experience during level 2, bringing a depth and breadth of perspective to the trainee. Here, the trainee illustrates an ability to plan and conduct effective treatments. Practitioners at level 3, though often not fully achieved, are typically considered experts by their colleagues and function creatively and fully across domains.

Rønnestad and Skovholt (2003) presented a model using data-driven research, with 100 counsellors showing development within six phases, as a formulation of 14 themes. These phases include: (1) lay helper (pre-training period), (2) beginning student (assigned to the first clients), (3) advanced student (practicum placement), (4) novice professional (first years after graduation), (5) experienced professional (more years of practice with various clients in different settings), and (6) senior professional (established professional who is regarded as a senior by others). Here are four themes: (1) professional development involves an increasing higher order of integration of the professional self and the personal self, (2) the focus of functioning shifts dramatically over time from external to internal, (3) continuous training is a prerequisite for optimal learning and professional development at all levels of experience, and (4) an intense commitment to learn propels the developmental process.

These characteristics of development show the movement from novice to experienced practitioner. Although novice practitioners feel anxious, doubt their abilities, and depend on their supervisors, the experienced practitioner becomes more client-centred and aware of the needs of oneself and others, which moulds better relationships with clients. Researchers in applied sport psychology reported similarities (e.g., Tod et al., 2007, 2009) and differences (e.g., Hutter et al., 2015) between sport psychology and counselling practitioners' development. Hutter et al. (2015) analysed the issues brought by 11 students in a European sport psychology post-master's degree programme. Though there were common supervisory issues (i.e., competence, purpose and direction, and professional ethics), they reported low frequencies and inter-rater agreement for emotional awareness, autonomy, theoretical identity, respect for individual differences, personal motivation, supervisory relationship, and personal issues.

Professional development

Most people reading this book hold an interest in practising as applied sport psychology practitioners and will find themselves somewhere on the continuum from neophyte to experienced practitioner. These practitioners represent the instruments for service delivery, and their developing competence relates directly to the person behind the practitioner (Poczwardowski & Sherman, 2011; Poczwardowski, 2017). The person and the practitioner set off on a journey to gain self-awareness and self-knowledge, to reveal their beliefs, and to explore their core values. This groundwork generates a congruent philosophy of practice (Lindsay et al., 2007), a coherent professional identity (Tod et al., 2017), and a sense of authenticity in who they are and what they do (Friesen & Orlick, 2010; Wadsworth et al., 2021). Without deep reflection, however, the opportunity to challenge and change one's beliefs about themselves, others, and the world when opportunities present themselves might be lost. These opportunities, moments, or critical moments (Nesti et al., 2012) represent the richness of life and professional experiences which permit us to make sense, and take stock of, who we are as people. In short, critical moments offer the chance to confront one's anxiety about one's identity (Nesti et al., 2012). Perhaps more critically, critical moments might reflect stages of professional development.

Professional structures for support

Supervision

Supervision usually includes more experienced practitioners supervising or working with less experienced practitioners to help them improve their knowledge, skills, and ethical practice. This partnership ought to ensure an ethically informed and effective service delivery. The nature and frequency of supervision varies; however, supervisees learn from reflection, conceptualisation (thinking), planning, and concrete experiences (feeling and doing) (Milne, 2009). Supervisees need opportunities to practise learning theory and practice and a meaningful space to reflect on development. Van Raalte and Andersen (2000) suggested that "supervision is something sport psychology practitioners need to be giving and receiving as long as they practise" (p. 154). The evidence from the research, however, suggests supervision might not hold the firm foundation it should have. Watson et al. (2004) and Winstone and Gervis (2006) reported that more than 75% of Association of Applied Sport Psychology (AASP) professional accredited/certified practitioners were not being formally supervised, and 33% of UK-accredited sport psychology consultants (SPCs) had never received formal supervision. McEwan and Tod (2015) noted that the SPCs within their investigation had discontinued formal supervision after competing training and certification. With formal training routes for practitioners in sport and exercise psychology expanding, it is likely that trainees who graduate from training programmes will continue the supervision process in their professional careers. Professional supervision offers a framework of challenge and support that cultivates a practitioner's personal and professional development to ensure effective professional practice (Winstone & Gervis, 2006). To believe that one's supervision finishes after accreditation misses the point of supervision and the significance of supervision as long as we practise.

Supervision gives opportunities for the supervisee and the supervisor to learn, grow, and practise better than before. At the outset of one's training, a supervisor helps separate the wheat from the chaff – what matters from what does not matter. For example, we can learn to identify feelings from personal issues and those stimulated by clients (i.e., client's behaviour) and the mix between the two (Hill, 2020). We can learn along with our supervisor by establishing supervision sessions to stimulate learning and development. If a client gives us consent to record a session, we can play back recordings in our supervision session. The recordings stimulate a moment-by-moment reflection on our actions and our intentions with the client and the client's response to our interventions as a sport psychology practitioner. Some university doctoral programmes set process reports as an assessment of training and client work to understand the theory, skills, and practices of the trainee. Trainees write process reports, which are descriptions of the practitioner's method, techniques, and metacommunication of a therapeutic encounter (Bor & Watts, 2017; Moffat & McCarthy, 2023).

What is supervision? Supervision includes a range of activities, like quality assurance of practice, management of service delivery, and case supervision. The bottom line is that supervisors oversee the work of supervisees with clients. Carroll (1996) presented seven key tasks of supervision: (1) creating a learning relationship, (2) teaching, (3) counselling, (4) evaluation, (5) consulting, (6) monitoring administrative aspects, and (7) professional and ethical issues. Each supervisor supervises according to the needs of the supervisee with a mix of personal and professional development to help the supervisee make sense of their experiencing. Although one supervisor might lean towards teaching a therapeutic approach (e.g., CBT), another might lean towards a reflection on one's therapeutic practice.

McCann (2017) presented examples of models of supervision (the master/apprentice model, the collaborative model, the consultative model). All these models contain the developmental trajectory of the supervisee (Page & Woskett, 1994), the tasks and functions of supervision (Holloway, 1995), and the social role of a relationship between a supervisor and the supervisee. A good supervisor creates a trusting working alliance to meet the needs of the supervisee, which translates into increasing the effectiveness of the trainee's relationships with clients. Developing a worthwhile alliance means establishing clear roles, responsibilities, and duties for each party. This equal footing pushes towards parity in the relationship rather than a power dynamic favouring the supervisor. Supervisees might reflect upon the following questions to judge the quality, strength, and value of the supervisor-supervisee relationship (McCann, 2017):

1. Do our theoretical approaches fit well together?
2. Does my supervisor know how I learn best?
3. Are we clear on our goals of learning?
4. Do we hold a shared understanding of evidence-based practice?
5. Is my supervisory relationship collaborative or driven from the position of expertise?
6. Is there a compatibility in the evolving relationship?
7. Is the trainee's voice heard in the evaluation report?

Some of these questions form part of early discussions with a supervisor before drawing up a supervision contract, and others unfold as supervision unfolds across the supervisory process.

Group supervision

Some doctoral training programmes and independent supervisors run group supervision sessions, usually involving several trainees and one or more qualified practitioners. There are also group supervision sessions for qualified practitioners and trainees facilitated by one or more supervisors. In a typical university setting for trainees, the supervisor leads the session officially, gradually yielding the reins to the group as the trainees mature in their personal and professional development.

A surprising yet reassuring feature of group supervision lies in appreciating that others also experience the high and lows of training and practising as a sport psychology practitioner. This commonality and similar footing means each member gains from sharing experiences and support offered by the group, such as feedback, guidance, and reassurance. In supportive group supervision, one develops competence, confidence, creativity, and compassion (Proctor, 2008).

Although the learning outcomes might be set for the group supervision sessions, the group members and supervisor set the ground rules, time management parameters, supervisee participation, and session structure to maximise engagement and learning that matches the developmental needs of the members. The members might choose to follow a case-based approach for some sessions whereby a trainee shares a case from their caseload (e.g., 10 minutes). Next, the group asks questions about the case for detail or clarification (e.g., 10 minutes). Then, the group discuss the case while the presenter takes notes (15 minutes). Finally, the presenter summarises their learning from the experience (10 minutes). This method involves all trainees in presenting, questioning, discussing, summarising, and reflecting with each week's case. The supervisor offers their observations and summarises the themes emerging from the discussions.

Group supervision, though valuable, does not always meet the individual needs of the trainees. We also encourage one-to-one supervision, so the training needs of each supervisee are protected. Trainees on practicum placement might have a supervisor on site (e.g., at the organisation's headquarters) and group supervision at university. This model of supervision typically caters to the trainee when organised and reviewed regularly.

Two other support structures that criss-cross with supervision and practice-based evidence are research-informed practice and evidence-based practice.

Research-informed practice

Being a research-informed practitioner is distinguished from being a research-driven or a research-absent practitioner. Alongside being informed by research, we need to understand how other parts fit together to establish us as practitioners. The personal qualities we might overlook in the research process come to the fore in our work with a client, such as sense and sensibility, being oneself, openness, reading non-verbal cues, sensitivity to others' needs, and so much more. These personal qualities and relational skills form the foundation of a good practitioner in applied sport psychology. We might witness others eschew sensitivity in sport settings, yet this perceived weakness remains a strength. Like all strengths and weaknesses, we need to realise when a strength can be a weakness and when a weakness can be a strength. The ethos in sport settings might be "Keep calm" or "Keep a cool head" or "Stay strong" regardless of how one feels. So as a sport psychology practitioner, our work might involve sensitively enquiring about how one truly feels, and this experiential learning coalesces with the research-informed practice rather than one trumping the other.

One issue we witness in doctoral training programmes is first-class students with excellent research and writing skills who exhibit in their assessments the academic skills to gather knowledge, understand, analyse, synthesise, and evaluate psychological theories, processes, and human development – but who in their skills practice classes are beginning a learning journey unlike anything in their previous academic experience. Dealing with facts seems easy, whereas processing feelings (personal or others) seems overwhelming. Often the realisation that one's skills with a client fall below one's academic skills shocks and saddens trainees who are used to the upper end of the grading rubric. We need to learn how to be with people in a genuine, empathic, non-judgemental way with openness to help the client share their thoughts and feelings at the deepest level. Learning how we are in session with a fellow trainee humbles us because we realise how we relate to others. We cannot possibly know how another person thinks, feels, and acts because of the infinite possibilities based on their unique social, cultural, economic, and developmental experiences. It is our skills in relating to others that matter to allow us to use our professional and academic skills at the right moments. Our life experiences, coping with our plights, overcoming adversity, and working with others form assets in our relational work with clients.

Research-informed practice means leaning on the research to inform your practice, but equally, understanding how the research fits within your chosen processes from assessment through to evaluation. Equally, without research, it would be difficult to know what works best for whom, how and when, as sport psychology practitioners, so we reduce our chances of helping clients as much as possible. This delicate balance between research and practice means acknowledging the ethical challenges, advantages, and disadvantages of research to inform practice in applied sport psychology. Service users (e.g., clients, club managers, performance directors) wish to know how effective our work with them might be while considering their time and money invested. The culture of research, while strong in the university sector, remains negligible in most practice settings – so as we move into an era with many more sport psychology practitioners working in the field, we could learn about the effectiveness of our work with individuals, teams, squads, and staff for the betterment of our field and services.

Locating the evidence to suggest what things are happening or not happening in our work with clients is vital because it tells us what works for whom and why. Those who fund sport, especially Olympic sport, and policymakers want to know how best to allocate funding and resources for groups and communities. One way to do so is through evidence-based practice, allowing policymakers to judge how much to spend on which projects for different clients. The spread of evidence-based practice from medicine to nursing, social care, education, and the helping professions (e.g., counselling) is also in sport. It makes sense to learn from the best research and clinical expertise to help clients.

Evidence-based practice

The idea of evidence-based practice makes sense in applied sport psychology and many other fields of practice in psychology, but the weight of evidence often depends on the quality – or perceived quality – of the research design. For example, randomised controlled trials (RCTs) appear to carry more weight than case studies in sport and exercise psychology (Ivarsson & Andersen, 2016), but the name of a design (e.g., RCT) does not guarantee best practice in its use (Spring & Neville, 2011). For practitioners in sport and exercise psychology, we explore efficacy (i.e., the measurable effects of the intervention) and effectiveness (i.e., whether treatments have measurable effects in real-world settings). Efficacy studies help to identify and determine evidence-based treatments and represent the gold standard of studies to evaluate the effects of psychotherapy mostly using RCT designs (Andersen, 2011). In an efficacy study, the researcher randomly assigns participants to different conditions following a strict protocol to implement the treatment, creating strong internal validity. Despite its strengths, efficacy studies come with their weaknesses, too – for instance, how well do the results of the efficacy study transfer to real-world conditions in professional practice? – and with all the elements influencing the effectiveness of the intervention in real-world settings, efficacy studies often show biased intervention effects (Singal et al., 2014).

What is needed, therefore, is effectiveness studies or clinical utility studies (APA Presidential Task Force on Evidence-Based Practice, 2006) which explore the feasibility and effects of treatments across populations in real-world settings like high-performance sport. APA Presidential Task Force on Evidence-Based Practice (2006, p. 274) listed nine categories of research that might supply evidence for efficacy/effectiveness:

- Clinical observation (including individual case studies) and basic psychological science are valuable sources of innovations and hypotheses (the context of scientific discovery).
- Qualitative research can be used to describe the subjective, lived experiences of people, including participants in psychotherapy.
- Systematic case studies are particularly useful when aggregated – as in the form of practice research networks – for comparing individual patients with others with similar characteristics.

- Single-case experimental designs are particularly useful for establishing causal relationships in the context of an individual.
- Public health and ethnographic research are especially useful for tracking the availability, utilisation, and acceptance of mental health treatments, as well as suggesting ways of altering these treatments to maximise their utility in a given social context.
- Process outcome studies are especially valuable for identifying mechanisms of change.
- Studies of interventions as these are delivered in naturalistic settings (effectiveness research) are well suited for assessing the ecological validity of treatments.
- RCTs and their logical equivalents (efficacy research) are the standard for drawing causal inferences about the effects of interventions (context of scientific verification).
- Meta-analysis is a systematic means to synthesise results from multiple studies, test hypotheses, and quantitatively estimate the size of effects.

What we know from the research evidence is that the treatment method (Nathan & Gorman, 2002), the psychologist (Wampold, 2001), the treatment relationship (Norcross, 2002), and the patient/client (Bohart & Tallman, 1999) are all contributors to the success of psychological practice (APA Presidential Task Force on Evidence-Based Practice, 2006).

Some practitioners assume that they can rely on informal clinical observations to judge whether treatments are effective. We can all be fooled into believing that a treatment works even when it does not because of causes of spurious therapeutic effectiveness (CSTEs). CSTEs can make ineffective or even harmful interventions appear effective (Hall, 2011; Lilienfeld et al., 2013, 2014). Lilienfeld et al. (2014) shared a taxonomy of CSTE. The following are some of the most fundamental.

- **Placebo effects:** these effects capture the improvements occurring from the mere expectation of improvement (Shapiro & Shapiro, 1997). Expectancies of improvement seem reasonable when one engages in therapeutic support; however, these expectancies can lead practitioners and researchers to conclude that the specific ingredients of a treatment are efficacious when they are not.
- **Spontaneous remission:** originating in medicine, this term describes cases in which diseases improve or resolve on their own (Beyerstein, 1997). For example, Posternak and Zimmerman (2000) described a spontaneous remission rate of 52% among patients with major depressive disorder. The longer a person remains in therapy, the greater the likelihood extratherapeutic factors (e.g., natural healing process, coping, social support, and positive experiences in everyday life) contribute to observed or perceived enhancement (Lilienfeld et al., 2014).

- **Regression to the mean:** this is the statistical finding that extreme scores tend to become less extreme upon re-testing (Kruger et al., 1999). Most people enter treatment when their symptoms are most severe, so regression to the mean effects are maximised. In treatment, a regression to the mean might dupe the psychologist and client into believing that a treatment is effective when it is not. Campbell and Kenny (1999) commented, "it seems likely that regression toward the mean leads people to believe in the efficacy of the scientifically unjustified regimens. Many a quack has made a good living from regression toward the mean" (p. 48).
- **Effort justification:** this effect captures the psychological need of clients to justify the commitment of effort, energy, money, and time in treatment (Cooper, 1980; Cooper & Axsom, 1982). They may persuade themselves the therapy was beneficial, considering all their investment.
- **Multiple treatment interference:** as the name suggests, when clients choose to seek a treatment, they often obtain other interventions simultaneously, so it becomes impossible to attribute client change to the active ingredients of the chosen intervention.

It seems reasonable that clients and organisations want to know whether sport psychology services work. A client might wonder: "Which type of sport psychology practitioner best meets my needs? How many sessions do I need?" An organisation providing services to Olympic squads might wonder which type of service delivery is most cost-effective – how many sessions are optimum for each client over a quadrennial cycle? A student choosing to follow an independent route or a university training programme might wonder: "Which training (e.g., CBT) and training route (e.g., doctoral training) best leads me to employment?"

As scientist-practitioners, for example, we can add to the research base to answer these questions. The service users, carers, and providers discussed in the previous paragraph harbour their own motives for the answers research offers. Our encouragement here – alongside the guidance of our professional training bodies – means contributing to the research process, keeping up to date with what is happening in the field, and seeking to do our best work, always. Those who research and practice in applied sport psychology know we have answers to some of the questions posed, but we also have much to understand about how service delivery works and its overall cost-effectiveness, and why some clients improve and some clients do not improve.

We are always learning in our field of applied sport psychology and also from other fields like counselling, psychotherapy, and clinical psychology. For example, Cooper (2008) presented research from counselling and psychotherapy that captured how vital clients are to their own positive outcomes (especially their motivation) alongside hope and encouragement. A client's expectations ought to be high, yet not too high. Also, good outcomes for the client also depend on the qualities of the therapist (e.g., empathy) and the quality of the therapeutic relationship. When the client can offer feedback on how things are going during therapy, the feedback process improves outcomes for the client. In short, the feedback helps the therapist to tailor their services to meet the client's needs and expectations.

We need to know more about our field in applied sport psychology practice, and the gathering research from the field of practice means we are moving towards the answers we need, but without our research endeavour, there is a likihood that we cannot improve our understanding of the process of service delivery and the therapeutic outcomes for services and therefore build our professional recognition and credibility in the world of sport, exercise, and physical activity. Professional bodies across the world (e.g., APA, BPS, APS) work to promote research through seed funding for research projects, conferences, awards, bursaries for research, and its dissemination and publication of research journals.

The field of research in applied sport psychology thrives despite its relatively small community across the globe. Despite the usual research challenges (e.g., gathering research participants such as practitioners and clients) added to the ethical challenges of confidentiality, privacy, privilege, and consent in any research project, researchers continue to explore the factors that contribute to service delivery: client characteristics, practitioner characteristics, service delivery context, and the service delivery experience.

Reading and using research findings

Research forms one pillar of most training programmes in applied sport psychology, and although not all practitioners value being active researchers, research findings offer much for personal and professional development, especially the quality of service offered to clients. Reading research, however, forms one part of the process, with critical thinking about the research as a fundamental underpinning. When we read research but do not study it, it is likely that we will not translate the meaning of the research for practical use. For example, if we read a study illustrating the value of pre-therapy to the effectiveness of service delivery for clients, it might prompt us to read further about pre-therapy to answer other questions. How does pre-therapy work? Where, when, and how is it best undertaken? Which elements of pre-therapy are most critical? Are there specific questions to ask clients during the pre-therapy session? These questions and their answers allow us to act (i.e., change our way of working or stick with current practice) on the research we read and critically consume.

Summary

Taking care of ourselves as people and as practitioners forms the final chapter of this book; however, it is truly the first chapter of your work in the field.

We need to recognise how critical it is to care for ourselves as people and as practitioners by exploring the professional structures that support us, from supervision to group supervision, and leaning on research-informed practice and evidence-based practice to offer the best service possible to the community while ensuring that we maintain our fitness to practise and live flourishing lives.

References

Ainsworth, M. D. S., Blehar, M. C., Waters, E., & Wall, S. (1978). *Patterns of attachment: A psychological study of the strange situation.* Erlbaum.

Allen, M., & McCarthy, P. J. (2016). Be happy in your work: The role of positive psychology in working with change and performance. *Journal of Change Management, 16*(1), 55–74. https://doi.org/10.1080/14697017.2015.1128471.

American Psychological Association, Presidential Task Force on Evidence-Based Practice. (2006). Evidence-based practice in psychology. *American Psychologist, 61*(4), 271–285. https://doi.org/10.1037/0003-066X.61.4.271

Anastasi, A. (1992). What counsellors should know about the use and interpretation of psychological tests. *Journal of Counselling and Development, 70*(5), 610–615. https://doi.org/10.1002/j.1556-6676.1992.tb01670.x

Andersen, M. B. (2005). Touching taboos: Sex and the sport psychologist. In M. B. Andersen (Ed.), *Sport psychology in practice* (pp. 171–191). Human Kinetics.

Andersen, M. B. (2011). Who's mental, who's tough, and who's both? Mutton constructs dressed up as lamb. In D. J. Gucciardi, & S. Gordon (Eds.), *Mental toughness in sport: Developments in research and theory* (pp. 66–85). Routledge.

Andersen, M. B. (2020). Identity and the elusive self: Western and Eastern approaches to being no one. *Journal of Sport Psychology in Action, 11*(4), 243–253. https://doi.org/10.1080/21520704.2020.1825026.

Andersen, M. B., Aldridge, T., Williams, J. M., & Taylor, J. (1997). Tracking the training and careers of graduates of advanced degree programs in sport psychology, 1989 to 1994. *The Sport Psychologist, 11*, 326–344. https://doi.org/10.1123/tsp.11.3.326.

Andersen, M. B., & Mannion, J. (2011). If you see the Buddha on the football field – Tackle him. In D. Gilbourne, & M. B. Andersen (Eds.), *Critical essays in applied sport psychology* (pp. 173–192). Human Kinetics.

Andersen, M. B., Van Raalte, J. L., & Brewer, B. W. (2001). Sport psychology service delivery: Staying ethical while keeping loose. *Professional Psychology: Research and Practice, 32*, 12–18.

Anderson, A., Knowles, Z., & Gilbourne, D. (2004). Reflective practice for sport psychologists: Concepts, models, practical implications, and thoughts on dissemination. *The Sport Psychologist, 18*(2), 188–203. https://doi.org/10.1123/tsp.18.2.188.

Anderson, A., Miles, A., Robinson, P., & Mahoney, C. (2004). Evaluating the athlete's perception of the sport psychologist's effectiveness: What should we be assessing? *Psychology of Sport and Exercise, 5*, 255–277. https://doi.org/10.1016/S1469-0292(03)00005-0.

Angus, L. E., & Greenberg, L. S. (2011). *Working with narrative in emotion-focused therapy: Changing stories, healing lives.* American Psychological Association. https://doi.org/10.1037/12325-000.

Anshel, M. H., & Brinthaupt, T. M. (2014). Best practices for the use of inventories in sport psychology consulting. *Journal of Clinical Sport Psychology, 8*(4), 400–420. https://doi.org/10.1123/jcsp.2014-0045.

Aoyagi, M. W., Portenga, S. T., Poczwardowski, A., Cohen, A. B., & Statler, T. (2012). Reflections and directions: The profession of sport psychology past, present, and future. *Professional Psychology: Research and Practice, 43*(1), 32–38. https://doi.org/10.1037/a0025676.

Ardito, R. B., & Rabellino, D. (2011). Therapeutic alliance and outcome of psychotherapy: Historical excursus, measurements, and prospects for research. *Frontiers in Psychology.* https://doi.org/10.3389/fpsyg.2011.00270.

Baljon, M., & Pool, G. (2013). Hedgehogs in therapy. Empathy and insecure attachment in emotion-focused therapy. *Person-Centered & Experiential Psychotherapies, 12*(2), 112–125. https://doi.org/10.1080/14779757.2013.804652.

Ballantyne Dykes, F., Postings, T., De Winter, A., & Crouch, A. (2017). *Counselling skills and studies.* SAGE Publications.

Baltes, P., & Smith, J. (2004). Lifespan psychology: From developmental contextualism to developmental biocultural constructivism. *Research in Human Development, 1*(3), 123–144. https://doi.org/10.1207/s15427617rhd0103_1.

Barkham, M., Guthrie, E., Hardy, G. E., & Margison, F. (2017). *Psychodynamic-interpersonal therapy: A conversational model.* Sage.

Barkham, M., Mellor-Clark, J., Connell, J., & Cahill, J. (2006). A core approach to practice-based evidence: A brief history of the origins and applications of the CORE_OM and CORE system. *Counselling and Psychotherapy Research, 6*(1), 3–15. https://doi.org/10.1080/14733140600581218

Barnett, J. E., Lazarus, A. A., Vasquez, M. J. T., Moorehead-Slaughter, O., & Johnson, W. B. (2007). Boundary issues and multiple relationships: Fantasy and reality. *Professional Psychology: Research and Practice, 38*, 401–410.

Basevitch, I., Filho, E., Shipherd, A., Rossato, C., Gutierrez, O. (2016, September). *Apply, adapt, and achieve: Tips for a successful transition from graduation to the job market.* Symposium presented at the annual conference of the Association for Applied Sport Psychology, Phoenix, AZ.

Beaulieu, D. (2006). Impact techniques: Applying our knowledge of human memory systems to psychotherapy. *Annals of the American Psychotherapy Association, 9*(4), 23–29.

Beck, A. T. (1976). *Cognitive therapy and the emotional disorders.* International University Press.

Beck, A. T., Rush, A. J., Shaw, B. F., & Emery, G. (1979). *Cognitive therapy of depression.* Guildford.

Beckman, J., & Kellmann, M. (2003). Procedures and principles of sport psychological assessment. *The Sport Psychologist, 17*(3), 338–350. https://doi.org/10.1123/tsp.17.3.338.

Belar, C. D., & Perry, N. W. (1992). The national conference on scientist-practitioner education and training for the professional practice of psychology. *American Psychologist, 47*(1), 71–75. https://doi.org/10.1037/0003-066X.47.1.71.

Bernard, J. M. (1979). Supervisory training: A discrimination model. *Counselor Education and Supervision, 19*, 60–68.

Bernard, J. M. (1997). The discrimination model. In C. E. Watkins, Jr (Ed.), *Handbook of psychotherapy supervision* (pp. 310–327). John Wiley & Sons Inc.

Beyerstein, B. L. (1997). Why bogus therapies seem to work. *The Skeptical Inquirer, 21*(5), 29–34.

Bifulco, A., Moran, P. M., Ball, C., & Bernazzani, O. (2002). Adult attachment style. I: Its relationship to clinical depression. *Social Psychiatry and Psychiatric Epidemiology, 37*(2), 50–59. https://doi.org/10.1007/s127-002-8215-0.

Bohart, A., & Tallman, K. (1999). *How clients make therapy work: The process of active self-healing.* American Psychological Association.

Bohart, A. C., Elliott, R., Greenberg, L. S., & Watson, J. C. (2002). Empathy. In J. C. Norcross (Ed.), *Psychotherapy relationships that work: Therapist contributions and responsiveness to patients* (pp. 89–108). Oxford University Press.

Bond, T., & Mitchels, B. (2008). *Confidentiality and record keeping in counselling and psychotherapy.* SAGE Publications.

Bor, R., & Watts, M. (2017). *The trainee handbook.* SAGE Publications.

Borders, L. D., Brown, L. L. (2022). *The new handbook of counselling supervision.* Taylor and Francis.

Bordin, E. S. (1979). The generalizability of the psychoanalytic concept of the working alliance. *Psychotherapy: Theory, Research & Practice, 16*(3), 252–260. https://doi.org/10.1037/h0085885.

Bowlby, J. (1969). *Attachment and loss: Vol. 1. Attachment.* Basic Books.

Bowlby, J. (1973). *Attachment and loss: Vol. 2. Separation: Anxiety and anger.* Basic Books.

Bowlby, J. (1979). *The making and breaking of affectional bonds.* Tavistock.

Bowlby, J. (1982). Attachment and loss: Retrospect and prospect. *American Journal of Orthpsychiatry, 52*(4), 664–678. https://doi.org/10.1111/j.1939-0023.1982.tb01456.x.

Bowlby, J. (1988). *A secure base.* Basic Books.

Brackenridge, C. (2001). *Spoilsports: Understanding and preventing sexual exploitation in sports.* Routledge.

Brackenridge, C., & Fasting, K. (2005). The grooming process in sport. *Auto/Biography: An International and Interdisciplinary Journal, 13*, 33–52.

Brewer, B. W., Caldwell, C. M., Petitpas, A. J., Van Raalte, J. L., Pans, M., & Cornelius, A. E. (2021). Development and preliminary validation of a sport-specific self-report measure of identity foreclosure. *Journal of Clinical Sport Psychology, 15*(2), 105–120. https://doi.org/10.1123/jcsp.2019-0057.

British Psychological Society. (2018). Code of ethics and conduct. Retrieved from: https://www.bps.org.uk/sites/bps.org.uk/files/Policy%20-%20Files/BPS%20Code%20of%20Ethics%20and%20Conduct%20%28Updated%20July%202018%29.pdf.

Brown, D., Pryzwansky, W. B., & Schulte, A. C. (2011). *Psychological consultation and collaboration: Introduction to theory and practice* (7th ed.). Pearson Education.

Brown, J. L., & Cogan, K. D. (2006). Ethical clinical practice and sport psychology: When two worlds collide. *Ethics & Behavior, 16*, 15–23.

Bruner, M. W., Erikson, K., Wilson, B., & Cote, J. (2010). An appraisal of athlete development models through citation network analysis. *Psychology of Sport and Exercise, 11*(2), 133–139. https://doi.org/10.1016/j.sportpsych.2009.05.008.

Buckley, W. (2005, July 10). Black knight of the fairway. *Sunday Independent* (Sport), p. 12.

Bucknell, G. (2015). A big new world: A sport psychology placement student's findings. *Sport & Exercise Psychology Review, 11*(2), 82–85.

Butler, R. J., & Hardy, L. (1992). The performance profile: Theory and application. *The Sport Psychologist, 6*(3), 253–264. https://doi.org/10.1123/tsp.6.3.253.

Campbell, D. T., & Kenny, D. A. (1999). *A primer on regression artifacts.* Guilford Press.

Carless, D., & Douglas, K. (2013). Living, resisting, and playing the part of athlete: Narrative tensions in elite sport. *Psychology of Sport and Exercise, 14*(5), 701–708. https://doi.org/10.1016/j.psychsport.2013.05.003.

Carlstedt, R. A. (2013). *Evidence-based applied sport psychology: A practitioner's manual.* Springer.

Carroll, M. (1996). *Counselling supervision: Theory, skills and practice.* Cassell.

Castillo, E. A. (2022). A comprehensive and updated review of the performance profile technique. *The Sport Psychologist, 36,* 206–216. https://doi.org/10.1123/tsp.2022-0003.

Castillo, E. A., & Bird, M. D. (2021). The strengths-based performance profile (SBPP): A method for strengths-spotting and application in single-session consultations with athletes. *Journal of Sport Psychology in Action.* https://doi.org/10.1080/2152070 4.2021.1988782.

Castillo, E. A., Bird, M. D., & Chow, G. M. (2020). Implementation and evaluation of a standardized performance profile intervention with collegiate athletes: A comparison of the original and revised techniques. *Journal of Applied Sport Psychology,* Advanced online publication. https://doi.org/10.1080/10413200.2020.1862358.

Castillo, E. A., & Chow, G. M. (2020). Implementation and evaluation of a performance profile intervention with college dancers. *The Sport Psychologist, 34*(1), 1–10. https://doi.org/10.1123/tsp.2018–0138.

Castonguay, L. G., Eubanks, C. F., Goldfried, M. R., Muran, J. C., & Lutz, W. (2015). Research on psychotherapy integration: Building on the past, looking to the future. *Psychotherapy Research, 25,* 365–382. https://doi.org/10.1080/10503307.2015. 1014010.

Chow, G. M., & Gilson, T. A. (2018). Inventories using objective measures. In J. Taylor (Ed.), *Assessment in applied sport psychology* (pp. 83–100). Human Kinetics.

Committee on Professional Practice and Standards. (2003). Legal issues in the professional practice of psychology. *Professional Psychology: Research and Practice, 34,* 595–600.

Cooper, J. (1980). Reducing fears and increasing assertiveness: The role of dissonance reduction. *Journal of Experimental Social Psychology, 16,* 199–213. http://dx.doi.org/ 10.1016/0022–1031(80)90064–5.

Cooper, J., & Axsom, D. (1982). Effort justification in psychotherapy. In G. W. Weary, & H. Mirels (Eds.), *Integrations of clinical and social psychology.* Oxford University Press.

Cooper, M. (2008). *Essential research findings in counselling and psychotherapy: The facts are friendly.* Sage.

Cooper, M., & Norcross, J. C. (2016). A brief, multidimensional measure of clients' therapy preferences: The Cooper-Norcross inventory of preferences (C-NIP). *International Journal of Clinical and Health Psychology, 16*(1), 87–98.

Corrie, S., & Lane, D. A. (2017). Developing skills in formulation. In R. Bor, & M. Watts (Eds.), *The trainee handbook: A guide for counselling and psychotherapy trainees.* SAGE Publications.

Cote, J., Strachan, L., & Fraser-Thomas, J. (2007). Participation, personal development and performance through sport. In N. L. Holt (Ed.), *Positive youth development through sport* (pp. 34–45). Routledge.

Cote, J., Turnnidge, J., Murata, A., Mcguire, C. S., & Martin, L. J. (2020). Youth sport research: Describing the integrated dynamic elements of the personal assets framework. *International Journal of Sport Psychology, 51,* 562–578. https://doi.org/10.7352/IJSP.2020.51.562.

Cozolino, L. (2014). *The neuroscience of human relationships: Attachment and the developing social brain* (2nd ed.). W. W. Norton & Company.

Cripps, B. (2017). *Psychometric testing: Critical perspectives.* Wiley.

Cruickshank, A., & Collins, D. (2015). Illuminating and applying "the dark side": Insights from elite team leaders. *Journal of Applied Sport Psychology, 27,* 249–267. http://dx.doi.org/10.1080/10413200.2014.982771.

Culley, S., & Bond, T. (2011). *Integrative counselling skills in action.* SAGE Publications.

Cutts, L. A. (2013). Considering a social justice agenda for counselling psychology in the United Kingdom. *Counselling Psychology Review, 28*(2), 8–16.

Danish, S. J. (1985). Psychological aspects in the care and treatment of athletic injuries. In P. F. Vinger, & E. F. Hoerner (Eds.), *Sports injuries: The unthwarted epidemic* (2nd ed., pp. 345–353). John Wright.

Danish, S. J., Petitpas, A. J., & Hale, B. D. (1993). Life development intervention for athletes: Life skills through sports. *The Counselling Psychologist, 21,* 352–385. https://doi.org/10.1177/0011000093213002.

Davies, A. (2018). From 'disorder' to 'challenge': Using lifespan development theories to reframe distress. *Counselling Psychology Review, 33*(1), 24–32.

de Bressy de Guast, V., Golby, J., Van Wersch, A., & d'Arripe-Longueville, F. (2013). Psychological skills training of an elite wheelchair water-skiing athlete: A single-case study. *Adapted Physical Activity Quarterly, 30,* 351–372.

Deci, E. L., & Ryan, R. M. (1985). *Intrinsic motivation and self-determination in human behavior.* Plenum.

Deci, E. L., & Ryan, R. M. (2002). Self-determination research: Reflections and future directions. In E. L. Deci, & R. M. Ryan (Eds.), *Handbook of self-determination research* (pp. 431–441). University of Rochester Press.

Douglas, K., & Carless, D. (2006). Performance, discovery, and relational narratives among women professional tournament golfers. *Women in Sport and Physical Activity Journal, 15*(2), 14–27.

Dryden, W. (2017). *Single-session integrated CBT.* Taylor and Francis.

Dryden, W. (2020). Help yourself with single-session therapy. Taylor & Francis.

Egan, G. (1984). People in systems: A comprehensive model for psychosocial education and training. In D. Larson (Ed.), *Teaching psychological skills: Models for giving psychology away.* Brooks/Cole.

Egan, G., & Reese, R. J. (2021). *The skilled helper: A client-centred approach* (3rd ed.). Cengage.

Ekman, P. (1993). Facial expression and emotion. *American Psychologist, 48*(4), 384–392. https://doi.org/10.1037/0003-066X/48/4/384.

Ekman, P., & Friesen, W. V. (1969). The repertoire of nonverbal behaviour: Categories, origins, usage, and coding. *Semiotica, 1,* 49–98. https://doi.org/10.1515/semi.1969.1.1.49.

Elliott, R., & Greenberg, L. (2021). *Emotion-focused counselling in action.* SAGE Publications.

Embleton Tudor, L., Keemar, K., Tudor, K., Valentine, J., & Worrall, M. (2004). *The person-centred approach: A contemporary introduction.* Palgrave.

Epstein, R. S., & Simon, R. I. (1990). The exploitation index: An early warning indicator of boundary violations in psychotherapy. *Bulletin of the Menninger Clinic, 54*(4), 450–465.

Equality Act. (2010). *Equality act.* The Stationary Office: S.N. Retrieved from: https://www.legislation.gov.uk/ukpga/2010/15/contents.

Erikson, E. H. (1959). Identity and the life cycle: Selected papers. *Psychological Issues, 1*, 1–171.

Erikson, E. H. (1963). *Childhood and society* (2nd ed.). Newton.

Eubank, M., Nesti, M., & Cruickshank, A. (2014). Understanding high performance sport environments: Impact for the professional training and supervision of sport psychology. *Sport and Exercise Psychology Review, 10*, 30–37.

Feltham, C., & Dryden, W. (2006). *Brief counselling: A practical, integrative approach.* Open University Press.

Feltham, C., Hanley, T., & Winter, LA. (2017). *The SAGE handbook of counselling and psychotherapy.* SAGE Publications.

Fernández-Álvarez, H., Consoli, A. J., & Gómez, B. (2016). Integration in psychotherapy: Reasons and challenges. *American Psychologist, 71*, 820–830. https://doi.org/10.1037/amp0000100.

Fifer, A. M., Henschen, K., Gould, D., & Ravizza, K. (2008). What works when working with athletes. *The Sport Psychologist, 22*(3), 356–377. https://doi-org.gcu.idm.oclc.org/10.1123/tsp.22.3.356.

Fitzpatrick, S. J., Monda, S. J., & Wooding, C. B. (2016). Great expectations: Career planning and training experiences of graduate students in sport and exercise psychology. *Journal of Applied Sport Psychology, 28*, 14–27. doi: 10.1080/10413200.2015.1052891.

Fletcher, D., & Wagstaff, C. R. D. (2009). Organizational psychology in elite sport: Its emergence, application and future. *Psychology of Sport & Exercise, 10*, 427–434. doi: 10.1016/j.psychsport. 2009.03.009.

Fogaca, J. L., Watson, J. C., & Zizzi, S. J. (2020). The journey of service delivery competence in applied sport psychology: The arc of development for new professionals. *Journal of Clinical Sport Psychology, 14*, 109–126. https://doi.org/10.1123/jcsp.2019-0010.

Fonagy, P. (2001). The human genome and the representational world: The role of early mother-infant interaction in creating an interpersonal interpretative mechanism. *Bulletin of the Menninger Clinic, 65*, 427–448.

Fonagy, P., & Target, M. (2002). Early intervention and the development of self-regulation. *The Psychoanalytic Inquiry, 22*, 307–335.

Forrest, K. A. (2008). Attachment and attention in sport. *Journal of Clinical Sport Psychology, 2*, 242–257.

Frankel, Z. E., Holland, J. M., & Currier, J. M. (2012). Encounters with boundary challenges: A preliminary model of experienced psychotherapists' psychotherapists' working strategies. *Journal of Contemporary Psychotherapy, 42*, 101–112.

Friesen, A., & Orlick, T. (2010). A qualitative analysis of holistic sport psychology consultants' professional philosophies. *The Sport Psychologist, 24*(2), 227–244. doi: 10.1123/tsp.24.2.227.

Frost, R. (2015). A servant to servants. Retrieved from https://www.robertfrost.org/a-servant-to-servants.jsp.

Gardner, F. L. (2001). Applied sport psychology in professional sports: The team psychologist. *Professional Psychology, Research and Practice, 32*, 34–39. doi: 10.1037/0735- 7028.32.1.34.

Gardner, F. L. (2009). Efficacy, mechanisms of change and the scientific development of sport psychology. *Journal of Clinical Sport Psychology, 3,* 139–155.

Gardner, & Moore, Z. E. (2004). The multi-level classification system for sport psychology (MCS-SP). *The Sport Psychologist, 18*(1), 89–109. https://doi.org/10.1123/tsp.18.1.89.

Gardner, F. L., & Moore, Z. E. (2006). *Clinical sport psychology.* Human Kinetics.

Gendlin, E. T. (1996). *Focusing-oriented psychotherapy: A manual of the experiential method.* Guilford Press.

Giges, B. (1998). Psychodynamic concepts in sport psychology: Comment on Strean and Strean (1998). *The Sport Psychologist, 12,* 223–227.

Gill, E. L. (2008). Mental health in college athletics: It's time for social work to get in the game. *Social Work, 53,* 85–88. PubMed doi: 10.1093/sw/53.1.85.

Glosoff, H. L., Herlihy, S. B., Herlihy, B., & Spence, E. B. (1997). Privileged communication in the psychologist–client relationship. *Professional Psychology: Research and Practice, 28,* 573–581.

Gnacinski, S., Post, P., Simpson, D., & Christensen, D. (2016, September). *Looking to the next generation of professionals: Student members' needs, interests, and perceived value of AASP membership.* Poster presented at the annual conference of Association for Applied Sport Psychology, Phoenix, AZ.

Gollwitzer, P. M., & Wicklund, R. A. (1985). Self-symbolizing and the neglect of others' perspectives. *Journal of Personality and Social Psychology, 48,* 702–715.

Govindji, R., & Linley, P. A. (2007). Strengths use, self-concordance and well-being: Implications for strengths coaching and coaching psychologists. *International Coaching Psychology Review, 2,* 143–153.

Grange, P. (2010). Professional athletes. In S. J. Hanrahan, & M. B. Andersen (Eds.), *Routledge handbook of applied sport psychology: A complete guide for students and practitioners* (p. 396–413). Routledge.

Greenberg, L. S. (2002). *Emotion-focused therapy: Coaching clients to work through their feelings.* APA Press.

Greenberg, L. S., & Pascual-Leone, A. (2006). Emotion in psychotherapy: A practice-friendly research review. *Journal of Clinical Psychology, 62*(5), 611–630.

Greenberger, D., & Padesky, C. A. (1995). *Mind over mood: A cognitive therapy treatment manual for clients.* Guilford Press.

Guggenbuhl-Craig, A. (1971). *Power in the helping professions.* Spring.

Guthiel, T., & Gabbard, G. (1993). The concept of boundaries in clinical practice: Theoretical and risk management dimensions. *American Journal of Psychiatry, 150,* 188–196.

Haberl, P., & Peterson, K. (2006). Olympic-sized ethical dilemmas: Issues and challenges for sport psychology consultants on the road and at the Olympic games. *Ethics & Behavior, 16,* 25–40.

Hall, H. (2011). Evidence-based medicine, tooth-fairy science, and Cinderella medicine. *Skeptic, 17*(1), 4–5.

Hanley, T., & Amos, I. (2017). The scientist-practitioner and the reflective-practitioner. In V. Galbraith (Ed.), *Topics in applied psychology: Counselling psychology.* Wiley.

Hanley, T., Cutts, L., Gordon, R., & Scott, A. (2013). A research-informed approach to counselling psychology. In G. Davey (Ed.), *Applied psychology.* Wiley.

Hannan, T., Hanrahan, S., Andersen, M., & Gordon, S. (2010). Postgraduate training in sport psychology: Challenges and future directions. *Journal of Science and Medicine in Sport, 12*(2), E196. doi: 10.1016/j.sams,2009.10.409.

Hanrahan, S. J. (2010). Culturally competent practitioners. In S. J. Hanrahan, & M. B. Andersen (Eds.), *Routledge handbook of applied sport psychology: A comprehensive guide for students and practitioners* (pp. 460–468). Routledge.

Hanrahan, S. J. (2015). Psychological skills training for athletes with disabilities. *Australian Psychologist, 50*(2), 102–105. https://doi.org/10.1111/ap.12083.

Hanrahan, S. J., & Andersen, M. B. (2010). *Routledge handbook of applied sport psychology: A comprehensive guide for students and practitioners.* Taylor and Francis.

Harper, R. G., Wiens, A. N., & Matarazzo, J. D. (1978). *Nonverbal communication: The state of the art.* Wiley.

Hartveit, M., Thorsen, O., Biringer, E., Vanhaecht, K., Carlsen, B., & Aslaksen, A. (2013). Recommended content of referral letters from general practitioners to specialised mental health care: A qualitative multi-perspective study. *BMC Health Services Research, 13*(1), 329.

Hayes, J. A. (2004). The inner world of the psychotherapist; a program of research on countertransference. *Psychotherapy Research, 14*(1), 21–36. https://doi.org/10.1093/ptr/kph002.

Hays, K. F. (2006). Being fit: The ethics of practice diversification in performance psychology. *Professional Psychology, Research and Practice, 37,* 223–232.

Hays, K. F., & Brown, C. H. (2004). *You're on! Consulting for peak performance.* American Psychological Association.

Hays, R., Spike, N., Gupta, T. S., Hollins, J., & Veitch, J. (2002). A performance assessment module for experienced general practitioners. *Medical Education, 36*(3), 258–260. https://doi.org/10.1046/j.1365-2923.2002.01145.

Hawkins, P., & McMahon, A. (2020). *Supervision in the helping professions* (5th ed.). McGraw-Hill Education.

Health Care and Professions Council. (2016). Standards of conduct, performance, and ethics. Retrieved from: https://www.hcpc-uk.org/publications/standards/index.asp?id=38.

Hedberg, A. (2010). *Forms for the therapist.* Academic.

Henriksen, K., Stambulova, N., & Roessler, K. K. (2010). Holistic approach to athletic talent development environments: A successful sailing milieu. *Psychology of Sport and Exercise, 11*(3), 212–222. https://doi.org/10.1016/j.psychsport.2009.10.005.

Henschen, K., & Tenenbaum, G. (2005). Introduction. In G. D. Hackfort, J. L. Duda, & R. Lidor (Eds.), *Handbook of research in applied sport and exercise psychology: International perspectives.* Fitness Information Technology.

Hesse, E. (1999). The adult attachment interview: Historical and current perspectives. In J. Cassidy, & P. R. Shaver (Eds.), *Handbook of attachment: Theory, research and clinical applications.* Guilford Press.

Hesse, E., & Main, M. (2000). Disorganized infant, child, and adult attachment: Collapse in behavioral and attentional strategies. *Journal of Psychoanalytic Association, 48,* 1097–1127.

Hill, A. P. (2023). *The psychology of perfectionism in sport, dance, and exercise.* Routledge.

Hill, C. E. (2020). *Helping skills: Facilitating exploration, insight, and action* (5th ed.). American Psychological Association.

Hill, C. E., Gelso, C. J., Chui, H., Spangler, P. T., Hummel, A., Huang, T., . . . Miles, J. R. (2014). To be or not to be immediate with clients: The use and perceived effects of immediacy in psychodynamic/interpersonal psychotherapy. *Psychotherapy Research, 3,* 299–315. http://dx.doi.org/10.1080/10503307.2013.812262.

Holloway, E. (1995). *Clinical supervision: A systems approach.* Sage.

Horvath, S., & Rothlin, P. (2018). How to improve athletes' return of investment: Shortening questionnaires in the applied sport psychology setting. *Journal of Applied Sport Psychology, 30*, 241–248. doi: 10.1080/10413200.2017.1382020.

Hunter, M., & Struve, J. (1998). *The ethical use of touch in psychotherapy*. Sage Publications. https://doi.org/10.4135/9781483328102.

Hutter, R. I., Oldenhof-Veldman, T., & Oudejans, R. D. (2015). What trainee sport psychologists want to learn in supervision. *Psychology of Sport and Exercise, 16*, 101–109. doi: 10.1016/j.psychsport.2014.08.003.

Ivarsson, A., & Andersen, M. B. (2016). What counts as "evidence" in evidence-based practice? Searching for some fire behind all the smoke. *Journal of Sport Psychology in Action, 7*(1), 11–22. doi: 10.1080/21520704.2015.1123206.

Ivey, A. E., Ivey, M., & Zalaquett, C. (2018). *Intentional interviewing and counseling: Facilitating client development in a multicultural society* (9th ed.). Cengage Learning.

Jansen, J., van Weert, J. C. M., de Groot, J., van Dulmen, S., Heeren, T. J., & Bensing, J. M. (2010). Emotional and informational patient cues: The impact of nurses' responses on recall. *Patient Education and Counselling, 79*, 218–224.

Johns, H. (2012). *Personal development in counsellor training*. SAGE.

Johnson, S. M. (2018). *Attachment theory in practice*. Guilford Publications.

Johnson, U., & Andersen, M. (2019). On the Swedish road to becoming a professional practitioner in sport and exercise psychology: Students' views, hopes, dreams, and worries. *The Sport Psychologist, 33*(1), 75–83. https://doi.org/10.1123/tsp.2017-0137.

Johnstone, L., & Dallos, R. (2013). *Formulation in psychology and psychotherapy: Making sense of peoples problems*. Routledge.

Jones, G. (1993). The role of performance profiling in cognitive behavioural interventions in sport. *The Sport Psychologist, 7*(2), 160–172.

Karpman, S. (1976). Fairy tales and script drama analysis. *Transactional Analysis Bulletin, 7*(26), 39–43.

Kelly, G. A. (1955/1991). *The psychology of personal constructs: A theory of personality* (Vol. 1). Routledge. (Original work published 1955).

Kennerley, H., Kirk, J., & Westbrook, D. (2017). *An introduction to cognitive behaviour therapy: Skills and applications*. SAGE Publications.

Kipp, L. E. (2018). Developmental considerations for working with young athletes. In C. J. Knight, C. G. Harwood, & D. Gould (Eds.), *Sport psychology for young athletes*. Routledge.

Kitchener, K. S. (1984). Intuition, critical evaluation and ethical principles: The foundation for ethical decisions in counselling psychology. *Counselling Psychologist, 12*, 43–55.

Knapp, S., & Slattery, J. M. (2004). Professional boundaries in nontraditional settings. *Professional Psychology: Research and Practice, 35*, 553–558.

Knowles, Z., Gilbourne, D., Cropley, B., & Dugdill, L. (2014). *Reflective practice in the sport and exercise sciences: Contemporary issues*. Routledge.

Korzybski, A. (1933/1958). *Science and sanity: An introduction to non-Aristotelian systems and general semantics*. Institute of General Semantics.

Kruger, J., Savitsky, K., & Gilovich, T. (1999). Superstition and the regression effect. *The Skeptical Inquirer, 23*, 24–29.

Lama, D. (1984). Altruism and the six perfections. In J. Hopkins, & E. Napper (Ed. & Trans.), *Kindness, clarity and insight* (pp. 43–56). Snow Lion.

Lambert, M. J., & Simon, W. (2008). The therapeutic relationship: Central and essential in psychotherapy outcome. In S. F. Hick, & T. Bien (Eds.), *Mindfulness and the therapeutic relationship* (pp. 19–33). Guilford.

Lazarus, R. S. (1991). Progress on a cognitive-motivational-relational theory of emotion. *American Psychologist, 46,* 819–834.

Lazarus, R. S. (2000). Toward better research on stress and coping. *American Psychologist, 55,* 665–673.

Leahy, T. (2008). Editor's note: Understanding and preventing sexual harassment and abuse in sport: Implications for the sport psychology profession. *International Journal of Sport and Exercise Psychology, 6,* 351–353.

Leahy, T. (2010). Working with adult athlete survivors of sexual abuse. In S. J., Hanrahan, & M. B. Andersen (Eds.), *Routledge handbook of applied sport psychology: A comprehensive guide for students and practitioners* (pp. 303–312). Routledge.

Leahy, T., Pretty, G., & Tenenbaum, G. (2003). Childhood sexual abuse narratives in clinically and non-clinically distressed adult survivors. *Professional Psychology: Research and Practice, 34,* 657–665.

Leahy, T., Pretty, G., & Tenenbaum, G. (2004). Perpetrator methodology as a predictor of traumatic symptomatology in adult survivors of childhood sexual abuse. *Journal of Interpersonal Violence, 19,* 521–540.

Leary, M. R. (2004). *The curse of the self: Self-awareness, egotism, and the quality of human life.* Oxford University Press.

LeUnes, A. (2008). *Sport psychology* (4th ed.). Psychology Press.

Lilienfeld, S. O., Ritschel, L. A., Lynn, S. J., Cautin, R. L., & Latzman, R. D. (2013). Why many clinical psychologists are resistant to evidence-based practice: Root causes and constructive remedies. *Clinical Psychology Review, 33*(7), 883–900. https://doi.org/10.1016/j.cpr.2012.09.008.

Lilienfeld, S. O., Ritschel, L. A., Lynn, S. J., Cautin, R. L., & Latzman, R. D. (2014). Why ineffective psychotherapies appear to work: A taxonomy of causes of spurious therapeutic effectiveness. *Perspectives on Psychological Science, 9*(4), 355–387. https://doi.org/10.1177/1745691614535216.

Lindsay, P., Breckon, J. D., Thomas, O., & Maynard, I. W. (2007). In pursuit of congruence: A personal reflection on methods and philosophy in applied practice. *The Sport Psychologist, 21*(3), 335–352. doi: 10.1123/tsp.21.3.335.

Linley, P. A., & Burns, G. W. (2010). Strengths spotting. In G. W. Burns (Ed.), *Happiness, healing, enhancement: Your casebook collection for applying positive psychology in therapy* (pp. 3–14). Wiley.

Linnemeyer, R. M., & Brown, C. (2010). Career maturity and foreclosure in student athletes, fine arts students, and general college students. *Journal of Career Development, 37*(3), 616–634. doi: 10.1177/0894845309357049.

López, R., & Levy, J. (2013). Student athletes' perceived barriers to and preferences for counsellor counseling. *Journal of College Counseling, 16,* 19–31. doi: 10.1002/j.2161-1882.2013.00024.x.

Lubker, J. R., Visek, A. J., Geer, J. R., & Watson, J. C. (2008). Characteristics of an effective sport psychology consultant: Perspectives from athletes and consultants. *Journal of Sport Behavior, 31,* 147–165.

Luepker, E. T. (2010). Records: Purposes, characteristics, and contents for protecting our clients and ourselves. In S. J. Hanrahan, & M. B. Andersen (Eds.), *Routledge handbook of applied sport psychology: A comprehensive guide for students and practitioners.* Taylor and Francis.

Luepker, E. T. (2022). *Record keeping in psychotherapy and counseling: Ethics, practice, and supervision*. Routledge.

Luft, J., & Ingham, H. (1955). *The Johari Window: A graphic model for interpersonal relations*. University of California, Western Training Lab.

Mack, R. J., Breckon, J. D., O'Halloran, P. D., & Butt, J. (2018). Enhancing athlete engagement in sport psychology interventions using motivational interviewing: A case study. *The Sport Psychologist*, *33*(2), 159–168. doi: 10.1123/tsp.2018-0053.

Main, M. (2000). The organized categories of infant, child, and adult attachment: Flexible vs. inflexible attention under attachment-related stress. *Journal of the American Psychoanalytic Association*, *48*, 1055–1096.

Maniar, S. D., Curry, L. A., Sommers-Flanagan, J., & Walsh, J. A. (2001). Student-athlete preferences in seeking help when confronted with sport performance problems. *The Sport Psychologist*, *15*, 205–223.

Marcia, J. (1966). Development and status of ego-identity status. *Journal of Personality and Social Psychology*, *3*(5) 551–558. PubMed ID: 5939604. doi: 10.1037/h0023281.

Marshall, D., Quinn, C., Child, D., Shenton, D., Pooler, J., Forber, S., et al. (2016). What IAPT services can learn from those who do not attend. *Journal of Mental Health*, *25*, 410–415.

Martens, R., Vealey, R. S., & Burton, D. (1990). *Competitive anxiety in sport*. Human Kinetics.

Martin, D. R. F., Quartiroli, A., & Wagstaff, C. R. D. (2021). An exploration of sport psychology professional quality of life in British neophyte practitioners. *The Sport Psychologist*, *35*(4), 329–339. https://doi.org/10.1123/tsp.2021-0062.

Martin, D. T., Andersen, M. B., & Gates, W. (2000). Using profile of mood states (POMS) to monitor high-intensity training in cyclists: Group versus case studies. *The Sport Psychologist*, *14*, 138–156. doi: 10.1123/tsp.14.2.138.

Martin, E. A., Winter, S., & Holder, T. (2017). An exploration of trainee practitioners' experiences when using observation. *The Sport Psychologist*, *31*(2), 160–172. doi: 10.1123/tsp.2016-0019.

Martin, E. A., Winter, S., & Holder, T. (2020). Land ahoy! Guidelines for navigating the choppy waters of observation practice. *Journal of Sport Psychology in Action*, *11*(1), 34–44. doi: 10.1080/21520704.2019.1678536.

Martindale, A., & Collins, D. (2010). But why does what works work? A response to Fifer, Henschen, Gould, and Ravizza, 2008. *The Sport Psychologist*, *24*(1), 113–116. https://doi.org/10.1123/tsp.24.1.113.

Martindale, A., & Collins, D. (2013). The development of professional judgment and decision making expertise in applied sport psychology. *The Sport Psychologist*, *27*(4), 390–399. https://doi.org/10.1123/tsp.27.4.390.

Maslach, C., & Leiter, M. P. (2008). Early predictors of job burnout and engagement. *Journal of Applied Psychology*, *93*(3), 498. https://doi. org/10.1037/0021-9010.93.3.498.

Maslow, A. (1943). A theory of human motivation. *Psychological Review*, *50*, 370–396.

Maslow, A. (2013). *A theory of human motivation*. Wilder Publications.

May, R. (1993). *The art of counselling*. Souvenir Press Ltd.

McCann, D. (2017). Supervision: Making it work for you. In R. Bor, & M. Watts (Eds.), *The trainee handbook; A guide for counselling and psychotherapy trainees* (pp. 346–368). SAGE Publications.

McCann, S. C. (2000). Doing sport psychology at the really big show. In M. B. Andersen (Ed.), *Doing sport psychology* (pp. 209–222). Human Kinetics.

McCarthy, P. J., Gupta, S., & Burns, L. (2023). *Cognitive behaviour therapy in sport and performance: An applied practice guide*. Routledge.

McCarthy, P. J., & Jones, M. V. (2013). *Becoming a sport psychologist*. Routledge.

McCarthy, P. J., & Moffat, Z. L. (2023). *Counselling skills in applied sport psychology*. Routledge.

McEwan, H. E., & Tod, D. (2015). Learning experiences contributing to service-delivery competence in applied psychologists: Lessons for sport psychologists. *Journal of Applied Sport Psychology, 27*(1), 79–93. https://doi.org/10.1080/10413200.2014.952460.

McEwan, H. E., Tod, D., & Eubank, M. (2019). The rocky road to individuation: Sport psychologists' perspectives on professional development. *Psychology of Sport and Exercise, 14.* https://doi.oeg/10.1016/j.psychsport.2019.101542

McLeod, J. (1997). *Narrative and psychotherapy*. Sage.

McLeod, J. (2019). *An introduction to counselling and psychotherapy: Theory, research and practice*. McGraw-Hill Education.

McLeod, J., & McLeod, J. (2014). *Personal and professional development for counsellors, psychotherapists and mental health practitioners*. McGraw-Hill Education.

McLeod, J., & McLeod, J. (2022). *Counselling skills: Theory, research and practice* (3rd ed.). McGraw-Hill Education.

McNair, D. M., Lorr, M., & Droppleman, L. (1992). *Revised manual for the profile of mood states*. Educational and Industrial Testing Service.

Mearns, D. (2004). Problem-centered is not person-centered. *Person-Centered & Experiential Psychotherapies, 3*(2), 88–101. https://doi.org/10.1080/14779757.2004.9688335.

Mearns, D., & Cooper, M. (2018). *Working at relational depth in counselling and psychotherapy* (2nd ed.). SAGE Publications.

Meichenbaum, D., & Turk, D. C. (1987). *Facilitating treatment adherence: A practitioner's guidebook*. Plenum.

Meijen, C., Turner, M., Jones, M. V., Sheffield, D., & McCarthy, P. J. (2020). A theory of challenge and threat states in athletes: A revised conceptualisation. *Frontiers in Psychology: Movement Science and Sport Psychology, 11*(126). doi: 10.3389/fpsyg.2020.00126.

Merry, T., & Haugh, S. (2020). *Learning and being in person-centred counselling* (3rd ed.). PCCS.

Meyer, A. (1935). The material of human nature and conduct. *American Journal of Psychiatry, 92,* 271–274.

Mikulincer, M., & Shaver, P. R. (2016). *Attachment in adulthood: Structure, dynamics, and change* (2nd ed.). Guilford Press.

Milne, D. (2009). *Evidence-based clinical supervision and practice*. BPS Blackwell.

Moffat, Z. L., & McCarthy, P. J. (2023). Process reports in applied sport psychology: A tool for professional development. *Journal of Sport Psychology in Action.* https://doi.oeg/10.1080/21520704.2023.2195813.

Moffat, Z. L., McCarthy, P. J., Burns, L., & McCann, B. (2023). A lifespan approach to understanding and managing choking with a youth athlete. *The Sport Psychologist, 37*(1), 69–77. https://doi.org/10.1123/tsp.2022-0103.

Moore, Z. E. (2003). Ethical dilemmas in sport psychology: Discussion and recommendations for practice. *Professional Psychology, Research and Practice, 34*(6), 601–610. https://doi.org/10.1037/0735-7028.34.6.601.

Moran, A. P. (2018). *Managing your own learning at university: A practical guide* (3rd ed.). UCD Press.

Moran, A. P., & Toner, J. (2017). *A critical introduction to sport psychology.* Taylor & Francis.

Mytton, J., & Sequeira, H. (2017). Cognitive therapy. In C. Feltham, T. Hanley, & L. A. Winter (Eds.), *The SAGE handbook of counselling and psychotherapy.* SAGE Publications.

Nathan, P. E., & Gorman, J. M. (Eds.). (2002). *A guide to treatments that work* (2nd ed.). Oxford University Press.

Nelson-Jones, R. (2012). *Introduction to counselling skills* (4th ed.). SAGE Publications.

Nelson-Jones, R. (2016). *Basic counselling skills: A helper's manual* (4th ed.). SAGE.

Nesti, M., Littlewood, M., O'Halloran, L., Eubank, M., & Richardson, D. (2012). Critical moments in elite premiership football: Who do you think you are? *Physical Culture and Sport. Studies and Research, 56*(1), 23–32. doi: 10.2478/v10141-012-0027-y.

Nideffer, R. M. (1976). The Test of Attentional and Interpersonal Style. *Journal of Personality and Social Psychology, 34,* 394–404. doi: 10.1037/0022-3514.34.3.394.

Nideffer, R. M. (1993). *Predicting human behavior: A theory and test of attentional and interpersonal style.* Assessment Systems International.

Norcross, J. C. (Ed.). (2002). *Psychotherapy relationships that work: Therapist contributions and responsiveness to patient needs.* Oxford University Press.

Norcross, J. C. (2012). *Changeology.* Simon & Schuster.

Norcross, J. C., & Farber, B. A. (2005). Choosing psychotherapy as a career: Beyond "I want to help people". *Journal of Clinical Psychology, 61*(8), 939–943. doi: 10.1002/jclp.20175.

Norcross, J. C., & Lambert, M. J. (2011). Psychotherapy relationships that work II. *Psychotherapy, 48*(1), 4–8. https://doi.org/10.1037/a0022180.

Olivera, J., Braun, M., Penedo, M. G., & Roussos, A. (2013). A qualitative investigation of former clients' perception of change, reasons for consultation, therapeutic relationship, and termination. *Psychotherapy, 50,* 505–516.

Orlick, T., & Partington, J. (1987). The sport psychology consultant: Analysis of critical components as viewed by Canadian Olympic athletes. *The Sport Psychologist, 1,* 4–17.

Owton, H., Bond, K., & Tod, D. (2014). It's my dream to work with Olympic athletes: Neophyte sport psychologists' expectations and initial experiences regarding service delivery. *Journal of Applied Sport Psychology, 26,* 241–255.

Owton, H., & Sparkes, A. C. (2017). Sexual abuse and the grooming process in sport: Learning from Bella's story. *Sport, Education and Society, 22*(6), 732–743. https://doi.org/10.1080/13573322.2015.1063484.

Page, S., & Woskett, V. (1994). *Supervising the counsellor: A cyclical model.* Routledge.

Pearson, M., & Bulsara, C. (2016). Therapists' experiences of alliance formation in short-term counselling. *European Journal of Psychotherapy and Counselling, 18*(1), 75–92.

Pennebaker, J. W. (1995). *Emotion, disclosure and health.* American Psychological Association.

Petitpas, A. J., & France, T. (2010). Identity foreclosure in sport. In S. J. Hanrahan, & M. B. Andersen (Eds.), *Routledge handbook of applied sport psychology: A comprehensive guide for students and practitioners* (pp. 471–480). Routledge.

Petitpas, A. J., Giges, B., & Danish, S. J. (1999). The sport psychologist-athlete relationship: Implications for training. *The Sport Psychologist, 13*(3), 344–357. https://doi.org/10.1123/tsp.13.3.344.

Poczwardowski, A. (2017). Deconstructing sport and performance psychology consultant: Expert, person, performer, and self-regulator. *International Journal of Sport and Exercise Psychology, 17*(5), 427–444. doi: 10.1080/1612197X.2017.1390484.

Poczwardowski, A., Aoyagi, M., Fritze, T., & Laird, M. (2020). Revisiting "gaining entry": Roundtable discussion 25 years later. *The Sport Psychologist, 34*(2), 153–161. https://doi.org/10.1123/tsp.2018-0189.

Poczwardowski, A., & Sherman, C. P. (2011). Revisions to the sport psychology service delivery (SPSD) heuristic: Explorations with experienced consultants. *The Sport Psychologist, 25*(4), 511–531. doi: 10.1123/tsp.25.4.511.

Poczwardowski, A., Sherman, C. P., & Henschen, K. P. (1998). A sport psychology service delivery heuristic: Building on theory and practice. *The Sport Psychologist, 12*(2), 191–207. https://doi.org/10.1123/tsp.12.2.191.

Pope, K. S., & Keith-Spiegel, P. (2008). A practical approach to boundaries in psychotherapy: Making decisions, bypassing blunders, and mending fences. *Journal of Clinical Psychology, 64,* 638–652.

Portenga, S. T., Aoyagi, M. W., & Statler, T. A. (2012). Consulting on the run: Performance psychology and the preparation of USA track and field athletes for the Olympics. *Journal of Sport Psychology in Action, 3,* 98–108.

Posternak, M. A., & Zimmerman, M. (2000). Short-term spontaneous improvement rates in depressed outpatients. *The Journal of Nervous and Mental Disease, 188*(12), 799–804.

Postings, T. (2022). *Counselling skills.* SAGE Publications.

Proctor, B. (2008). *Group supervision: A guide to creative practice* (2nd ed.). SAGE Publications.

Quartiroli, A., Etzel, E. F., Knight, S. M., & Zakrajsek, R. A. (2019a). The multifaceted meaning of sport psychology professional quality of life. *Journal of Clinical Sport Psychology, 13*(4), 645–667. https://doi. org/10.1123/jcsp.2017-0048.

Quartiroli, A., Etzel, E. F., Knight, S. M., & Zakrajsek, R. A. (2019b). Fostering and sustaining sport psychology professional quality of life: The perspectives of senior-level, experienced sport psychology practitioners. *The Sport Psychologist, 33*(2), 148–158. https://doi.org/10.1123/tsp.2017-0140.

Quartiroli, A., Vosloo, J., Fisher, L., & Schinke, R. (2020). Culturally competent sport psychology: A survey of sport psychology professionals' perception of cultural competence. *The Sport Psychologist, 34*(3), 242–253. https://doi.org/10.1123/tsp.2019-0075.

Quartiroli, A., Wagstaff, C. R. D., & Etzel, E. F. (2019c). The professional quality of life of sport psychologists: Development of a novel conceptualization and measure. *Professional Psychology: Research and Practice, 50*(3), 155. https://doi. org/10.1037/pro0000213.

Råbu, M., & Haavind, H. (2018). Coming to terms: Client subjective experience of ending psychotherapy. *Counselling Psychology Quarterly, 31*(2), 223–242. https:// doi.org/10.1080/09515070.2017.1296410.

Ravizza, K. (1988). Gaining entry with athletic personnel for season-long consulting. *The Sport Psychologist, 2*(3), 243–254. https://doi.org/10.1123/tsp.2.3.243.

Reeves, A., & Bond, T. (2021). *Standard and ethics for counselling in action* (5th ed.). Sage Publications.

Reik, T. (1948). *Listening with the third ear.* Grove.

Rice, L. N., & Kerr, G. (1986). Measures of client and therapist vocal quality. In L. S. Greenberg, & W. M. Pinsof (Eds.), *The psychotherapeutic process: A research handbook* (pp. 73–105). Guilford Press.

Richards, M., & Bedi, R. P. (2015). Gaining perspective: How men describe incidents damaging the therapeutic alliance. *Psychology of Men and Masculinity, 16,* 170–182.

Rippere, V., & Williams, R. (Eds.). (1985). *Wounded healers: Mental health workers' experiences of depression*. Wiley.

Rogers, C. R. (1951). *Client-centered therapy*. Houghton Mifflin.

Rogers, C. R. (1959). A theory of therapy, personality, and interpersonal relationships, as developed in the client-centered framework. In S. Koch (Ed.), *Psychology: A study of a science. Vol. 3: Formulations of the person and the social context* (pp. 184–256). McGraw-Hill.

Rønnestad, M. H., & Skovholt, T. M. (2003). The journey of the counselors and therapist: Research findings and perspectives on professional development. *Journal of Career Development, 30*, 5–44. https://doi.org/10.1177/089484530303000102.

Rosenzweig, S. (1936). Some implicit common factors in diverse methods of psychotherapy. *American Journal of Orthopsychiatry, 6*(3), 412–415. https://doi.org/10.1111/j1939-0025.1936.tb05248.x.

Rothbaum, F., Weisz, J. R., & Snyder, S. S. (1982). Changing the world and changing the self: A two-process model of perceived control. *Journal of Personality and Social Psychology, 42*(1), 5–37. https://doi.org/10.1037/0022-3514.42.1.5.

Ryba, T. V., Stambulova, N. B., Si, G. Y., & Schinke, R. J. (2013). ISSP position stand: Culturally competent research and practice in sport and exercise psychology. *International Journal of Sport & Exercise Psychology, 11*(2), 123–142. https://doi.org/10.1080/1612197X.2013.779812.

Sasaki, J. Y., & Kim, H. S. (2017). Nature, nurture, and their interplay: A review of cultural neuroscience. *Journal of Cross-Cultural Psychology, 48*(1), 4–22. https://doi.org/10.1177/0022022116680481.

Schinke, R. J., Stambulova, N. B., Si, G., & Moore, Z. (2017). International society of sport psychology position stand: Athletes' mental health, performance, and development. *International Journal of Sport and Exercise Psychology, 16*(6), 622–639. https://doi.org/10.1080/1612197X. 2017.1295557.

Schore, A. N. (2014). The right brain is dominant in psychotherapy. *Psychotherapy, 51*(3), 388–397. https://doi.org/10.1037/a0037083.

Schön, D. (1991). *The reflective practitioner: How professionals think in action*. Arena.

Segal, J. C. (1985). *Phantasy in everyday life*. Pelican Books.

Segal, J. C. (2017). Psychodynamic psychotherapy. In C. Feltham, T. Hanley, & L. A. Winter (Eds.), *The SAGE handbook of counselling and psychotherapy* (pp. 205–209). SAGE Publications.

Sexton, T. L., & Whiston, S. C. (1994). The status of the counselling relationship: An empirical review, theoretical implications and research directions. *The Counselling Psychologist, 22*(1). https://doi.org/10.1177/0011000094221002.

Shapiro, A. K., & Shapiro, E. (1997). *The powerful placebo: From ancient priest to modern physician*. Johns Hopkins University Press.

Shapiro, E. L., & Ginzberg, R. (2003). To accept or not to accept: Referrals and the maintenance of boundaries. *Professional Psychology: Research and Practice, 34*(3), 258–263.

Sharp, L., & Hodge, K. (2011). Sport psychology consulting effectiveness: The sport psychology consultant's perspective. *Journal of Applied Sport Psychology, 23*(3), 360–376. https://doi.org/10.1080/10413200.2011.583619.

Sharp, L., & Hodge, K. (2013). Effective sport psychology consulting relationships: Two coach case studies. *The Sport Psychologist, 27*, 313–324.

Sharp, L. A., Hodge, K., & Danish, S. (2015). Ultimately it comes down to the relationship: Experienced consultants' views of effective sport psychology consulting. *The Sport Psychologist, 29*(4), 358–370. https://doi.org/10.1123/tsp.2014-0130.

Simms, J. (2011). Case formulation with a person-centred framework: An uncomfortable fit? *Counselling Psychology Review, 26*(2), 24–37.

Simons, J. P., & Andersen, M. B. (1995). The development of consulting practice in applied sport psychology: Some personal perspectives. *The Sport Psychologist, 9*(4), 449–468. https://doi.org/10.1123/tsp.9.4.449.

Singal, A. G., Higgins, P. D. R., & Waljee, A. K. (2014). A primer on effectiveness and efficacy trials. *Clinical and Translational Gastroenterology, 5*, e45. http://dx.doi.org/10.1038/ctg.2013.13.

Singer, R. N., & Anshel, M. H. (2006). Assessment, evaluation and counselling in sport. In J. Dosil (Ed.), *The sport psychologists handbook: A guide for sport-specific performance enhancement* (pp. 89–117). John Wiley & Sons.

Sly, D., Mellalieu, S. D., & Wagstaff, C. R. D. (2020). "It's psychology Jim, but not as we know it!": The changing face of applied sport psychology. *Sport, Exercise, and Performance Psychology, 9*(1), 87–101. https://doi.org/10.1037/spy0000163.

Smith, B., & Sparkes, A. C. (2009). Narrative inquiry in sport and exercise psychology: What can it mean, and why might we do it? *Psychology of Sport and Exercise, 10*, 1–11. https://doi.org/10.1016/j.psychsport.2008.01.004.

Smith, R. E., Schutz, R. W., Smoll, F. L., & Ptacek, J. T. (1995). Development and validation of a multidimensional measure of sport-specific psychological skills: The athletic coping skills inventory-28. *Journal of Sport & Exercise Psychology, 17*, 379–398. https://doi.org/10.1123/jsep.17.4.379.

Sparkes, A. C. (2004). Bodies, narratives, selves, and autobiography: The example of Lance Armstrong. *Journal of Sport and Social Issues, 28*, 397–428.

Spring, B., & Neville, K. (2011). Evidence-based practice in clinical psychology. In D. H. Barlow (Ed.), *The Oxford handbook of clinical psychology* (pp. 128–149). Oxford University Press.

Stafford, M. R., & Bond, T. (2020). *Counselling skills in action*. Sage.

Stambulova, N. B., Ryba, T. V., & Henriksen, K. (2020). Career development and transitions of athletes: the International Society of Sport Psychology Position Stand. *International Journal of Sport and Exercise Psychology, 19*(4), 524–550. https://doi.org/10.1080/1612197X.2020.1737836.

Stapleton, A. B., Hankes, D. M., Hays, K. F., & Parham, W. D. (2010). Ethical dilemmas in sport psychology: A dialogue on the unique aspects impacting practice. *Professional Psychology: Research and Practice, 41*(2), 143–152. http://dx.doi.org/10.1037/a0017976.

Stevens, L. M., & Andersen, M. B. (2007). Transference and countertransference in sport psychology service delivery: Part I. A review of erotic attraction. *Journal of Applied Sport Psychology, 19*(3), 253–269. https://doi.org/10.1080/10413200701314003.

Stoltenberg, C. D., & McNeil, B. (2009). *IDM supervision: An integrated developmental model for supervising counselors and therapists*. Jossey-Bass. doi: 10.4324/9780203893388.

Storch, E. A., Storch, J. B., Killiany, E. M., & Roberti, J. W. (2005). Self-reported psychopathology in athletes: A comparison of intercollegiate student-athletes and non-athletes. *Journal of Sport Behavior, 28*, 86–97.

Strawbridge, S., & Woolfe, R. (2004). Counselling psychology in context. In R. Woolfe, W. Dryden, & S. Strawbridge (Eds). Hand*book of counselling psychology* (2nd ed.). Sage.

Sutton, J., & Stewart, W. (2017). *Learning to counsel: How to develop the skills, insight and knowledge to counsel others* (3rd ed.). Little, Brown Book Group.

Talmon, M. (1990). *Single session therapy: Maximizing the effect of the first (and often only) therapeutic encounter.* Jossey-Bass.

Taylor, J. (2018). *Assessment in applied sport psychology.* Human Kinetics.

Thomas, P. R., Murphy, S. M., & Hardy, L. (1999). Test of performance strategies: Development and preliminary validation of a comprehensive measure of athletes' psychological skills. *Journal of Sports Sciences, 17,* 697–711. https://doi.org/10.1080/026404199365560.

Tod, D. (2007). The long and winding road; professional development in sport psychology. *The Sport Psychologist, 21*(1), 94–108. https://doi.org/10.1123/tsp/21/1/94.

Tod, D., Andersen, M. B., & Marchant, D. B. (2009). A longitudinal examination of neophyte applied sport psychologists' development. *Journal of Applied Sport Psychology, 21*(Suppl 1), S1–S16.

Tod, D., Andersen, M. B., & Marchant, D. B. (2011). Six years up: Applied sport psychologists surviving (and thriving) after graduation. *Journal of Applied Sport Psychology, 23,* 93–109.

Tod, D., & Bond, K. (2010). A longitudinal examination of a British neophyte practitioner's development. *The Sport Psychologist, 24,* 35–51.

Tod, D., Eubank, M., & Hutter, R. I. (2017). Professional development for sport psychology practice. *Current Opinion in Psychology, 16,* 134–137. https://doi.org/10.1016/j.copsyc.2017.05.007.

Tod, D., & Lafferty, M. (2020). Developing an integrated approach. In D. Tod, & M. Eubank (Eds.), *Applied sport, exercise, and performance psychology: Current approaches to helping clients.* Routledge.

Tod, D., Marchant, D., & Andersen, M. B. (2007). Learning experiences contributing to service-delivery competence. *The Sport Psychologist, 21*(3), 317–334. https://doi.org/10.1123/tsp.21.3.317.

Tryon, W. W., & Tryon, G. S. (2011). No ownership of common factors. *American Psychologist, 66*(2), 151–152. https://doi.org/10.1037/a0021056.

Tudor, K. (2011). Understanding empathy. *Transactional Analysis Journal, 41*(1), 39–57. https://doi.org/10.1177/036215371104100107.

Tudor, K. (2017). Person-centred therapy. In C. Feltham, T. Hanley, & L. A. Winter (Eds.), *The SAGE handbook of counselling and psychotherapy* (pp. 280–284). SAGE Publications.

Van Raalte, J. L., & Andersen, M. B. (2000). Supervision I: From models to doing. In M. B. Andersen (Ed.), *Doing sport psychology* (pp. 153–165). Human Kinetics.

Vealey, R. S., Cooley, R., Nilsson, E., Block, C., & Galli, N. (2019). Assessment and the use of questionnaires in sport psychology consulting: An analysis of practices and attitudes from 2003 to 2017. *Journal of Clinical Sport Psychology, 13*(4), 505–523. https://doi.org/10.1123/jcsp.2019-0012.

Vealey, R. S., & Garner-Holman, M. (1998). Applied sport psychology: Measurement issues. In J. L. Duda (Ed.), *Advances in sport and exercise psychology measurement* (pp. 433–446). Fitness Information Technology.

Wadsworth, N., McEwan, H., Lafferty, M., Eubank, M., & Tod, D. (2021). Stories of critical moments contributing to the development of applied sport psychology practitioners. *The Sport Psychologist, 35*(1), 11–21. https://doi.org/10.1123/tsp.2020-0085.

Wadsworth, M. H., Lafferty, M., Eubank, M., & Tod, D. (2021). A systematic review exploring the reflective accounts of applied sport psychology practitioners.

International Review of Sport and Exercise Psychology, 1–27. https://doi.org/10.10 80/1750984X.2021.1975304.

Waho, R. S., Swift, J. K., & Whipple, J. L. (2016). The role of stigma and referral source in predicting college student-athletes' attitudes towards psychological help-seeking. *Journal of Clinical Sport Psychology*, *10*, 85–98. http://dx.doi.org/10.1123/JCSP.2015-0025.

Waite, B. T., & Pettit, M. E. (1993). Work experiences of graduates from doctoral programs in sport psychology. *Journal Of Applied Sport Psychology*, *5*, 234–250. https://doi.org/10.1080/10413209308411317.

Walls, J., McLeod, J., and McLeod, J. (2016). Client preferences in counselling for alcohol problems: A qualitative investigation. *Counselling and Psychotherapy Research*, *16*, 109–118.

Wampold, B. E. (2001). *The great psychotherapy debate: Models, methods, and findings.* Erlbaum.

Watson, J. C., & Greenberg, L. S. (2000). Alliance ruptures and repairs in experiential therapy. *Journal of Clinical Psychology*, *56*, 175–186.

Watson, J. C., Zizzi, S. J., Etzel, E. F., & Lubker, J. R. (2004). Applied sport psychology supervision: A survey of students and professionals. *The Sport Psychologist*, *18*(4), 415–429. https://doi.org/10.1123/tsp.18.4.415.

Wells, M. I. (2000). Beyond cultural competence: A model for individual and institutional cultural development. *Journal of Community Health Nursing*, *17*(4), 189–199.

Weston, N. J. V., Greenlees, I. A., & Thelwell, R. C. (2010). Applied sport psychology consultant perceptions of the usefulness and impacts of performance profiling. *International Journal of Sport Psychology*, *41*, 360–368.

Weston, N. J. V., Greenlees, I., & Thelwell, R. (2013). A review of Butler and Hardy's (1992) performance profiling procedure within sport. *International Review of Sport & Exercise Psychology*, *6*(1), 1–21. https://doi.org/10.1080/17509 84X.2012.674543.

Wicklund, R. A., & Gollwizter, P. M. (1982). *Symbolic self-completion.* Erlbaum.

Wilkins, P. (2010). *Person centred therapy: 100 key points.* Routledge.

Wilkins, P., & Gill, M. (2003). Assessment in person-centred therapy. *Person-Centred & Experiential Psychotherapies*, *2*(3), 172–187. https://doi.org/10.1080/14779757 .2003.9688310.

Williams, D. E., & Andersen, M. B. (2012). Identity, wearing many hats, and boundary blurring: The mindful psychologist on the way to the Olympic and Paralympic games. *Journal of Sport Psychology in Action*, *3*(2), 139–152. https://doi.org/10.1 080/21520704.2012.683090.

Williams, J. M., & Scherzer, C. B. (2003). Tracking the training and careers of graduates of advanced degree programs in sport psychology, 1994–1999. *Journal of Applied Sport Psychology*, *15*, 335–353. http://dx.doi.org/10.1080/714044201.

Winstone, W., & Gervis, M. (2006). Countertransference and the self-aware sport psychologist: Attitudes and patterns of professional practice. *The Sport Psychologist*, *20*(4), 495–511. https://doi.org/10.1123/tsp.20.4.495.

Winter, L. A., Guo, F., Wilk, K., & Hanley, T. (2016). Difference and diversity in pluralistic therapy. In M. Cooper, & W. Dryden (Eds.), *The handbook of pluralistic counselling and psychotherapy.* Sage.

Winter, S., & Collins, D. J. (2016). Applied sport psychology: A profession? *The Sport Psychologist*, *30*, 89–96. https://doi.org/10.1123/tsp.2014-0132.

Wolanin, A., Hong, E., Marks, D., Panchoo, K., & Gross, M. (2016). Prevalence of clinically elevated depressive symptoms in college athletes and differences by gender and sport. *British Journal Of Sports Medicine, 50*, 167–171. PubMed. https://doi.org/10.1136/bjsports-2015-095756

Wylleman, P. (2019). A developmental and holistic perspective on transitioning out of elite sport. In M. H. Anshel, T. A. Petrie, & J. A. Steinfeldt (Eds.), *APA Handbook of sport and exercise psychology, Vol 1* (pp. 201–216). American Psychological Association. https://doi.org/10.1037/0000123-011.

Wylleman, P., & Lavallee, D. (2004). A developmental perspective on the transitions faced by athletes. In M. R. Weiss (Ed.), *Developmental sport and exercise psychology: A lifespan perspective* (pp. 503–523). Fitness Information Technology.

Zarbo, C., Tasca, G. A., Cattafi, F., & Compare, A. (2016). Integrative psychotherapy works. *Frontiers in Psychology, 6*, article 2021. https://doi.org/10.3389/fpsyg.2015.02021.

Zizzi, S. J., & Andersen, M. B. (2010). An Eastern philosophical approach. In S. J. Hanrahan, & M. B. Andersen (Eds.), *Routledge handbook of applied sport psychology: A comprehensive guide for students and practitioners* (pp. 194–202). Routledge.

Zuroff, D. C., Koestner, R., Moskowitz, D. S., McBride, C., Marhsall, M., & Bagby, M. R. (2007). Autonomous motivation for therapy: A new common factor in brief treatments for depression. *Psychotherapy Research, 17*(2), 137–147. https://doi.org/10.1080/10503300600919380.

Appendix
Letters, contracts, case notes, and formulations

Letters, contracts, case notes, and forms are part of the written communication between sport psychology practitioners and clients. What we produced here are exemplars. You can change and adapt these to suit your circumstances and context. A contract, for example, helps to ensure a professional relationship unfolds between the client and the sport psychology practitioner. The ground rules typically include venue, time; fee, if appropriate; frequency of sessions; process of referral, if required; the nature of the therapeutic relationship; the duties and responsibilities of each party; goals and tasks of therapy; and boundaries and expectations in the working alliance. The following letters, sport psychology service delivery contract and supervision contract are adapted from Hedberg (2010), Sutton and Stewart (2017), and Kennerley et al. (2017), and thank you to Dr Scott Gladstone for exemplar cases to produce the client reflection and supervision notes exemplars.

Intake assessment confirmation letter/e-mail

Dr John Smith
BSc, MSc, PhD, CPsychol, HCPC No.
The Heronry Clinic, London
Telephone: 0900 090 090
E-mail: john.smith@theheronryclinic.com

Confidential

Date _____
Client's name and address

_____
_____
_____
_____

Dear Alexa,

This letter confirms your appointment for an initial assessment at **The Heronry Clinic on May 6 at 4 pm**. The initial assessment will last for 50 minutes. We shall, in this initial assessment, discuss whether sport psychology support is appropriate for your presenting issues and whether I am the right sport psychology practitioner with the relevant skills and experience to meet your needs. We can judge if the fit is right for each of us to proceed with sport psychology support.

Our work together requires privacy and confidentiality to work together safely with trust and respect. To honour these values and ways of working, please arrive on time for our session. If you do not wish to keep this appointment or you cannot attend, we would appreciate 24 hours' notice.

We offer a free initial consultation. If we decide that sport psychology support is right for you, following our consultation, we shall agree on a contract (no. of sessions, dates, time, fees, etc.). We shall also agree upon the face-to-face or remote (online) service delivery to suit each party. Our standard fee is £100 per 50-minute session for individuals. We are open to negotiating a sliding fee scale depending on income and circumstances. Directions to our premises are available at www.theheronrycliniclondon.com. You will also see more information about sport psychology and my approach to working with clients on the website.

I look forward to meeting you. If you have questions or queries in the meantime, please e-mail me or contact our receptionist on the telephone number at the top of this page.

Yours sincerely,
Dr John Smith

Sport psychology service delivery contract

Sample Contract

We draw up this contract between sport psychology practitioner Dr John Smith and (enter client's name) _____ on the (enter date) _____

Aims of service delivery

The aim of sport psychology service delivery is to provide you, the client, with a confidential opportunity to explore professional, personal, and relational issues in safety. I, Dr John Smith, work with cognitive behaviour therapy to help you through this process without judging or directing you about what to do. Occasionally, I offer some education or guidance. During service delivery, we set agreed goals and tasks. You, the client, agree to work towards our agreed goals. If I feel I can no longer help you, I will offer to refer you to someone who can better meet your needs and presenting issue(s).

Confidentiality

The sessions between us remain confidential. I, Dr John Smith, reserve the right to breach this agreement of confidentiality in exceptional circumstances. As an example: If you disclose information during our work together that you are at risk of harming yourself or others. Or, if during our work together, you committed a serious crime (e.g., arson, robbery) or express intent to do so. Or, if I am ordered by a court to disclose information about you. I will consult with my supervisor should I choose to breach confidentiality.

Supervision

Part of my ongoing professional development as a sport psychology practitioner means I attend supervision once each month to ensure the efficacy of my work. Part of this supervision means disclosing information about a case; however, we do not disclose names or possibly identifying details.

Number of sessions

We agree at this stage that you commit to (enter number of sessions) _____. Each session lasts for 50 minutes and will take place at (enter address) _____. If we decide to conduct sessions remotely, we shall use the digital platform (enter name) _____. To ensure continuity, we shall meet each week at (enter day and time) _____ beginning (enter date) _____. If any changes arise in our circumstances, we shall negotiate a new contract.

Fees

We agreed you will pay my standard fee of £ _____ per 50-minute session. We have also agreed that should your financial situation change during our contract, we will negotiate a reduced fee until your financial situation improves. You have agreed to pay all sessions in advance using my online payment system.

Missed or cancelled appointments

Our contract outlines the (enter number of sessions) _____ sessions allocated to you for your therapeutic work with (enter name) _____.
We assigned this time to you alone and will not assign your time to another client even if you cannot attend. I, Dr John Smith, will charge you my normal fee for non-attendance or cancelled sessions. Scheduled appointments start and finish on time. If you arrive late, the standard fee remains. We cannot extend sessions beyond the scheduled appointment. If, for whatever reason, I cannot attend (e.g., illness or other extenuating circumstances), you will receive as much notice as possible and I will offer an alternative appointment in the same week. If this rearrangement is not possible, I will not charge you for the session.

Keeping records

As part of my professional requirements, I keep notes of our sessions. I keep these notes in a secure system online. I will save any other notes or records shared with me by a third party (e.g., a referral from another health professional) to your record on the online system. Under GDPR (the General Data Protection Regulation of the European Union [EU]), your information (e.g., notes, letters) remains yours.

Ending service delivery

When we end service delivery, we experience challenges as clients and practitioners. Throughout our work together, we shall keep the end in mind so you can share thoughts and feelings about progress and the end of our work together. If you feel that our work together is not working, let us set aside time to consider the implications of an early termination and prepare a referral if it fits your needs. We seek two weeks' notice for terminating our contracted number of sessions. If we feel that a referral to another health professional is necessary and appropriate, we shall discuss options and write a referral letter together with sufficient detail for the health professional to decide about accepting a new client.

Accreditation

I am a chartered psychologist with the British Psychological Society and a registered practitioner psychologist with the Health and Care Professions Council (HCPC). You can search for my accreditation at www.hcpc-uk.org/check-the-register/ and if my work does not meet your satisfaction and we cannot resolve the issue, and should you wish to register a formal complaint, you can do so with the HCPC.

If the above terms satisfy you, please sign below.

Client's signature _____ Date_____

Practitioner's signature: _____ Date _____

Sample supervision contract

We draw up this supervision contract between sport psychology practitioner Dr John Smith and (enter supervisee's name) _____ on the (enter date) _____

Aims of supervision

The aim of supervision is to provide you, the supervisee, with a confidential opportunity to explore professional, personal, and relational issues in safety adhering to best professional and ethical practice. Our primary focus remains with the welfare and safety of the client through the supervisee's learning journey (i.e., gathering knowledge and skills, and refining attitudes for supporting service users). I, Dr John Smith, work with the cognitive behaviour therapy model of supervision. During supervision, we set agreed goals and tasks. You, the supervisee, agree to work towards our agreed goals. If I feel that I can no longer help you with your supervision needs, I will offer suggestions of alternative supervisors who can better meet your supervision needs.

Confidentiality

The supervision sessions between us remain confidential. I, Dr John Smith, reserve the right to breach this agreement of confidentiality in exceptional circumstances. As an example: If you disclose information during our work together that you are at risk of harming yourself or others. Or, if during our work together, you committed a serious crime (e.g., arson, robbery) or express intent to do so. Or, if I am ordered by a court to disclose information about you. I will consult with my supervisor should I choose to breach confidentiality.

Recording of sessions

All cases or professionals discussed during supervision must be made anonymous. A necessary part of our work together is to record sessions with clients. You, the supervisee, must have informed consent from the service user, carer, or professional to undertake any recordings. You, the supervisee, handle arrangements to erase any recordings.

Supervision

Part of my ongoing professional development as a sport psychology practitioner means that I attend supervision once each month to ensure the efficacy of my work. Part of this supervision means disclosing information about my supervisory processes; however, we do not disclose names or possibly identifying details.

Supervision session content

Supervision follows a cognitive behaviour therapy process and addresses four central themes. First, we seek to acquire knowledge, understanding, conceptualisation, and clinical skills within a cognitive-behavioural model. Second, any presenting cases that require immediate attention or referral shall be addressed as a matter of urgency. Third, we explore supervisee thoughts, feelings, actions, attitudes, values, beliefs, and the possible influence of these on therapeutic services and professional conduct. Finally, we shall explore the process aspects of our work together as supervisor and supervisee. More practically, we shall address:

1. Therapeutic relationships, strategies, risks, safety, and boundaries.
2. Case presentations and assessments.
3. Case conceptualisation.
4. Therapeutic strategies (i.e., interventions, simulations, role play).
5. Homework.
6. Therapeutic evaluations and endings.
7. Review of audio and video recordings.
8. Direct observation of practice.
9. Explore supervisee thoughts, feelings, actions, attitudes, values, beliefs, and the possible influence of these on therapeutic services and professional conduct.
10. Review current clinical practice guidelines, psychoeducational material, and current research relating to presenting cases.

Agreed supervision goals

1. _____

   _____

   _____

2. _____

   _____

   _____

3. _____

   _____

   _____

4. _____

   _____

   _____

Number of supervision sessions

We agree at this stage that you commit to (enter number of sessions) _____ .
Each session lasts for 50 minutes and will take place at (enter address) _____
_____. If we decide to conduct supervision sessions remotely,
we shall use the digital platform (enter name) _____ . To ensure
continuity, we shall meet fortnightly at (enter day and time) _____
beginning (enter date) _____. If any changes arise in our circumstances, we shall negotiate a new supervision contract.

Fees

We agreed you will pay my standard fee of £ _____ per 50-minute session.
We have also agreed that should your financial situation change during
our contract, we will negotiate a reduced fee until your financial situation
improves. You have agreed to pay all supervision sessions in advance using
my online payment system.

Missed or cancelled sessions

Our contract outlines the (enter number of sessions) _____ sessions
allocated to you for your supervision with (enter name) _____. We
assigned this time to you alone and will not assign your time to another
supervisee even if you cannot attend. We, Dr John Smith, will charge
you my normal fee for non-attendance or cancelled sessions. Scheduled
appointments start and finish on time. If you arrive late, the standard fee
remains. We cannot extend sessions beyond the scheduled appointment.
If, for whatever reason, I cannot attend (e.g., illness or other extenuating
circumstances), you will receive as much notice as possible and I will offer
an alternative appointment in the same week. If this rearrangement is not
possible, I will not charge you for the session.

Keeping records

As part of my professional requirements, I keep notes of our sessions. I keep
these notes in a secure system online. I will save any other notes or records
shared with me by a third party (e.g., a referral from another health professional) to your record on the online system. Under GDPR (the General Data
Protection Regulation of the European Union [EU]), your information (e.g.,
notes, letters) remains yours.

Ending service delivery

When we end service delivery, we experience challenges as clients and practitioners. Throughout our work together, we shall keep the end in mind so

you can share thoughts and feelings about progress and the end of our work together. If you feel that our work together is not working, let us set aside time to consider the implications of an early termination and prepare a referral if it fits your needs. We seek two weeks' notice for terminating our contracted number of sessions.

Accreditation

I am a chartered psychologist with the British Psychological Society and a registered practitioner psychologist with the Health and Care Professions Council (HCPC). You can search for my accreditation at www.hcpc-uk.org/check-the-register/ and if my work does not meet your satisfaction and we cannot resolve the issue, and should you wish to register a formal complaint, you can do so with the HCPC.

Anti-discriminatory practice

Our supervision work shall follow the policy of the _____
_____ (professional body)
If the above terms satisfy you, please sign below.

Supervisee's signature _____ Date_____

Practitioner's signature: _____ Date _____

Intake and treatment proposal

Name: _____ D.O.B. _____

Address:

_____

_____

_____

_____

Telephone: Home:_____ Work: _____ Mobile: _____

E-mail _____

Gender: _____ Age: _____

Marital status: _____ Children: _____

Ethnicity: _____

Employment:_____

Course of study: _____

Source of referral: (Name, address, and contact e-mail and telephone)

_____

_____

_____

_____

Reasons for referral

_____

_____

_____

Presenting issue(s)

_____

_____

_____

_____

Suggested basis of the presenting issue(s)

_____

_____

_____

_____

Goals and desired outcome

_____

_____

_____

_____

Follow-up plan

_____

_____

_____

_____

Client No. _____

Sample session notes form 1

Client No. _____ Session No. _____ Date: _____

Length of session: _____
Client's reflections since the last meeting (including homework)

_____

_____

_____

_____

Review of previous session

_____

_____

_____

_____

Current issues

_____

_____

_____

_____

New issues

_____

_____

_____

_____

Homework tasks

_____

_____

_____

_____

Date/time/venue for next session

_____

Signature (of practitioner) _____ Date: _____
Additional notes

_____

_____

_____

_____

Sample session notes form 2

Client No. _____ Session No. _____ Date: _____

Client's reflections since the last meeting (including homework)

_____

_____

_____

_____

Issues addressed in today's meeting

_____

_____

_____

_____

Homework activities set for next session

_____

_____

_____

_____

Brief reflections on session

_____

_____

_____

_____

_____

Issues for supervision

_____

_____

_____

_____

Date and time of next session

_____

Signature (of practitioner) _____ Date: _____

Sample brief session notes form 3

Client No. _____ Session No. _____ Date: _____

PACE Notes: Presentations – Assessment – Comments – Expectations

Presentations (client's reflections since the last meeting)

_____

_____

_____

_____

Assess (client's behaviour and progress)

_____

_____

_____

_____

Comments (about the client's behaviour and presenting issues in today's meeting)

_____

_____

_____

_____

Expectations (homework activities set for the next session)

_____

_____

_____

_____

Signature (of practitioner)_____Date:_____

Sample case notes to share with others (e.g., health professionals)

Client Name: _____ Client No. _____ Date: _____

Presenting issues

_____

_____

_____

_____

Treatment recommendations

_____

_____

_____

_____

Client's consent to disclose _____ (Yes/No)

Sample group therapy notes form

Group Reference _____ Session No. _____ Date: _____

Group therapy time: _____

No. of group members attending: _____ No. of group members
  missing _____

Today's topic

_____

_____

_____

_____

Issues raised

_____

_____

_____

_____

Observations about the group

_____

_____

_____

_____

_____

Next week's topic

_____

_____

Signature (of practitioner)_____ Date: _____

Client contact reflection notes

Background and assessment

Adele is a woman in her mid-20s who currently lives with her parents in a village in the Scottish Borders. Recently, Adele returned to university to complete a postgraduate degree in English, having taken time to train full-time as a triathlete following her undergraduate degree in veterinary medicine. Adele returned to the same university to complete her postgraduate degree because her old coach trained the triathlon squad, allowing her to combine her studies with her training. Adele self-referred for psychological therapy after being signposted to the service by her coach because she was experiencing low mood and performance anxiety since returning to university and training with the triathlon squad. Adele shared that she previously used to control her food intake as a coping mechanism while a teenager, but stated that she currently has no thoughts of self-harm or suicide. Adele described her parents as supportive, but noted that they have been worrying more about her recently, which leads to more arguments at home. Her partner is also a triathlete with the men's squad. Like her friends, he is supportive; however, his training base is 200 miles away, where Adele used to live and train. Adele's goals for therapy were to understand her low mood and reduce her performance anxiety in competitive triathlons.

Though Adele reflected on her past and present, she focused intently on the expectations of others (i.e., performance director, coaching staff) to continue progressing and performing for the upcoming Olympic trials and selection. I felt able to offer the core conditions of empathy, congruence, and unconditional positive regard, and Adele appeared to perceive these responding to empathic reflections and clarifying questions. Taking these considerations – alongside Adele's goals for sport psychology support – suggests that she was suitable for present-centred therapy (PCT) (Merry & Haugh, 2020; Wilkins & Gill, 2003).

Formulation – developed collaboratively over therapy

During childhood and adolescence, Adele excelled at school, music, and especially running and swimming, receiving praise from her teachers, parents, and coaches regarding the grades she achieved, awards she won, and the national coverage in print and social media rather than the effort to achieve these outcomes. As Adele grew older, she realised how much more effort was required to maintain these standards and continue to receive praise and recognition, contributing to a condition of worth regarding academic and sporting achievement (Rogers, 1951; Tudor, 2011). She felt worthwhile as long as she was achieving. At the beginning of her undergraduate degree in veterinary medicine, Adele dropped her music to focus on her degree and her training. She kept a strict training and studying regime from 5 am until 10 pm. Adele withdrew from her friends to make enough time for studying and training. At one national trial, she underperformed drastically, becoming highly distressed. Adele used restrictive eating to cope with self-critical thoughts, low mood, and expectations from her team. She appeared to experience 'incongruence'

(Rogers, 1959; Wilkins, 2010) between her organismic (genuine) experiences (struggling with the training volume and academic assessments) and her self-concept (academically and athletically able and focused on outcomes). Adele attended our service delivery regarding this 'incongruence' and focused on reconnecting with her friends and cherished pastimes to promote connection, enjoyment, and pleasure (Allen & McCarthy, 2016).

After completing her undergraduate degree, Adele began training full-time as a triathlete in England for three years before choosing to return to Scotland and to pursue a postgraduate degree. Her national coach felt that this move was a backward step in her pursuit of Olympic glory. Knowing how dissatisfied her coach and support staff were with her decision, Adele focused intently on improving her times in the pool, on the bike, and running to show them she was right (Rothbaum et al., 1982) and could make the right decisions. Though it appeared Adele made this decision, the strings attached had an external focus of evaluation (Rogers, 1959), placing the greatest importance on proving her worth to her coaches and support staff. This increased psychological demand and training load meant Adele withdrew from her cherished pastimes, including spending time with her friends, walking in the countryside, and visiting cafés to read and relax, leading to a low mood and rumination about competing at the highest level. Adele's low mood and worry dismissed any sense of loss regarding these sources of social support, engagement, and pleasure and altering from her awareness of the worry, self-criticism, and self-denial about not meeting her conditions of worth (Rogers, 1951, 1959) she has held since late childhood. Again, Adele experienced psychological distress because of 'incongruence'. Athletes sometimes confide that they know something is wrong but they cannot put their finger on precisely what is wrong. So how can one tell if one has an emotional problem? Perhaps the simplest answer is that you have an emotional problem if you think you have one, but there might also be a few other pieces to the problem jigsaw. When an athlete feels stuck, the athlete might experience painful emotions, though they are not necessarily a problem. An emotional problem comprises pain plus stuckness (Dryden, 2020). Maybe the athlete is engaging in self-defeating behaviours which increase one's stuckness, which seems to be the case for Adele. Athletes sometimes avoid the opportunities to tackle the problem or address the problem, but work in ways that worsen it. Sometimes, the thoughts and attitudes one holds underpin the self-defeating emotions and dysfunctional behaviours, which means that the athlete cannot arrive at emotional problem-solving. Finally, taking steps to prevent feeling the extent of an emotional problem helps briefly – but the athlete is preventing themself from handling it.

Session 1: first session

I began the first session by informing Adele about the purpose of the session, to explore her reasons for attending sport psychology services and to discuss contracting. Adele completed the intake assessment two weeks previously, outlining her presenting issues and reasons for attending therapy. I began by explaining that although I held the information from the assessment session, I also wished to discuss this information with her to ensure I had a thorough understanding of her experience and any change in the meantime. Adele appreciated this clarification and setting the scene because, although she spoke about the past, she felt much less comfortable discussing her feelings and, especially, her presently experienced feelings (Bohart et al., 2002).

I also felt that I needed to use some assessment tool regarding Adele's level of distress. I had settled on the CORE-10 as the most accessible and meaningful tool that fitted with the organisation's requirements for assessment. Adele scored 'moderate' on the level of psychological distress according to the CORE ratings. Adele felt that fitted about right. I was aware how coarse it might feel to use such an assessment tool rather than to foster the therapeutic relationship. I focused on attending, listening, and – when possible – to use open questions, though not too many, following Adele's lead to show openness and paraphrasing or summarising as the need presented itself (McCarthy & Moffat, 2023). Adele appreciated the soft, understanding tone of my voice, and pauses after she spoke: "You give me space and time to speak and I don't feel so nervous or rushed now sharing my . . . eh, my . . . eh, my feelings".

Session 2: second session

Adele completed a CORE-10 measure. Her clinical score indicated a 'mild' level of psychological distress. Adele felt that this rating was about right. Adele explained that she felt much better after the first session and during the week. She disclosed, "I'm just not used to anyone listening to me; they're usually telling me what to do. It's strange, but it feels good". This session focused on continuing discussing themes from our previous session regarding Adele's perception that the adults around her growing up had expected excellence in everything, and she felt that she had to meet these needs, showing a condition of worth related to scholastic and sporting achievement.

Though Adele recognised the perfectionistic drive, she welcomed how it helped her to improve; yet, in the intervening years since starting university, she had tempered her distress if assessments or performances did not go her way – but she felt like she was going back to being 17 or 18 years old again. What seemed unsettling for me in the session was Adele's 'foot on the pedal' to get somewhere. I sensed an unease and felt there was sufficient trust in the therapy relationship, so I offered this point as a congruent reflection and asked if Adele was also experiencing this urgency.

Adele dropped her head, slumped her shoulders, and sank into the chair. After a long pause, Adele said, "I need to take a moment", so we sat in silence. Then she said, "I said I was back feeling like I was 17 or 18 years old again. I feel that is right, and it's here in the room with me. I'm jumping up and down inside to get fixed quickly and I can't even relax in here". Acknowledging this point, the pace of Adele's speech fell and a mutual understanding emerged (McCarthy & Moffat, 2023). I experienced a sense of relational depth (Mearns & Cooper, 2018) which I felt Adele reciprocated because she said at the end of the session, "I feel even better right now. I didn't want to share the jumpiness inside my body and the wild horses inside my mind. Thank you – that session was most helpful".

Session 3: late cancellation

Adele did not attend this session, but had contacted reception staff to say she could not make the session but would like to reschedule. Though I was initially feeling concerned about Adele missing the session, I was unsure about my congruent reflection in our previous session regarding the ongoing presence of perfectionism in her sport training and competition. I was also concerned that Adele wished to prove everyone wrong and herself right. According to the self-completion theory, when people experience a threat to a part of their self-concept they value, they become highly motivated to seek social recognition for that identity (Wicklund & Gollwizter, 1982; Gollwitzer & Wicklund, 1985). I felt like I might have added myself to the team of doubters and our session reflected a failure for Adele. With the self-completion theory, perhaps Adele would actively seek to seek an opportunity to show and restore her sense of self as capable and independent.

While writing these notes, an e-mail popped up from Adele explaining why she could not attend the session. She had taken a day off training (which she never does) to head to Edinburgh and missed the train back. She had spent the morning relaxing with friends and in the afternoon, she sat in a comfy chair in her favourite bookshop reading "A River Runs through it" by Norman Maclean. She shared a line from the book: "Help", he said, "is giving part of yourself to somebody who comes to accept it willingly and needs it badly". Then explained, "this is you, you're trying to help me. I got that in the last session, thank you".

Rather than feeling guarded and vulnerable after my congruent reflection, Adele felt empowered. I feel it would be helpful to discuss Adele's experience during the last session, and I will discuss this experience with my supervisor.

Session 6: final session

I began this session by reviewing Adele's CORE-10 scores. Her clinical score showed a 'low' level of psychological distress according to CORE ratings. I discussed Adele's experience of ending our sessions. Adele said she felt "sanguine" about ending our sessions. I felt that Adele had considered this word and truly meant it. Sanguine means 'confident and inclined to hopefulness'. Adele's mood certainly resonated with her low level of psychological distress. She reflected on how the day off in Edinburgh about one month previously helped her to realise that those things she avoided (e.g., days off, being with friends, reading in a bookshop or café) were her fuel source and her ballast.

Please do not misunderstand me. I still want to go to the Olympics. I still want to do well, but you know, I know where they fit now. There's a store cupboard in my mind for all those things I want to achieve. They have a place in my mind and now I can close the store cupboard while I relax and recharge; it feels good – no, it feels right.

This reflection showed a further wilting in her condition of worth regarding achievement.

I ended the session by discussing details about how Adele could re-access the service in the future and the possibility of booster sessions (McCarthy et al., 2023).

Closing summary

Adele's change in CORE-10 scores from a 'moderate' to 'low' level of psychological distress showed a reliable and clinically significant change (Barkham et al., 2006) in her psychological distress across sessions. Adele felt that her mood had improved, and she felt more relaxed while training and competing. The sense of performance anxiety waned and she could distinguish between a challenge and a threat state more readily (Meijen et al., 2020). She felt that she had progressed well in her goals for therapy.

Though I'm not sure what to do with my pleased feelings regarding the process and progress of sessions with Adele, I know that congruence has been my friend. I have developed my ability to be congruent in sessions (e.g., handling contracts, psychometrics, missed sessions, and endings), and also how I can make use of – when appropriate – sharing aspects of my process as part of helping my client reflect on their process, such as in our second session.

Though I read much about perfectionism (Hill, 2023), I struggled with holding my theoretical knowledge to one side while remaining attuned to Adele. I struggle to remain empathically attuned when I know I am working on a time-limited model. I feel as if I ought to do something more; however, this set of sessions reinforced how I can work with a client experiencing perfectionism amongst other elements of 'stuckness' while focusing on offering the core conditions rather than experiential tasks (e.g., two-chair technique), which has made me more confident in using PCT. I am fitting the therapeutic modality (i.e., PCT) alongside my theoretical knowledge, research, and practice experience while remaining with the client's frame of reference (Tudor, 2011).

Supervision reflection notes

Supervision session 3

This session focused on my initial sessions with Adele and using psychometrics in intake assessment. My overriding concern focused on assessment. I shared with my supervisor that I felt unsure about the place for assessment in person-centred therapy because I (might) equate assessment with diagnosis (Wilkins & Gill, 2003; Tudor, 2011). The difficulty with diagnosis assumes that there is an underlying problem (disease) and that we might treat – and therefore cure – this problem. This view places the problem first, the person second.

My supervisor reiterated the position of Mearns (2004), who explained this point by clarifying that different clients experience a problem (e.g., perfectionism) differently because they symbolise and experience their past, present, and future differently.

Diagnosis and assessment fall into different categories here because diagnosis might reflect 'labelling' a person with a particular problem based on a set of criteria, whereas assessment draws on the mutuality of the client and the sport psychology practitioner in the therapeutic relationship working together to reach a conclusion about the client's difficulties. One assessment the person-centred practitioner makes is the likelihood of offering a relationship to a client, including Rogers' six conditions. What is under consideration here is the potential relationship, rather than the client – it is the sport psychologist's ability to fulfil those conditions. In this assessment, the sport psychologist judges the necessary and sufficient conditions (e.g., "Can I and my potential client establish and maintain contact?") to arrive at an answer. Where there are shortcomings, one can take these to supervision.

I also shared Adele's case regarding her low mood, performance anxiety, and the role of her coach and support team. I felt Adele may be at a stage 2 level of process, because although Adele accepted things are not quite right in her life, she placed herself as a victim in this hostile world and the faults with others (i.e., her coach and support team). My only hint that Adele may be at a stage 3 level of process related to her disclosing the differences between one's idealised self and one's reality: "I'm trying too hard to be the perfect triathlete but it doesn't work. I fail again and again". Although there might be the glimmer of different possibilities, the strictness of good or bad and right or wrong remains.

Through our discussions, my supervisor and I considered the possibility of remaining with primary empathic reflection and clarifying questions about Adele's beliefs and experiences, which could help to build trust in the relationship. I felt Adele would be reluctant to respond well to advanced empathy. We finished by revisiting a selection of assessments (e.g., CORE-10) as a method of identifying change across sessions with clients presenting with low mood, for example. Rather than presenting the assessment tool as a requirement, it could be a collaborative discussion. This way of working felt more congruent. My supervisor suggested reading a few specific chapters regarding critical perspectives on psychometrics in sport exercise contexts, as well as for applied practice (Cripps, 2017).

Client referral for mental health support services

Dr John Smith
The Heronry Clinic
London
Telephone: 0900 090 090

Confidential

01.05.23
Dear Dr Johnson.
Re: Adam Smith (Date of birth: 29.02.92)
221b Baker Street, London.

Reason for referral

The client and I present this referral request seeking treatment for a history of disordered eating, bulimia, and binge eating that is impairing the client's mood, self-worth, eating and exercise behaviours, and functioning at home and especially at work

Case history and social situation

Adam, a 31-year-old male, works as a professional jockey. He lives with his girlfriend in a small village in Berkshire. Adam has been employed as a professional jockey for 12 years. There is no family history of mental illness disclosed so far with perceived normal social family functioning. There is no history of abuse and no history of substance abuse; however, exercise dependence was identified through self-disclosure.

Present state

The client completed the CORE-10, an accessible and meaningful tool that fitted with the organisation's requirements for assessment. Adam scored 'moderate' on the level of psychological distress, according to the CORE ratings. Adam felt that fitted about right. Adam disclosed that he was feeling more tense as the season progressed because he expected to win or at least be placed in races, but his current form was worse than predicted. Although he had support from his agent and family, he was unsure about how to cope when things go wrong on race day. He had difficulty getting to sleep and staying asleep. He sometimes felt hopeless about his current situation and often felt unhappy.

Past treatment and ongoing formulation and treatment

The client and I met for (state number of sessions) between (state dates) at (state premises). I began working with the client using a person-centred approach to help the client explore and understand his incongruence and factors underpinning his poor performances over the previous two months. Upon the client sharing more of his psychological considerations, and after conducting and sharing a psychological formulation, the client disclosed a history of disordered eating, bulimia, and binge eating for which the client never sought medical or psychological support. I consulted with Dr Thomas Hardy, PhD, MSc, BSc, CPsychol (BPS), HCPC practitioner psychologist, and read the new eating disorders guidance by NICE (the National Institute for Health and Care Excellence), and therefore recommend that the client accesses the specialist service for his presentations and disorders.

Reason for referral

The disorders noted above cause significant impairment in the client's mood, self-worth, eating and exercise behaviours, and functioning at home and especially at work, and he seeks treatment to diminish these impairments. He would need access to a clinical psychologist specialising in treating eating disorders.

Recommendations

The issues presented lie outside my competency and experience as a sport psychology practitioner. The recommended service to support this client is a clinical psychologist who specialises in eating disorders.

If you have questions, contact me at the address at the top of the page.

Yours sincerely,
John

Example person-centred case formulation

This is an example of a theoretical framework for client material in a person-centred case formulation of psychological difficulties adapted from Simms (2011).

Conditions of worth laid down in childhood

Emotion is a sign of weakness.
Your best is your best, if you win.
There's always more in you.
Happiness comes from success.
Parents know what is best and they are never wrong.

Introjected values and beliefs

Trust no one.
Failure is not an option.
I must be strong.
When I don't win, it's my fault.

Denial and distortion of experience
Unworthy of success.
Blaming himself for his poor form.
Need for close relationships.
Need for a close relationship with parents.

*Critical
Incidents:*

Recent poor
performances.
Increasing
dissatisfaction
from racing.

State of incongruence
Achievement still feels unfulfilling.
Blaming self for current poor performance.
Great career but getting no satisfaction from horse racing.
Need to confide in others.

Psychological difficulties
(Emotional –behavioural –cognitive –interpersonal)
Low mood.
Social withdrawal.
Low self-worth.
Poor self-care.
Constant self-criticism.
Severely restricting food intake then bingeing.

Index

Note: Numbers in **bold** indicate tables and numbers in *italics* indicate figures on the corresponding page.

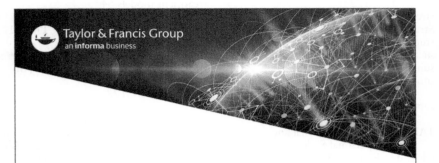